The Red Apprentice

The Red Apprentice

OLE GUNNAR SOLSKJÆR: THE MAKING OF MANCHESTER UNITED'S GREAT HOPE

Jamie Jackson

**SIMON &
SCHUSTER**

London · New York · Sydney · Toronto · New Delhi

First published in Great Britain by Simon & Schuster UK Ltd, 2020

Copyright © Jamie Jackson, 2020

The right of Jamie Jackson to be identified as the author of
this work has been asserted in accordance with the
Copyright, Designs and Patents Act, 1988.

1 3 5 7 9 10 8 6 4 2

Simon & Schuster UK Ltd
1st Floor
222 Gray's Inn Road
London WC1X 8HB

www.simonandschuster.co.uk
www.simonandschuster.com.au
www.simonandschuster.co.in

Simon & Schuster Australia, Sydney
Simon & Schuster India, New Delhi

The author and publishers have made all reasonable efforts
to contact copyright-holders for permission, and apologise
for any omissions or errors in the form of credits given.
Corrections may be made to future printings.

A CIP catalogue record for this book
is available from the British Library

Hardback ISBN: 978-1-4711-8784-1
Trade Paperback ISBN: 978-1-4711-8785-8
eBook ISBN: 978-1-4711-8786-5

Typeset in Bembo by M Rules

Printed and bound by CPI Group (UK) Ltd, Croydon, CR0 4YY

For Sonny, Martha and Gaynor – always XXX

CONTENTS

Part Three: The Dream Job

The Red Apprentice

'Elvis.'

OLE GUNNAR SOLSKJÆR – WHEN ASKED
WHO HE'D LIKE TO MEET

THE FOOTBALL MADRIGALS . . .

Football can be hyper-real. Events occur in fast-forward, games are executed at lightning speed, judgements are breathless, romantic, knee-jerk and reflexive. Here is a galaxy of short-termism, a universe of the instant. A zillion experts making a zillion declarations. The first and last verdict on players, teams, matches and managers zooming at all angles on a 24/7, 365-days-a-year loop.

On 19 December 2018 Ole Gunnar Solskjær's appointment as Manchester United interim manager is announced. The verdict: *wow, really??*

After a record start of eight consecutive wins in all competitions and OGS's subsequent appointment as full-time manager – the verdict: *inspirational.*

And, after a run of only two wins in the season's final 14 matches and no Champions League qualification – the verdict: *told you so; the jury is out; the 2019-20 season will tell all.*

Crystal clear is *this:* the tale of how Ole Gunnar Solskjær, the goalscoring hero of Manchester United's 1999 Champions League triumph, came to return to the club as manager would read as syrupy cliché if not true. Because here is the real-life story of a boy from a Norwegian fishing village on the shores of the Atlantic with a sparkly persona, who bounced through the tribal world of football to take the ultimate job. This is a tale of joy and reversal, revival and determination. Of a man with boundless belief, smart enough to understand his accusers and their accusations that he was callow and inexperienced. That he lacked the requisite gravitas and footballing imagination to lead the global behemoth that is Manchester United. Who despite – or *because* – of this remains at centre a man with an innocent love of the sport. Who touched the lives of his boyhood friends when managing their street team and who has touched the lives of the players and staff of all the clubs he has managed as well as people beyond the football cabaret.

Ole Gunnar Solskjær became a Manchester United immortal when he scored the dying-seconds winner in the 1999 Champions League final against Bayern Munich to earn the club a second European Cup. He became the stuff of fairytale, the man who entered a dream of his own making, followed by team-mates and fans and anyone else tuned in to sport's poetry. Its ability to synthesise glitz and glory into the glamour of folklore.

After losing virtually three of his last four seasons as a player to a knee injury and fading into the background as United reserve-team manager, Ole Gunnar became the most successful number one in Molde FK's history. Yet, after bombing as Cardiff City manager to *then* return to Old Trafford as caretaker boss was characteristic of his ability to rewrite the narrative of his personal movie.

Occasionally, a story occurs that is a reminder of why, in essence, sport is sport, and draws us back to its spectacle. When José Mourinho was sacked by Manchester United on

18 December 2018, he left a club listing in a funk of backbiting and negativity. Morale was sub-zero, players disaffected and treading water. There were 11 points between the team and Champions League qualification – the absolute minimum demand for any season. Manchester United was an unhappy, dismal place. The staff, football and non-football, were struggling to enjoy life in what should have been a vibrant environment.

This was the Mourinho effect. The cheesed-off one's mood pervaded all areas of the club: the field of play, the training ground, the locker room, media department, the club's administrative and financial arms and its hierarchy, all the way to executive vice-chairman Ed Woodward. Solskjær reversed this instantaneously. He made Manchester United buoyant again. He was the kid-faced assassin as a striker. He was the still kid-faced caretaker who reminded players that football should be fun. For a two-month, eight-win streak in all competitions, Old Trafford became a place of joy for supporters once more; watching their team invigorating. Solskjær closed the gap to a top-four place to three points. He reversed a 2-0 home deficit to Paris Saint-Germain to progress to the Champions League quarter-final.

Then, after a run of just one defeat in 17 matches, the road became bumpier – 'a rollercoaster', as Solskjær said. Defeats came against Wolverhampton Wanderers in the FA Cup and in the Premier League, to Barcelona in the Champions League. More losses followed, at Everton – a 4-0 nadir that left OGS despairing – and to Manchester City: part of a run which, following the 2-1 win over West Ham United on 13 April, meant the team went winless in the league for a month, until the end of the campaign. The tilt at a top-four berth lasted until the penultimate game, then failed. 'We just fell short of what would be a miraculous target of fourth back in December,' Ole Gunnar said.

The old frailties that have plagued Manchester United since the genius Sir Alex Ferguson stepped away in May 2013 resurfaced. The defence required an overhaul. The midfield lacked subtlety and options. The attack needed two or more prolific goalscorers. Away from the field United had to advance, re-tailor its recruitment and scouting, build a bespoke operation for the 21st century in which Liverpool, their fiercest rivals, have been exemplars of what a world-class club, from bottom to top, stadium to boardroom, should look and perform like.

This is Ole Gunnar's challenge. He signed a three-year deal when made permanent manager in March 2019 and may need all of this (and more) to achieve what David Moyes, Louis van Gaal and José Mourinho failed to do: make Manchester United formidable again.

Can he do it? How smart is he? How able to husband the disparate forces that swirl around the club into a unified mass of irresistible energy? This is what *The Red Apprentice* examines. Who Ole Gunnar Solskjær is. What formed him. How he thinks and acts. What moves him.

This is his story; this is the book before you.

PROLOGUE

Stavanger, Rogaland Province, 10 October 1995

'He could've gone to Spurs – no Manchester
United fairytale.'

John Moncur, Tottenham Hotspur
chief scout

This is the cold winter evening when fate and romance
began tangoing. Norway Under-21s v England Under-21s
in south-west Norway on 10 October 1995. When Ole
Gunnar Solskjær diced with an alternative reality.

This is the night when the 22-year-old Molde FK centre-
forward could have been rubber-stamped as perfect for
Tottenham Hotspur. Two of the 2,640 crowd in the stands
at Viking FK Stadion were Gerry Francis, manager of
Tottenham Hotspur, and John Moncur, his chief scout. They
were watching Solskjær: Francis for the first time, Moncur for
what was to be the last of many times. Scouting the young,
goal-glutton striker.

Moncur, whose son John (junior) was a Tottenham and
West Ham United midfielder, was impressed whenever

watching Ole Gunnar. 'He stood out,' Moncur says. 'I thought he had the potential to be a top player. And had a chance to go straight into our first team, to be honest. We were looking for players. It began because Steve Perryman rang me from Norway and told me about Ole.'

Steve Perryman, who remains Tottenham Hotspur's record appearance maker, had become IK Start's manager in late August 1995 and had spotted OGS on *Forball Extra* and *Sportsrevyen*, Norway's answers to *Match of the Day* as the country's highlights shows. Perryman was assistant to Tottenham Hotspur manager Ossie Ardiles until the previous year when Alan Sugar, the owner, eased them out of the club. Despite feeling sore at this, Perryman remained fond of Spurs, a sentiment that was a prevailing factor in the near-transfer of Ole Gunnar to Tottenham in the winter of 1995.

Perryman wanted to take Stephen Carr, a 19-year-old Irish right-back, and two other players on loan from Spurs to IK Start. So, when John Moncur asked Perryman to be Tottenham's 'eyes in Norway' – be on the lookout for any fresh potential talent – Perryman told Moncur, sure, as long as he could take Carr and the others on loan. When Moncur concurred, Perryman told him about Ole Gunnar, but played the recommendation down, as he had never seen Solskjær play live, or even for a whole 90 minutes on TV.

Moncur says, 'Steve went to Norway because he'd always had contacts in the country. He began managing out there at Start and rang me one day because we were friends and said, "You got to come and see this boy."'

Perryman, who became Start manager mid-way through the season due to the illness of his predecessor, first saw Ole on TV the night after his first match in charge. Perryman caught the centre-forward scoring and was instantly intrigued because of Ole's youth. On initial viewing, he sighted a player who had the potential for development, an impression confirmed when he again saw the highlights shows the following weekend. He told friends that Ole's style and cold-eyed finishing reminded him of the great Jimmy Greaves, a Tottenham team-mate when Perryman's 17-year career in the first team commenced in 1969.

On Perryman's recommendation, John Moncur came to assess Ole, saw him play for the first time, and sent a fax to Gerry Francis that told the Spurs manager: 'We don't need to scout this player again, we should just sign him.'

Yet Francis did want another assessment of Ole Gunnar. 'I told Gerry about him,' says John. 'And Gerry said, "Well, look. There is an international game on the Saturday in Oslo between France and Norway. Watch that and then fly to Molde the next morning and watch the game up there." So I did that.'

Moncur, 25 years at Spurs and an expert in youth development, was impressed. 'When I saw Ole again, you could see what a good player he was. He was only young. He was top scorer in Norway in that league. He just stood out – on set pieces, everything he did – potentially a top player.'

By then Moncur had even agreed a price with Molde for Solskjær. 'I'll never forget it, because I was the only person in the hotel, in Molde. I lay there all night because it never got dark – it was the time of year there where it doesn't get dark and I went to see him play. I still have a cutting of Molde's local paper and on the front page is me sitting there – a photo of me watching him. It was front-page news at the time. Someone from Spurs watching Ole Gunnar Solskjær.

I went back and reported to Gerry that I had spoken to the Molde president about a price. What they asked for, what they wanted, I said to Ger I would jump at it.'

Francis still wasn't convinced. 'Gerry sent someone else who went and had a look at Solskjær who came back and wasn't as enthusiastic as me,' says Moncur. 'I won't tell you who that is because he's a name in football now. So then I said, "Well, look, Ger, I'm telling you, I think he's different class." He says, "Well, go and have another look."'

Moncur, again, went to watch Ole and became even more confident that here was a boy worth buying. 'They were playing in the European Cup Winners' Cup at the time – September 1995 – playing PSG and lost 3-1.' But the ever-prolific Solskjær registered the opener for Molde. 'Ole scored so I came back, raving about him again,' Moncur says. 'Gerry said, "Right, I'll tell you what to do. Get a game for me and you to go and watch together, but it's got to be a midweek game."'

'The only game I could find midweek was a Norway Under-21 game. It was in Stavanger, so I booked the flights and we went.'

Fate, Lady Fortune, and the selection policy of Nils Johan Semb, the Under-21 coach: all were to step in and ensure Solskjær would not go to Spurs and instead fulfil his name-in-lights, hero-status destiny at United.

For his Norway Under-21 attack, Semb chose Steffen Iversen on the right in a 'free role', Tore André Flo at centre-forward and Solskjær on the left, 'but not wide left', says Semb, 'close to the inside'. Dave Sexton's England side would feature a substitute appearance from an 18-year-old Phil Neville, who four years later watched on from the bench at the Camp Nou when Ole Gunnar joined the

Manchester United pantheon by scoring *that* winner against Bayern Munich.

Semb went on to manage the senior Norway team and select the same front three in the successful Euro 2000 qualification campaign when 'available'. But the goal Ole Gunnar struck in front of Gerry Francis and John Moncur did not convince the Tottenham manager. John, who has a slightly different recollection of Solskjær's playing position, says: 'Unfortunately, when we got there, Ole was playing on the left wing because Norway at that time only played with one front player. That was the big boy Flo, who was at Chelsea. When you play out on the left and you're a striker, you have to rely on people getting you the ball, and you know how it goes in football: it didn't work out that good for him.'

This was despite Solskjær's finish, Ole registering the opener. Moncur says, 'We came away and I said: "Well, look, Ger, I can only tell you what I saw when he played as a front player." He said: "Don't worry."'

Moncur laughs. 'You *can* only go on what you see and that was it, the move died a death. The following pre-season an agent took Ole to Manchester United and after a couple of days Alex Ferguson signed him straight away. If he had come to Spurs, who knows? He might have been a different type of player; it might not have worked for him. I don't know. Someone's got to have a crystal ball to say what would happen. He was a good player. You could see, potentially, he could be a top player. That's what I thought and I've spent years and years in youth development. I've seen young players and you just get a feel for it. When you've got a watching brief, that's what you have, isn't it? He could've gone to Spurs and still been a great player, but it wouldn't have been the fairytale that you've got now. With him going back to Man U as manager.'

Told the story about Francis deeming Solskjær not good enough, Nils Johan Semb laughs. 'I have not heard this, but you have to remember at that time Ole Gunnar had to work a lot, run a lot from box to box. As a team we had to run a lot. And he is at his best, of course, staying in the box. In the box, he was a top international, the top level there because he always had to know how to score,' says Semb, who offers scant surprise at Solskjær's subsequent success as a United centre-forward. 'There are a lot of chances for a striker in a team like that.'

Solskjær ended 1995 as top scorer for Molde in Norway's top division, the country's season running from spring to early winter due to the weather. OGS was the spearhead in the heralded, so-called Three S's strike force, alongside fellow attackers Arild Stavrum and Ole Bjørn Sundgot.

The following summer, on 2 June 1996, Ole scored a memorable volley for Norway's senior team, the first of two goals against Azerbaijan as Jim Ryan, a coach of Alex Ferguson's at Manchester United, there to scout centre-back Ronny Johnsen, watched on in what ended as a 5-0 win. Ryan recommended OGS to Ferguson, who called Åge Hareide, Solskjær's manager at Molde, to ask if he thought Ole could play for Manchester United. Hareide had no doubt and informed Ferguson that, yes, Solskjær was of the quality required.

This proved a particularly prescient prediction.

PART ONE

Childhood, the Starlet Striker, and Manchester United

CHAPTER 1

The Solskjærs

'He takes the family to Grip where they
have a cabin.'

BRITA SOLSKJÆR

Ole Gunnar Solskjær grew up on Norway's west coast in
Kristiansund, a stunning fishing village of four inter-linked
islands fringed by mountain peaks on the shores of the
Atlantic Ocean.

This is where his heart remains, a storied life is centred.
Where Ole Gunnar met and fell in love with his future
wife, Silje. Where the football-mad street player immersed
himself in English football. Where he made his bow in the
senior game – for Clausenengen FK as a teenager. Where
the name Ole Gunnar Solskjær first broke into Norway's
football consciousness.

For Scandinavia, Kristiansund's climate is mild, hitting freezing or just below in January and December, and

maximum highs do not generally reach above 17°C in summer. 'The climate is coastal. Rain and wind, a little snow. Ole and I, all of us, played all year round,' Arild Stavrum, his childhood friend, says.

Growing up as one of Kristiansund's roughly 25,000 inhabitants, Ole Gunnar's obsession with football meant inclement weather was part of the fun, as in the comical moment when one opposition goalkeeper attempted to kick the ball out, only to see it stall in mid-air and blow back towards him. Then, when he tried a second clearance, the wind blew the ball again and a corner was conceded.

The elements never stopped matches. 'That is all we did. We played,' says Arild. 'It is a saying in Norway that kids are born with skis. Not in Kristiansund – winter sports have no place. It was only football, and basically that was it. We didn't have time for much more.'

Ole Gunnar's parents, Brita and Øyvind, have their home in the neighbourhood of Karihola, where a 10-year-old Ole would first be a 'manager', taking charge of a street team that included many friends who would also grow up to enjoy careers in the game.

Ole's childhood was contented and safe and secure. Øyvind worked for the local council for over half a century, and Brita at a communications company for 30 years. A room in their house is devoted to Ole's career, where pictures of their son, Manchester United annuals and other memorabilia of an ever-evolving life have prominence. Both of Ole Gunnar's parents have his kind-eyed demeanour and calm outlook and are devoted to their son and his sister, Brit, who is four years younger.

Brita grew up in Bøfjorden, to the east of Kristiansund,

and moved there at high-school age. She once said, 'I'm from the country and after coming here I then lived in the town. After high school I got a job at what was then called Telecom. I've never been active in any sport, but we followed the kids when they got into football – lots of driving here and there and washing jerseys. Our daughter Brit has three children who are all enthusiastic about football, as are all three kids of Ole Gunnar.'

Øyvind was born on the island of Smøla, which is close to Kristiansund, and in the same Møre og Romsdal county as the village and Bøfjorden. He recalled: 'My dad was born on Smøla. His mother died when he was four years old, so he was placed with the sister of his father. She lived on Solskjel Island.'

The resemblance of 'Solskjel' to that of the family name is probably no coincidence as the island was formerly called Solskjær, though Øyvind is unsure whether this is where their surname originates. *Sol* can mean 'sun' and *kjær* 'reef' in Norwegian, but there are other meanings.

Odd Williamsen, a Kristiansund historian, offers clarification. 'Solskjel is a small island where up to 200 people lived in the old days. These were farmers and fishermen. A famous Viking battle took place here. Solskjel is north of Kristiansund, south of Smøla. When the Danish priests came here after the Reformation in 1536, they started to write what they thought they heard, a kind of audio-writing. So, the name of the biggest farm and most of the people became Solskjær. As of 2012, only 60 persons use Solskjær as a family name. Most people who descend from Solskjel use the name Solskjær.'

Williamsen describes the island's proximity to Ole Gunnar's hometown. 'You have to use two carriers. First, the car ferry. Then a small cable ferry rented out by the people living there in the summer, so everyone on this island has to have a certificate to drive this – 200 or so have a certificate that signifies the person has a captain's licence. It's run by cables and is the only way of going from the mainland to the island.'

Solskjel's Viking battles occurred less than a thousand years before the birth of OGS on 26 February 1973 in Kristiansund, into a family that he remains close to despite a life that has been played out in public since he was a young man. As Erik Nevland, a Norwegian striker who was at Manchester United with Ole, says: 'He protects himself, his family, and doesn't want to make a big fuss about it – this shows a little bit the person Ole is.'

Ole Gunnar's interest in English football as a child was mirrored by his hometown's historical bond with the United Kingdom. Kristiansund's oldest inhabitants can be traced to 800 BC and many current residents descended from the Scots who arrived in the 18th century to trade in cod, its dried form – *bacalhau* – and salt.

Williamsen says: 'From 1735 up into the 1800s, Kristiansund was dominated by British *bacalhau* merchants. They were mainly people from Cullen, in north-east Scotland, who had learned the trade in America and Newfoundland and took their business to Norway and started this processing of cod. But only for export, not for sale domestically.'

Ole Gunnar would grow up to be the village's – and his nation's – most famous export but historically there have been many others. Williamsen says: 'Kristiansund is based on this. First it was wood, timber and cheese in the old days, in the 1600s. Many old houses in London are built from timber – timber from Norway, including this area.' Modern-day Kristiansund's economy remains the same. 'It's still an export centre,' Williamsen adds. 'Today it's oil – which was found in the 1960s.'

Growing up in a cultured locale imbued in Ole Gunnar a rounded world-view. 'Kristiansund has had opera as long ago as 1805 because of the *bacalhau*,' Williamsen says. 'The export people were foreigners, and the traders here were very orientated to what the buyers were interested in. They wanted to have the same cultural things as they had seen in Spain, Portugal, England and Germany. So there was the local opera and theatre and literature. They even had English newspapers in something called the Club Society, which dates back to 1789.'

The young Ole Gunnar's society could simply be called Football, Football, Football. The stadium Solskjær began his career in – Clausenengen's 4,000-capacity Atlanten Stadion – is now a multi-purpose venue. To move around Kristiansund's many islands, Ole would take the tiny yellow-and-green Sundbåten ferry, a service that dates from 1876 and calls itself 'the world's oldest public transport service in uninterrupted use'.

Ole attended Dalabrekka skole from first to sixth grades – 1980-86 – where he was a quiet pupil who also did gymnastics, although football was already the obsession. Then, he was a pupil at Langveien ungdomsskole (seventh to ninth grades), before high school at Atlanten videregående skole. In the playgrounds of both these schools he would practise the finish that would gather him many goals when a professional player: a precise shot threaded just inside the post.

Teachers recall how, even at a very young age, Ole

Gunnar's talent and ability made him the star footballer, games in which he featured often having to be weighted so as to make them competitive. Classes could be small, perhaps only 13 boys, and in competitions teams would often be made up of 'Manchester United', 'Liverpool' and 'Tottenham Hotspur', Ole Gunnar virtually always enjoying the status of the standout player.

He met future wife, Silje, when they were both junior players at Clausenengen, where later his prolific goalscoring would precipitate a move to Molde FK in 1994. 'Silje was also a very good footballer,' Ole said once. 'We often trained together when we were younger. In Clausenengen we had a group in the morning that I really was too old to be part of, but I was allowed to be with anyway. Actually, I just wanted to because Silje did.'

Øyvind was a Greco-Roman champion wrestler and, though the young Ole tried the sport, he found a dislike for it, as the moves caused sickness and dizziness, making him the polar opposite of the natural his father was.

'Ole Gunnar himself wrestled for two years – between the ages of eight and 10. He was not really very good – not as good as he was at football. But he was a big part of that world and with his dad would go training, running up and down the highest mountain in the area, which is about 830 metres high. Up and down,' Tore Lovikis, director of the Kristiansund Atletklubb, told the BBC.

'It was football instead,' said Øyvind. Football, plus a liking for The King – not Denis Law or Eric Cantona, as each were christened by Manchester United fans – but the hip-swivelling Elvis Presley, the King of Rock and Roll, despite the superstar crooner having died when OGS was four.

'He was a very big fan,' Brita told Norway's *United Support* magazine. 'I have a *bursdagsbok* [notebook] where I write all important birthdays and there I discovered that many years ago he had written in it "Elvis Aaron Presley".'

When Ole became United's interim manager his parents, as they previously had, remained in the background – granting a single media interview only. This modesty, which is a kind of shyness, has been passed down to Ole Gunnar, who, despite the glare of the football world he has inhabited since a teenager, is more inclined to the quieter life.

What OGS is far more enthusiastic about is the sport he has adored from the first time he kicked a ball. His children, Noah, Karna and Elijah, share the love. Noah, 'tall and calm like Ole', according to Brita, is now at Kristiansund BK and made his debut against Manchester United on the club's summer 2019 tour – having previously trained at Carrington on occasion when visiting his father at the club.

This sporting pedigree derives from Øyvind, who was also a player for Clausenengen in the 1950s along with two elder brothers. 'When I was playing football and doing wrestling, I was a training junkie,' Ole Gunnar's father told *United Support*. 'Ole and the grandchildren have also always been keen on training. Exercise is important.' Øyvind, though, did not initially tell his parents just how talented a wrestler he was. 'One day they received a letter from the club – they were a bit surprised,' he said. 'Then I won the championship – in 1958, when I was 14 years old. I became Norwegian champion for juniors and from 1966 was Norwegian champion in wrestling for six consecutive years through to 1971.

'During that time, I competed in both the European Championships and World Championships, which were great experiences. We got to experience cities like Minsk, Bucharest and Calgary. The visit to Minsk made an impression – this was for the European Championships in 1967. At the hotel there were armed guards on every floor, so I understood how good we had it in Norway.'

Øyvind's success gave him a national profile that allowed interest and attention to seem natural to Ole when growing up. Tore Lovikis recalled: 'Øyvind has his own wrestling move named after him – it's one that he developed himself and that's very difficult to beat. It's an intelligent move, one that people never expect to happen. They would always be expecting one thing and he would do this something else. It's a big a reason why he won so many championships.'

The grounding Ole received from Øyvind and Brita, which accentuated his own natural level-headedness, has proved invaluable during his career. 'I will certainly point to the job Brita has done over the years to scrub suits and sports clothes, every day,' Øyvind said. 'The bag was thrown on the floor and clothes washed and dried the next day. I dare say that he appreciates the job that his mother has done in all those years. The same applies to food and diet.'

Brita said, 'It was very important for him to always get to training, so we made sure that everything was ready.'

Ole's paternal grandmother was also a vital part of the close family environment in which he thrived. 'She lived until she was 97 and was Ole Gunnar's nanny when he was little. They used to glue football cards into a book – at the time, he knew every player on every team in England,' Brita said. Young Ole's compulsion to soak up as much knowledge as possible about football remains unchanged, according to his mother. 'He is very quick to buy books on managers to read about how they lead their teams. Those about Ferguson, Mourinho, Klopp, the Liverpool manager, and City's Guardiola. He has read all of these. All about their approach to training, their systems of training, philosophy, so I think he has, in his own management, brought a part of all of these.'

In the warmth of his family home, Ole could follow where his passion took him. 'I used to write down all the team sheets and formations from *Match of the Day*. I think I knew everything about football in England. I watched tapes of Kenny Dalglish, Gary Lineker and Marco van Basten and tried to imitate them. I remember trying so hard to copy a Peter Beardsley trick,' he told the *Manchester Evening News*.

Brita remembers how Ole Gunnar, 'when smaller, sat in the middle of the floor and followed the game on television'. Then, according to Øyvind, 'after the game it was straight out to practise some tricks he had seen. At the time, he could recite all the names of all the teams. That's how Noah and Elijah are now.'

This contented, safe childhood in an unassuming area of Norway proved vital to the formation of Ole Gunnar the person, and thus the player and manager he would become. It gave him a sense of self-possession, an ability to handle the game's intense spotlight, and allowed him to harness his natural calmness and intelligence. All qualities that helped point the quiet young boy along a road that began in windblown Kristiansund, where kicking a ball became a life-altering obsession.

CHAPTER 2

Football Manager on the Streets

'We played a couple of hundred games
together as children.'

*ARILD STAVRUM, LIFELONG FRIEND AND
CLUB AND INTERNATIONAL TEAM-MATE*

From childhood to first career success at local club
Clausenengen, and leaving for Molde FK at the age of 21, Ole
Gunnar had a spectrum of defining influences.

To the fore was Øyvind, whose pedigree as a successful
wrestler drummed into OGS how vital practice and training
were, and who was a constant presence. Two coaches, Ole
Olsen and Ole Stavrum, were important mentors who developed Ole technically and physically as the schoolboy star rose
through the age groups at Clausenengen, up to his first-team
debut and beyond. There were also his friends and the teams
he founded and played for on the streets of Kristiansund, which
allowed a constant day-to-day fix of the game he adored.

None of these, though, would have had any effect if Ole Gunnar had not been desperate to improve, not been open to advice. Even when very young he understood instinctively the need to learn constantly.

Arild Stavrum was eight when he first met Ole, whose home was on Korallveien in Karihola, Arild's on Fredericiaveien in the adjacent neighbourhood, Brunsvika. Arild, whose own playing career would take in Clausenengen, Brann, Molde, Stabæk, Helsingborgs, Aberdeen, Beşiktaş, Mainz and Norway, before he became a teacher and writer, says of Ole: 'He was always there. We come from the same town, played for the same team – on the street and for Clausenengen.'

The pair were close from the start, Ole as effervescent as a kid as when older. 'We grew up together – I mean, we played together from the age of, I don't know, as long as I can remember,' Arild says. 'Maybe we were seven, eight years old and we played all the time until I went to become professional first – Ole Gunnar is a year younger than me. He was the same then as when he grew up. I suppose it's more difficult for you to think about when younger because you're just friends and I don't know how much you notice each other's personality.

'At the beginning, we were just joking and being around each other, being friends and playing together. Ole Gunnar and I were kind of the same – all we wanted was to play football and we trained all the time, played all the time. Just football all the time. We must have played a couple of hundred games together as children.'

Solskjær and Stavrum were a prolific partnership in their youth, playing for Clausenengen age teams. 'The one match that stands out is a game against Dahle – another team from

Kristiansund. We were about 13 and won 32-0, and me and Ole scored 22 combined. The game got mentioned in *Adresseavisen*, the biggest paper in mid-Norway,' says Stavrum, of a publication that dates from the 18th century. 'It is from Trondheim – I guess this is the first time Ole was written about outside Kristiansund.'

Ole Gunnar and Arild created a street team they named Brunsvika Sports Verein, while also at Clausenengen and attending the same primary and secondary schools. Of Brunsvika SV, Arild says: 'It was Ole Gunnar and me and a few other guys. We trained together and basically won every game. We played on small pitches, gravel pitches in the neighbourhood. Also in other parts of town and in competitions started by a lad who was a few years older than us, who arranged different cups.'

This was in an area called Røssern and the boy was called Kjetil Thorsen, who, still a friend of Ole Gunnar's, would become CEO of Kristiansund football club, which merged with Clausenengen in 2003 and is now in the Norwegian premiership. Stavrum says: 'Before the merger Kristiansund was only once a top-flight team – in the 1950s – and they basically lost every game then. Now, they are by far the best side that has been from the city and Kjetil is the main driver behind this.'

Kjetil, who is four years older than Ole Gunnar, describes how as a child he and friends sourced their own pitch, then built a clubhouse and stand for it. They were not the only ones. 'There were a few of these clubs run and established by kids,' he says. 'When I was about 10, my parents built a house a little outside of the centre of the city. And close to there was a spot where we could have a playground and some other free public space. So we built a small football ground and organised our own teams and had competitions for all the kids in the street who wanted to play. At that time, in the early 1980s, everyone was building new houses in this area of Kristiansund. We were going around every house and asking if they had materials we could use to do this. Then we invited kids from all around Kristiansund to make their own teams and have a club. I think there was about 70, 80 teams actually and we had adults helping us – our parents – but the kids, we organised it.'

'I met Ole Gunnar this way and later also played for Clausenengen in the same team as him,' Kjetil says. 'Ole Gunnar lived near Brunsvika and the name of his team, Brunsvika SV, was probably named after Hamburg SV. My team was Røssern and at first we played friendly games, then we started some cups.'

Ole Gunnar, Kjetil and their friends engaged in real-time *Football Manager* – for children. 'It was like a game where we thought we were chairmen and managers and players all at the same time,' Kjetil says. 'We had tournaments during the year, maybe three or four. It was very nice and there are a lot of those kids from that time, who ran these small clubs, now also in our professional game – they are chairmen or have other roles in clubs, or some work in the Football Association here in Norway. This was our education.'

Another childhood friend of Ole Gunnar's was Christian Michelsen, who is three years younger and who, like Kjetil, is now at Kristiansund BK, having been the manager since 2014. Ole Gunnar and Christian had their own side – a different one to Brunsvika SV. 'Ole actually started his managerial career by being the manager of our team – "Maranico", which was a merger of Maradona, Platini and Zico,' says Christian, whose family home was on the same street as Ole's and who also played with him at Clausenengen. 'I've had the pleasure of knowing Ole Gunnar since I was a little boy. Kristiansund is a small town so everybody lives close to each other – five minutes' walk and you are together. So, I've been fortunate to have Ole close. When he went out for extra football practice when he was young, it was natural for me to do the same and so did many other kids too.'

In Arild, Kjetil and Christian, Ole Gunnar had three friends whose love for football equalled his. It was a happy and – surely – telling coincidence that Ole grew up surrounded by boys whose dreams were also to turn the game of their youth into a professional life. Michelsen reflects on a hometown that was a football hotbed. 'For most of the history of Kristiansund we have created a lot of good players but not a good team,' he says. 'A lot of individuals who, like Ole Gunnar, have gone on elsewhere. Lately, we have also tried to keep the best players in the town.' Of his Kristiansund side, Christian adds: 'Now, we have a team in the top division in Norway – that's fantastic.'

Solskjær's parents comprehend how crucial this time was in their son's development. 'Ole started his own team and was both treasurer and had a leadership role,' said Øyvind once. 'They played a cup every Saturday and Sunday, set up the programme and arranged everything.' Brita identified the manager the young Ole would become: 'In the street football he was certainly a leader type, had a leading role in his team. He is very determined but treats everyone with respect – this is a great leadership quality.'

Playing not managing, though, was Ole's prime focus, and Kjetil recalls a boy who took time to develop physically. 'I've seen him play football from when he was a kid – Ole Gunnar was always a good football player. He scored a lot of goals in those tournaments, but when he reached 13, 14 years old, some of the other kids were much bigger,' he says. 'There were a couple of years where Ole was average as a player because of his size. But when he turned 17, 18, he became more physical, and then he was the number one. A "late bloomer".'

When Ole Gunnar was a junior player at Clausenengen he and Arild were schooled by Arild's father, Ole, and another coach, Ole Olsen, who would become a lifelong confidant and an assistant, working alongside OGS when he managed Molde. Ole and Arild trained at Clausenengen's various venues – a grass pitch at Engabanen, an Astroturf facility at Idrett, and at Kunstgressbanen in the centre of Kristiansund – for 12 years until Arild left at age 19.

Of Ole Gunnar's time at Clausenengen, Ole Olsen says: 'I coached him from 10 to 12 and from when he was 16 until 21. He was a natural goal-getter from an early age and understood football. At 10 years old he was shooting with both feet – it's very rare to see in young boys, that they use both feet. He was a natural.'

Ole was often accompanied by his father, and the champion wrestler impressed on his son the need to 'train to be good', says Ole Olsen. He points to an in-game intelligence that allowed OGS to squeeze the maximum from himself as a footballer and hinted at the coach and manager he would become. 'Ole could read the game and play everywhere on the field. The way he trained was very much to do with the influence of his father. And, Ole Gunnar was always very interested in the game – the tactical side of it – at a young age. He was also a cheerful and calm person. He caught the eye immediately – it looked like he slept with the ball in his bed.'

OGS's off-field persona was reflected when lacing up his boots and entering the field. 'He didn't get overexcited, even if he scored many goals – he was the same boy,' Olsen says, adding that Ole was popular and proved a natural mentor of younger boys as he grew older – again an augury of the astute man-manager many of his players would describe him as. 'I have a son called Kenneth; he is a year younger than Ole Gunnar, and Ole was good with him.'

Blond and curly-haired – and sporting a mullet as he grew up – Ole Gunnar could not stop scoring for Clausenengen's youth sides. One photograph shows him holding nine fingers up in celebration of the number registered against a beleaguered opposition team.

Solskjær broke into the Clausenengen first team at 17, playing his first game at the Atlanten Stadion in 1990, given his debut by the manager, Ole Einar Stavrum, Arild's father. 'It was a third division club,' says Olsen. 'An amateur one – we got crowds of between 500 and 600, and the last year before Ole left we played in the second division.'

During this period Ole worked on his physique. 'He scored a lot of goals every year but he was much smaller than the others and was hammered a bit. We trained his strength and when this began to work, he was pointing only one way. He was the best player I had but he was also a very good comrade with the other boys. He was the leader of the gang because of his ability and everyone looked up to him, but he didn't let that go to his head, never. He was very special as a footballer and as a person too,' Olsen told the BBC. 'I've been in football 50 years and I've never seen anything like him, never. He was one in a million.'

OGS was to prove prolific as a starlet striker for Clausenengen, while also serving mandatory national service during his third year at the club. In Norway national service is for 12 months at the age of 20, and Ole did his in the south of the country while still training at nearby clubs, taking advantage of the special dispensation given to athletes.

At his first club, OGS is still recalled as supremely dedicated and focused on improvement. 'He trained a lot,' John Marius Dybvik, the Clausenengen chairman, told the BBC. 'He was not satisfied by only going to organised training. He also trained by himself. He was highly motivated as well as extremely talented and he scored lots of goals for this club.'

Here, again, Øyvind's influence was key. 'Wrestling is a great sport for building up character, you learn how to take a hit, and it helps ground people,' Tore Lovikis said. 'Ole Gunnar's dad would tell him he must always train his weaknesses. In wrestling you must very much focus on that – improving what you are worst at, to make yourself a better person all round. So Ole Gunnar would train his weaker foot.'

Ole's incessant work yielded rich reward as he proved a revelation when moving from junior football to the senior game in Clausenengen's first team, scoring 109 times in 112 league appearances. When Clausenengen were promoted from the third tier in 1994 he scored 31 goals in what would be Ole's penultimate season at the club.

He was prolific throughout his decade-plus years at Clausenengen. 'I scored 14 in an indoor tournament, in the quarter-final of the Norwegian championship,' Ole told

FourFourTwo. 'Goals were my trademark, although if my team didn't create chances I wouldn't have been the one to stand out and dribble past three or four people. I was very dependent on my team-mates. We only had crowds of 50 or 100 at Clausenengen but we were best mates growing up together in the third and fourth tiers in Norway.'

Ahead of the 1994 domestic season came Ole Gunnar's breakthrough at international level as he made his Under-21 debut for Norway, a 10-minute substitute appearance – entering for Tore André Flo – on 2 February in a 3-3 friendly draw with Demark in Kuala Lumpur, the side also featuring soon-to-be Molde team-mate, Petter Rudi. This was the first of a run of 19 appearances at the level, ending the following year, in November 1995, with a 2-1 win over Holland in Herenveen, when he scored the last of his 13 goals for the Under-21s.

On selecting Ole Gunnar for that first Under-21 squad, the manager, Nils Johan Semb, says: 'Ole was 20 and playing for a very small club – Clausenengen – in the third level of Norwegian football. I saw him the first time when I had a small training camp on the west coast for which I just picked players from that part of Norway. Then I took him on a trip to Malaysia, where we had games against Malaysia, Denmark and Japan. Because we had some players that were injured, I gave him a chance. And he took his chance during that year.'

Ole made seven of his 19 appearances in 1994, scoring his maiden Under-21 strike in the 3-1 win over Malta on 13 December in Valletta, the island nation's capital. 'He scored his first goal in his sixth game for the Under-21s; after that he scored 12 times in the next 13 games,' Semb says. Solskjær's count of 13 goals still ranks him as the fourth highest scorer for the Under-21s more than two decades since his last outing, behind Steffen Iversen (14), Flo (15) and Trond Fredrik Ludvigsen (16).

While Ole was still at Clausenengen, Semb's Under-21 side faced Molde. Self-determination is a fundamental element of OGS's make-up, and by scoring he may have further convinced Åge Hareide, the manager, that he should sign the young player. 'We played a friendly game and he scored two goals,' Semb says. 'For that Under-21 team I used three strikers – Tore André Flo through the middle and Ole Gunnar left, Steffen Iversen coming from the right. They did really well, all of them, they were fantastic. And when I took over the national team, in 1998, I used the same three players for the qualification for Euro 2000, and we qualified and then they played all the games at the Euros.'

The month before Ole's final Under-21 appearance came his bow for the senior Norway side. This was in a friendly with Jamaica at Kingston's National Stadium on 26 November 1995, a month after the Under-21 match against Denmark in Stavanger watched by John Moncur and Gerry Francis. Ole started alongside Arild Stavrum in the Caribbean and scored the 80th-minute opener before a William Wilson equaliser just before the end, the XI of Egil Olsen (who would later coach Wimbledon), including Petter Rudi, Claus Lundekvam (soon to move to Southampton) and Frode Grodås (soon to join Chelsea).

At Clausenengen, in 1991 Ole met Jim Solbakken, who would become his advisor and close friend. It was a relationship that would develop, and became closer at the end of the decade when Solbakken helped broker a deal with the Norwegian Football Federation following a dispute over promotional rights with Ole and other international team-mates.

'I'm probably his best friend on a personal level,' Solbakken has said, having departed Clausenengen to work on an oil rig. 'I had the goal of becoming a platform manager in the North Sea when I played football with Ole Gunnar. I've often scolded him because he pulled me out of my dream and placed me in the world of football. But he needed help when he ended up in the spotlight after 1999. Then it was natural for him to use his buddy to protect him a little.'

At Clausenengen, Ole studied with another friend, Kjetil Thorsen, during the last summer they played together, in 1994. 'We started economics, but I applied for a job in another football club here in Kristiansund. They searched for a managing director; I was around 24 and got the position,' he says. 'Ole Gunnar was sold to Molde at the same time, so I was going to a club in the lowest level and he was going to the top level, but from 1994 to 2000, at my club we went from seventh level to the third level in Norway. That was my journey.'

After a prolific four years in the first team Ole Gunnar had outgrown Clausenengen and Molde moved for him at the close of the 1994 season – beating Rosenborg, among other suitors – his hometown team having finished sixth, and his record for the club ending with an impressive strike ratio of 1.05 goals per game. He departed for Molde, which was around 80 kilometres from Kristiansund and in Norway's top flight, ahead of the 1995 season. Molde's previous campaign had featured a Norwegian Cup triumph, the 3–2 victory over Lyn in the final at Oslo's Ullevaal Stadion with a side that included OGS's future Norway team- and room-mate Kjetil Rekdal, midfielder Petter Rudi and Arild. 'I played for Brann and then went to Molde in 1994 and Ole Gunnar came to Molde the next season,' he says. 'We joined up again after the couple of years we didn't play together.'

Ole Gunnar Solskjær's rise had begun. At Molde, Ole's career continued upwards, the trajectory now pointing towards the rarefied air of the elite professional game.

CHAPTER 3

The Three S's

'He was in the army, actually.'

ÅGE HAREIDE

Ole Gunnar left Clausenengen for Molde at the end of 1994 as a goal-machine centre-forward: the prime quality that moved the manager, Åge Hareide, to sign him. It was a transfer south for Ole from Kristiansund to a coastal neighbour in the same Møre og Romsdal county, Molde the capital and big brother to OGS's hometown.

'We were proud when he left for Molde,' said John Marius Dybvik, the chairman of Clausenengen FK. Yet Kristiansund and Molde are disparate towns, rivals due to their relative proximity, differing cultures and, of course, because of the football clubs. When Ole joined Molde it was the next stage of a life and career and he was cast as a kind of off-field 'diplomat' between the two, according to Mads Langnes, a curator at Romsdal Museum in the Molde municipality.

'It is interesting that the towns, only an hour's drive from each other, are so very different,' he says. 'Kristiansund is a lively place with a differing blend of people and a lot of colour – like a Latin city in Norway. But traditionally with problems – a lot of jobless people, health and social problems. Molde is at the other side of the scale, with the well-educated, good health and a good economy. But maybe also a bit more boring. It is a well-known truism that a funeral in Kristiansund is far more fun than a wedding in Molde. Also that you cannot tell if the football club in Molde has won or not. When the local supporters come out of the stadium after a match, they are so serious and well dressed, and no one roars in the streets. There has been a kind of "fight" between the two towns for centuries, as it often is between neighbours.

'In this case, Ole Gunnar Solskjær is an interesting person – because he has been a kind of diplomat between the two towns, and people in both Kristiansund and Molde think of him as "ours".'

Åge Hareide was very happy when the young striker became his, signing OGS in December 1994. 'It was the finishing,' says Hareide, who is 65 and a former Manchester City and Norwich City defender and the current Denmark manager. 'When he played in the second division for Clausenengen – actually the third highest level – we studied him for a while, had heard about him because we'd bought other players from the same club. They always have a very good youth system for players there. So, I went to see him. I was impressed with his finishing ability, really. He didn't look strong, was a bit tiny, but his technique was good and his finishing extremely good. That's why I wanted to have him.'

Norway's football bush telegraph buzzed about the boy

from Kristiansund. 'I heard he was a good lad but I never spoke to him. We had a need for new players when I came back as a coach in 1994, after the team got relegated in '93,' says Hareide, who previously managed Molde from 1986 to 1991. 'I first tried to sign him ahead of the 1994 season, but he said he wanted to play another year with Clausenengen.'

This last comment shows a maturity and self-possession within Ole, who would turn 21 in 1994. 'The clubs got in touch, but he had to go to the army – in Norway, at 20, you have to go for a year,' Hareide says. 'When I was a player, I had to try to find a club to train where the army was based, that was up north, you know, with bad facilities. But later on, the international players got a special dispensation – they were able to train with the team and be based in southern Norway where facilities are better. This was to allow players to stay fit.'

Solskjær ensured he remained in shape while on national service. 'Ole trained with some other clubs at the top level while in the army,' Hareide says. 'We got in touch with him again – several other bigger clubs had tried to get him, like Rosenborg, who had more money than us. I had a meeting with him in that winter of '94 and then we got him to sign for us just before Christmas – for the '95 season. I was very pleased because he had grown, had become stronger [as he matured] and still kept his touch for finishing, so that was good.'

The young Ole Gunnar knew his mind. 'He had been invited to train with Rosenborg,' says Bjarte Valen of the Norwegian supporters' club. 'But they wanted him to go and train with the youth team rather than the senior squad and he said, "No, I'm not interested in that." And when Åge Hareide wanted him to sign for Molde, well, even though there were other clubs interested, Solskjær was very sure that that was the right team to go to. He could stay near to his home. It was the right club and was also in the right location for him.'

He was still a relative unknown. 'Ole cost about 200,000 Norwegian kroner, which is, back then, around 16,000, 17,000 quid – ridiculous,' says Bjarte. 'It's hardly anything, really. He was one of these talents that had been looked at by different clubs, but I don't think it's right to say that all the top teams in Norway were desperate to sign him. That's probably going too far – he might have been one of those players who went a little bit under the radar. If people really knew how good he was, what kind of finisher he was, which he thoroughly showed in the upcoming season, they would have given Molde much more competition to sign him.'

Hareide now combined Ole Gunnar with two other forwards, Arild Stavrum and Ole Bjørn Sundgot, in attack for Molde. He describes the chemistry between them as instant: Ole was the No. 9, Stavrum and Sundgot forwards who operated either side of him, with Petter Rudi's creative influence from midfield also key.

'They were three different types of player, though they all had speed,' says Hareide. 'And Rudi, who we later sold to Sheffield Wednesday, was really central in feeding them because he was brilliant – he would be the player of the year in Norway in '96, a footballer who played three seasons for Wednesday. He provided a lot of goals and chances, was the assist maker.'

Solskjær's debut came at Brann on 22 April 1995 before 9,902 at Brann Stadion. The XI sent out by Hareide read: Morten Bakke; Petter Christian Singsaas, Knut Anders

Fostervold, Sindre Magne Rekdal, Trond Strande, Daniel Berg Hestad, Tarje Nordstrand Jacobsen, Rudi, Stavrum, Sundgot, Solskjær. Ole announced himself in predictable manner. Bjarte Valen says, 'I was there and remember he scored twice – and the interesting bit about that game really was that he had been scoring goals, lots of goals for Clausenengen, and he was undoubtedly a big talent and here he was continuing the same.'

It ended 6-0 to Molde, Ole's bow one to remember, as Bjarte notes, with Ole Sundgot also registering twice, Stavrum once. OGS had served notice of himself at the top of the Norwegian game, his very first strike at elite level coming 28 minutes in. 'That Brann team was actually quite good,' Bjarte says. 'It reached the quarter-finals of the Cup Winners' Cup, where they lost to Liverpool but they knocked out PSV Eindhoven on the way. Yet Molde were all over them in that game. They won 6-0 and it could've easily been more. They just completely outplayed Brann – I've never seen anything like it.

'Watching Solskjær live, seeing a player live for the first time, you think this guy is good, but you don't know for sure whether he's going to be a fantastic player five years down the line.'

The prolific start from the attack Ole spearheaded was no fluke. He and it were to prove a consistent menace to defences. His home debut came the following week where, at Molde Stadion in front of 4,430, Viking were beaten 5-4, OGS scoring a hat-trick (on 22, 26 and 75 minutes), Sundgot twice.

Solskjær, Sundgot and Stavrum were soon dubbed the Three S's. Hareide says: 'This combination liked attacking the space behind the defence and Ole would attack this way particularly well and he would often score – Ole was very clever at doing the right things and creating space for other players and, also, his movement in the box was fantastic. We worked a lot on that in training, basically because we were really poor defenders – as a team.'

Molde began the season in flying form. 'We won the first six games in a row and were top of the league.' In this run, Ole only failed to score in two games – against Lillestrøm and Stabæk – and he registered a second hat-trick when Hødd were beaten 7-2 on 16 May 1995, Stavrum also scoring three times.

Solskjær was rapidly proving a natural at Norway's highest level, Stavrum says. 'We had just been promoted from the second highest division in Norway, having won the cup final the previous season, too. It was a really talented team and Ole Gunnar came and after training for the first week Åge Hareide wanted us to play together, so he put me with Ole Gunnar and Ole Bjørn Sundgot.

'It must have been a nightmare to be striker number four in that team, as they never got a chance. We were playing the same three up front every game, every training session, because our manager was so certain that this was going to work. In the beginning when training it took some time before it did, and I think maybe if it was a different manager then it wouldn't have been successful. He kind of thought, "This will be great."

'[Ole Gunnar] had the same qualities at Molde as when he went on to play for Manchester United. He was absolutely the best at making sure his first touch put the ball in the right place. He was always taught as a kid how to get control over the ball. When you do that, he was easy to play with because

I would just play the ball up to him and he would control it – fast. And then he could play me in behind the defence or we could play the other striker in behind the defence or he would go for a shot.

'He was always so quick doing this. When you see a lot of the goals he scored for Man United – it's that control over the ball, and he then curls it in the top corner, fast and really precise. Those were the things that I think made his career, made him a brilliant striker: his ability to control the ball and shoot from both sides.'

Ole Gunnar was able to interchange positions, offering Molde a different option and illustrating his flexibility. 'Then, of course, when you play and play, things start to work,' says Stavrum. 'All of us got more confidence and it just exploded after the season started. We were winning games and Ole Gunnar was scoring goals and it was a fantastic thing to be a part of. The line-up was Ole Gunnar at centre-forward and me and Ole Bjørn outside of him, but during games we could change positions a lot so Ole Gunnar could suddenly be a winger and I could be a striker.'

Ole revelled in Molde's gung-ho style but the team could suffer defensively. 'Sometimes everything could go wrong because we attacked all the time. There was usually a big gap at the back,' Hareide says.

A nadir came in the 7–0 hammering suffered at home against Tromsø, who would finish sixth, nine points behind Molde, whose title challenge fell away. After the opening sequence of six consecutive victories, they won two consecutive matches once more only, though Ole and the team were never lower than second place. Yet if this was Molde's finishing position, there were 15 yawning points to the champions, Rosenborg – a fourth crown in a run of 13 titles on the bounce for the team from Trondheim.

'Better sides exploited us,' Hareide says. 'We finished second instead of winning the league that year. But I liked the way we worked – we had an average age of 22 in the team and there was so much spirit and joy to play. These guys played and ran and played. Sometimes they made a mistake but that doesn't matter when you're young. The three scored 49 goals that season and Ole scored 20 of them.'

Ole and company had impressed despite the fading challenge. 'When the season finished, Molde had fallen behind a little bit, but for the first half, Molde was playing some mesmerising football,' says Bjarte.

Molde's record was 14 wins from the 26 Tippeligaen matches, with seven defeats, and 60 goals. Ole's contribution of a third of this total made him the first Molde player to register 20 in Norway's top flight: a memorable elite-level debut season. He also scored twice in the Norway Cup in the 4-0 first-round win at Brattvåg. And on his European football debut, in the UEFA Cup Winners' Cup on 10 August 1995, an 85th-minute equaliser to secure a 1-1 draw at Belarus's (now defunct) Dinamo-93 Minsk and then the opener in the 2-1 return leg victory of the first qualifying round tie. The following month, in the first round proper, he scored again – in a 2-3 defeat at Paris Saint-Germain.

His goalscoring form alerted scouts across the continent, including those of Hamburg in Germany and Italy's Cagliari. And in England, too: Steve Perryman took over IK Start, the club based in Kristiansand on Norway's southern coast, and he would soon spot Ole on the country's football highlights shows and alert John Moncur at Tottenham Hotspur.

But for now, a fortnight after Tottenham's interest officially ended (for the time being anyway), OGS's first season at Molde ended with an impressive 29 goals in 34 appearances in all competitions, this by far the highest contribution to the Three S's total of 59. The rise of the street footballer from Kristiansund to Norway's elite level was complete, Ole Gunnar ending as third highest goalscorer in the Tippeligaen in his inaugural season.

What was the key to this continuing success? Åge Hareide is clear that Solskjær was a keen listener and supremely intent on learning and improving. 'What he did is the same, I think, as he's done later on as well in his career – he took notes on the exercises at Molde, the training we did: what we did, whenever we did it. He also did things on his own when training was finished. He had timetables for these sessions, would put a cone by the posts, and took shots aimed at them, the idea being he scored in off these.

'When he went to play for Man United that was fantastic, because his accuracy and the way he had worked paid off. He was so precise in everything he did. This shaped him as a player *and* as a manager. He was very fond of details. As he said, small details could change if that shot goes in or not, goes over the crossbar or outside the goal. He was so determined in his work. When I coached Ole, he said: "If you shoot this ball inside the post, it could always go in."

'He never missed the goal when he was shooting. All the players can shoot the ball everywhere, but Ole was so accurate in his work. That impressed me because he was young. It's what made him really good because he had this quality.'

Solskjær was easy to coach. 'He's a unique person in many ways because he's completely ideal in what you want from a footballer,' says Åge. 'You got questions from him, he always wanted to know about the team, would sit down and look at various situations that might occur during a match. In those days we didn't have the sophisticated equipment we have today, so you had to rewind and fast-forward the video tape back and forth to see how he finished, see his accuracy, or the technical movements or the pace of a move – all these kinds of things.'

This is more evidence of Ole's inner drive, a kind of X factor that allowed full realisation of potential. Ole Gunnar's determination to be the best he could be began as a kid in the school yard and as the young footballer with Clausenengen. When this brought him a move to Molde he became ever more ambitious, striving for excellence.

The next season Ole continued to be a force. There were 11 goals in 16 Tippeligaen appearances in 1996, starting with a hat-trick in an 8-0 trouncing of Moss FK in the first game of the campaign. Bjarte Valen says, 'You were looking at Solskjær and thought he was such a natural finisher. Sometimes, a lot of the goals he scored – he made it look easy, but I don't think they were. It's just a matter of being in the right position at the right time.'

There were only the 16 appearances in the league because of what happened just after the halfway mark of the term: the performance of a lifetime (so far) in Norway colours against Azerbaijan on 2 June. This was his competitive debut for the senior national team and Ole Gunnar took charge of the moment in a manner that might be dismissed as cornball Hollywood fare if it were not what actually happened.

This was no multiplex fictional flick. Some 14,012 souls were inside Oslo's Ullevaal Stadion, including Jim Ryan, the assistant of Alex Ferguson, Manchester United's manager. Ryan was there to watch Ronny Johnsen, then of Beşiktaş of Turkey. But cometh Manchester United's assistant manager, cometh OGS, who seized the narrative by scoring twice for Egil Olsen's team in a 5–0 rout of Azerbaijan in the World Cup qualifier.

Yet again, Ole Gunnar made himself unignorable. Particularly as his first strike was a scorcher of a volley that oozed class and quality. Olsen's XI was strong, featuring Henning Berg and Johnsen (later of United), Stig Inge Bjørnebye (later of Liverpool), Alf-Inge Håland (later of Manchester City), Øyvind Leonhardsen (later of Liverpool) and Petter Rudi. Ståle Solbakken, a Lillestrøm midfielder and 1995 Norwegian footballer of the year, had opened the scoring on eight minutes, when, after 37 minutes, the ball was hit towards Solskjær just inside the D of the Azerbaijan area.

In one graceful movement, Ole Gunnar first chested control of the ball before then, as the No. 11 began to drop to the ground, moving to strike it sweetly with his left boot, beating Aleksandr Zhidkov to the Azerbaijan goalkeeper's right. The finish is vintage Ole Gunnar: marginally inside Getman's crossbar, marginally inside the post – as he had practised from youth. The celebration is nonchalant as Solskjær turns in the Oslo sun to greet his jubilant team-mates.

This was goal number three of his 23 for Norway and he scored later to notch the fourth, this one – as became his custom for Manchester United – at the death. This time a long ball from Frode Grodås, the Norway goalkeeper who would win the FA Cup with Chelsea in 1997, is relayed to Solskjær and his left foot is again lethal, once more a triumph of timing, as he volleys past Zhidkov from just inside the area.

Ryan was impressed and told Ferguson all about the 23-year-old striker he had just seen. United had just won the Double, a second Premier League and FA Cup single-season triumph in three seasons.

What happened next was a fantasy for Ole Gunnar. He would recall to *Inside United*: 'I knew there was a United scout at my game, but I didn't think he was watching me. I thought he was there for one of my team-mates. I said, "Yes, yes, yes!" There was no way I would say "no" [to United].'

Åge Hareide describes how the £5.5m transfer occurred. 'Jim Ryan, Alex Ferguson's scout, was at the Azerbaijan game and afterwards Alex Ferguson phoned me – he had done that before, to ask me about Norwegian players. He phoned me this time about Ole Gunnar Solskjær and, just before that, Ole had said to me that his agent had a possibility, I think for Cagliari in Italy and Hamburg in Germany.

'He asked me about these clubs and I said, "Don't go there. Stay here. Be patient, stay." So Alex phoned and asked if Ole could be good enough for Man United. I said, "Yes" because he's such a good finisher and will be an even better player. Alex said, "Okay." I remember because I was in Amsterdam looking at Amsterdam Arena – Ajax's ground – for ideas as we were looking to build a new stadium in Molde. He phoned me when I was walking around and we talked about Ole.

'When I came back from Holland, Ole came to me and said, "Åge, what about Man United?" I said, "Yes, absolutely. I think you should have a go there. Do it." That was the summer of 1996, we didn't have many matches left before we had the summer break – I think we had one. We were second in the league and Ole asked me if he could come off if he scored a goal. I said, "You have to score the goal later in the game for me. I want to keep you on." He scored the last one, we won 5-1, and after he scored, off he went.'

Eight days later he signed for United: a lightning-quick deal in any era of the game. 'My agent said Manchester United were impressed and wanted to do something before Martin Edwards, the chairman, went on holiday,' Ole told *Inside United*. Here the owners of Molde, Kjell Inge Røkke and Bjørn Rune Gjelsten, two of Norway's richest men, were significant in ensuring his dream transfer went smoothly.

'Røkke and Gjelsten are important people in the life and career of Solskjær,' says Mads Langnes. 'When Ole Gunnar was to be sold to Manchester United, they agreed and flew him to Manchester in their private jet plane. From that time, OGS and Røkke and Gjelsten have enjoyed a special relationship.'

Ole said: 'They flew me to Manchester because they could see I wanted to go there. I'll always appreciate that.'

On arrival at the club to seal the deal there was a clear indication he was an unknown in English football. 'I got to Old Trafford and a tour guide thought I was going for a tour,' OGS old *FourFourTwo*. 'He was talking away, then at the end he asked me: "So what are you doing here?" I said I was going in to sign a contract. He was speechless. But he gave me his pen and I signed the contract with that pen.'

He was certainly the least heralded of the quintet of signings made by Ferguson that summer: Ronny Johnsen, Karel Poborský, Jordi Cruyff and Raimond van der Gouw were the others, yet Hareide believed Ole could prosper.

'To be honest, the only fear I actually had was the physical side of his game because of the Premier League, the tempo and everything else,' he says. 'If it was just about the finishing – no problem for him at all, because he will score goals. I think that happened because of how Ferguson played him; he didn't have to be a target man as he's not that type of player really. His movement and cleverness in the last third of the field made him still able to convert chances.'

Despite the decade being barely half completed when Ole signed for Ferguson, United were already the dominant force of the 1990s, of the new Premier League era that began with the 1992-93 season. That term had Ferguson's team of Giggs, Cantona, Paul Ince, Mark Hughes and Andrei Kanchelskis bridging a 26-year gap to the club's last championship of 1966-67. The following season the title was retained and the FA Cup won to give United a first Double, the side now featuring Roy Keane.

Two years later in 1995-96, and with Gary Neville, Nicky Butt and David Beckham now established in the XI, and Andy Cole a £7m British record signing, United had just completed their second Double when Solskjær landed. The one major trophy that continued to elude Ferguson and his scintillating side was the big one: the European Cup. On a May night in 1999 Ole Gunnar was to be the star turn in the most dramatic 90 minutes of Manchester United's history . . .

PART TWO

Manchester United's Darling

CHAPTER 4

Glory in Catalonia

26 May 1999

'I wish I had scored a goal like that – my
God, what a feeling.'

RAIMOND VAN DER GOUW

The dream is over – surely.

No second European Cup. No unprecedented, immortal
Treble for Manchester United. No place in football history for
Ole Gunnar Solskjær. The Premier League and the FA Cup
are already claimed by Manchester United, Ole a key player in
each triumph. But: Bayern Munich lead 1-0 through a sixth-
minute Mario Basler goal and the 32-game unbeaten streak
that began in mid-December is surely finished. Ole waits to
come on in the Champions League final with nine minutes
left and it looks desperate – United lack inspiration and more
vitally just cannot score, as heartbreaking defeat moves closer.

51

Except. Ole enters the final on 81 minutes and what fol-
lows is the stuff of fantasy. From his schoolboy dreams on the
Kristiansund streets to the home of Barcelona at the Camp
Nou in Catalonia.

It is the grandstand finish. The show-stopper. The
Hollywood blockbuster slowed down to a frame-by-frame,
millisecond-by-millisecond act; not just slowed but super-
slowed, like everything happens and sounds as if in a parallel,
hyper-real reality. Hyper-real edging towards the surreal.

Out in the sweet sultry Catalonia night. The Mediterranean
Sea is nearby. The Balearics lie south. And Ole Gunnar
Solskjær is here, now. David Beckham is here, now. The
rest of Ole's team-mates are here, now. Teddy Sheringham,
Dwight Yorke, Peter Schmeichel, Denis Irwin, Jaap Stam,
Gary Neville, Ronny Johnsen, Nicky Butt, Ryan Giggs.
They are all on the Camp Nou turf when it – it, *happens*.

Consciousness has never felt like this; not for the Bayern
Munich players about to be gut-punched and soul-destroyed.
Not for the Manchester United fans who surge with joy like
never before. Not for Alex Ferguson, a true phenomenon
of the game. Not for all adorers of sport and theatre and
sensation and those unadulterated moments that fix in the
memory. Become a permanent part of existence.

Not for Ole Gunnar Solskjær, the perma-twinkling man-
boy, touched by his own magic this eve.

Ninety minutes are gone and still Bayern Munich lead
1-0 when David Beckham wanders over to the left quadrant
to take a corner. Peter Schmeichel arrives in the Germans'
area, illustrating how desperate the team are. 'The big goalie's coming up,' says Ron Atkinson on co-commentary.
Beckham fires the delivery towards Schmeichel who is

between the penalty spot and the line of the six-yard box; the Dane challenges for the ball and it bounces through to Dwight Yorke. Ole is standing near the goal-line with Oliver Khan, the Bayern No. 1, in front of him, Mehmet Scholl on the right post, and when Yorke's header becomes a mis-kicked clearance that goes straight to Ryan Giggs, Scholl is about to regret departing his station. The Bayern substitute does so to try to play Teddy Sheringham offside but he fails, because when Giggs's mishit volley with his weaker right foot dribbles to the No. 10 he is onside and levels the final to the soundtrack of thousands of disbelieving United fans inside the stadium rending the Spanish night and Clive Tyldesley on commentary declaring of this remarkable Ferguson team: 'NAME ON THE TROPHY'. Cut to Ole raising his arms in celebration, then Ferguson and staff doing a jig on the bench.

Slow, *slow* motion.

Bayern kick off – stunned. And then a few more sec-onds pass before *this* occurs. Before Ole Gunnar Solskjær *occurs*. The Clive Tyldesley TV commentary – 'Is this their moment?' The David Beckham ball again, the Teddy Sheringham flick-on, and the right-footed/big-toe finish from Ole as Tyldesley's voice seems to slow to a slur: 'Where did you see Ole Gunnar Solskjær win it with virtually the last kick of the game?'

The winner comes from a second Beckham corner moments after the one taken by the United No. 7 that created Sheringham's equaliser. It is from the same left quadrant of the pitch, and when Beckham places the ball down he is sur-rounded by photographers: one lime-green- jacketed snapper has to quickly shift out of the way.

Beckham's delivery is a precise and dipping ball into the

near-post area where Sheringham this time is assist-maker, rising unmarked to head down and across Oliver Kahn's goal. 'A few seconds later we had another corner and Becks took it again,' Sheringham recalled to *The Guardian*. 'I went to the near post and got in front of my man but I got up a little bit early and realised I wouldn't be able to score, so I flicked it on to the far post into an area where I knew one of our players would be.' He is correct. Ole has placed himself in the supreme poacher's position, right in the six-yard box, right in front of Kahn, and he does not move, does not need to move as the *ball* moves towards him.

'Beckham into Sheringham,' says Tyldesley, and now time stretches, the 90,000 inside the stadium, the millions watching across the globe pause, as Ole Gunnar leans forward, sticks out his boot and spears the ball into the top left-hand corner past Kahn, the net rippling in the satisfying way it always does to signify a goal.

'AND SOLSKJÆR HAS WON IT!'

Ole Gunnar struggles to fathom what he has done but it is beautifully, undeniably true: he is transformed into the man who will for ever be the winning goalscoring hero of the 1999 Champions League final. Now he is sprinting past Kahn's right post, towards the advertising hoardings, the banks and banks of photographers, running arms aloft, then going down onto his knees for a surf across the turf, then back up on his feet to be mobbed by his team-mates, Dwight Yorke and Ronny Johnsen reaching him first, then Jaap Stam. Johnsen, the team-mate who was in the Norway side the day Jimmy Ryan watched him sparkle against Azerbaijan three years before. The day that began the journey to this moment, right here, right now.

'Manchester United have reached the promised land. The two substitutes have scored the two goals in stoppage time and nobody will ever win a European Cup more dramatically than this,' Tyldesley declaims. 'Champions of Europe, champions of England and winners of the FA Cup. Everything their hearts desire.'

Madness, pandemonium. The night stretches and tears. Things will never be the same again. Not for Ole Gunnar Solskjær. He has redefined Manchester United, redefined his team-mates and Ferguson. Redefined who he is and how he will be viewed from now and ever more.

He is 26 years old.

Nine minutes to change a life – actually, the extra three of added time, awarded by referee Pierluigi Collina at the end of the regulation 90.

On this hot night in Spain, Raimond van der Gouw was the reserve goalkeeper, the understudy to Peter Schmeichel, who, in Roy Keane's absence due to suspension, was Manchester United captain. What Van der Gouw witnessed he can hardly fathom, even two decades later. 'I was sitting on the bench next to Phil Neville and Phil asked me, "What do you think?" Well, my prediction had been 2-1 to us, and so the game went on and with 10 minutes to go we are 1-0 down, Lothar Matthäus went off, and at that time Phil said to me: "Well, Raimond, what do you think? Do you still think it will be like that – 2-1?"

'And I said, "Hmm, it will be really difficult now, but we'll see."'

Teddy Sheringham entered on 67 minutes for Jesper Blomqvist and, 14 minutes later, Ole for Andy Cole – he was not happy about having to wait so long. He was about to be *very* happy. Matthäus was superseded by Thorsten Fink on 79 minutes, Mehmet Scholl replaced Alexander Zickler on 70 minutes, and Hasan Salihamidžić came on for Basler on 89 minutes.

Van der Gouw recalls, 'Then we scored the first goal from Teddy, I think after the 90th minute, and all the subs – they came off the bench and were sprinting to the players and celebrating.'

Tyldesley says: 'Ole nearly scored with his first touch. Anything that I said in the buildup to the equalising goal was a reflection of something that had started to happen in the three or four minutes before it came. It wasn't solely down to Ole but there'd been just a slight change in the balance of the game. Part of that was that Ole had threatened their goal with literally his first involvement in the game.

'It was that gathering sense of destiny and fate.'

Van der Gouw: 'And then before we knew it, we were sitting down again on the bench and we scored the second one, from Ole, and to describe the feeling is really hard. I mean you can use so many words, but it's: "*Wow*".

'How can you say: happiness. It was the most exciting feeling; the game was over – the highest level of football. You have won the Champions League – and it was so special. And, also, when you think about it – 1-0 down, and we did it so many times that season – came back – and this was the last trophy after we won the Premier League, the FA Cup, and then the Champions League.'

The euphoria of Ole's goal even affected Tyldesley. 'At that moment I broke the cardinal rule of commentary: do not call the winner across the line until the line has appeared.'

The Treble. It has never been done before in English football. It has never been done since. It is Everest with a K2 on top, stretching to the stars, to conquer. Imagine scoring the goal that completes the shimmering trinity of League, FA Cup, European Cup?

Imagine being Ole Gunnar Solskjær.

The title was sealed 10 days earlier, on 16 May, via a 2-1 victory over Tottenham Hotspur at Old Trafford. Les Ferdinand opened the scoring after 24 minutes for the visitors before David Beckham equalised on 42 minutes and Andy Cole struck the sweetest of winners in the 47th minute to give Manchester United the crown. This was a Sunday, the Premier League season's final afternoon. The following Saturday, at Wembley, Newcastle United were beaten 2-0. Teddy Sheringham scored on 11 minutes, Paul Scholes seven minutes into the second half. Ole Gunnar played the whole final but this is not his moment.

Now, *now*, it is Ole's moment. Three minutes into added time. He bridges a 31-year gap to a second European Cup for Manchester United, from the 4-1 defeat of Benfica at Wembley on 29 May 1968. Bobby Charlton (twice), George Best and Brian Kidd score for United, Jaime Graça for Benfica.

Pierluigi Collina blows the whistle. The final is over. Time goes out of sync. The Treble is done. Ole Gunnar Solskjær, from street footballer and street manager, to *this*.

'So all the emotions came out,' says Van der Gouw. 'We decided the game in the last part of the game – we did it again. Ole did it so many times. His name made history. I wish I had scored a goal like that – my God, what kind of *feeling* to have had like that.'

Now comes the celebration. 'It was madness,' laughs Van der Gouw. 'We stayed for such a long time on the pitch. We had the cup in our hands, we walked around, we went to the supporters, we lifted the trophy there. There was cheering and shouting – we took a lot of pictures. And we were enjoying that time, and we went into the dressing room and started singing again and drinking – and drinking it in.

'Madness, I mean that was the final moment of a very top season. The feeling was: "Finally, yeah we did it, we got the Champions League." And, yes, Ole scored the most important goal. The most important goal of his career.'

Having joined the club at the same time as Ole Gunnar, along with Ronny Johnsen, and living near to OGS, travelling to training with him, Van der Gouw developed a particular bond with him. 'He stayed just the way he was, he never became arrogant. He was normal. Actually, it's not normal, of course, don't get me wrong. We had all the stars – Beckham, Roy Keane, Andrew Cole, Dwight Yorke, Jaap Stam, Schmeichel. Say the name – they were all stars and Solskjær was also one of them, but he was never arrogant, he stayed the same person. He deserved a lot of respect for the way he was.'

Arild Stavrum, Ole's childhood friend, says: 'It was an interesting experience watching my old friend score that goal. Of course, it's a highlight of his career. It's a fantastic thing that a Norwegian did that.'

Ole's take is to talk of wishing it to have been earlier in the game. 'I never get tired of answering questions about that match. I was a substitute and, to be honest, I was a little bit frustrated,' he told fifa.com. 'I was itching to get on and things weren't going well. I knew I could do something and I had an inkling that something big was going to happen for me. The manager put Teddy Sheringham on quite early, but I still felt that we needed something different.

'Jimmy Ryan said to me: "We're going to win tonight," and I responded, "Yes, I know. I'm going to come on and score." I can't remember too much about it, but when I see the video, I know that when I ran on the pitch, I was ready. As a striker, you have to be positive and think you're going to score, but I just had a feeling. And, thankfully, that's what happened.'

After Sheringham's equaliser Ole Gunnar's thought process was typically clear-eyed. 'It's two miskicks: Giggsy miskicks and Teddy finishes with a miskick I think, although he might not admit it! Everyone went mad. Everyone crowded round Teddy, even Peter Schmeichel, who was up for the corner – except me,' OGS told *Opus*. 'I headed back to the halfway line, concentrating. I was focused. I thought: "Now you're going to play another half an hour [of extra time] – don't waste your energy chasing Teddy."

'There's a long diagonal pass to the left wing. I run over from the right wing to reach it, [Sammy] Kuffour comes with me, I try to get past him with a step-over but he gets a foot in. It's a corner. We run into the box. He's [Kuffour] got a hold of me. He's grabbing me all the time. The cross comes and it's nowhere near us – it goes to the near post – so he lets go of me and looks at Teddy, and that just gives me the half-yard I need to move away from him.

'The goal? It's one of those that you score one time out of five if you're lucky, because you haven't practised that finish. You just do it. You just guide the ball on. More often than not it goes over the bar – and there's a man on the far post so, other times, you won't guide it above him. There were so many things that could have gone wrong with that finish. It was just instinct. Perhaps I'd done that finish once when I was younger. Perhaps there was some muscle memory there.

'Whether I'd scored 50 goals or 500 goals for Manchester United, that winning goal would have always been remembered as it won the Champions League in a very dramatic manner. There are so many people who have come up to me since and said: "That was the best night of my life – don't tell my wife." It seems like such a big moment for them to meet me. It was the same for me when I met Diego Maradona in 1986. We'd driven from Kristiansund to Oslo to watch Norway play Argentina, and after the game I stood there. Maradona finally came out and I just about managed to put my arm out and touch him.

'My first thought [about the winner] was: "Am I offside?" You're scared the referee is going to blow. But then it was just complete and utter chaos. You don't manage to think. I strained my ligaments sliding on my knees to celebrate and I missed a couple of games for Norway that summer because of it, but it was worth it. Winning the Champions League is the best thing you could ever do as a footballer.

'I'd scored the winning goal in the European Cup final so many times in my mind. I was on my own in the playground, commentating: "He's going through one-on-one with the goalkeeper!" and thinking: *If I hit the back of the net now, we win – if I miss, we lose.* But that was in my head. Realistically, though, I never thought it would really happen – no chance.'

Before the final, Ole's room-mate, Jaap Stam, had been snoring and OGS could not sleep. So, just as he told Jim

Ryan, Solskjær called a friend in Norway to explain the feeling he had. The friend was due to work during the final, but Ole told him to get his shift covered so he could watch.

'Sometimes,' OGS said, 'you just get a feeling.'

CHAPTER 5

The Big Debut

'Solskjær – he's got another chance, he's got a goal!'

MARTIN TYLER

If the understated atmospheres of Kristiansund and Molde and their football clubs mirror Ole Gunnar's nature, he encountered the diametric opposite in Manchester, the north of England capital and cultural powerhouse.

Kristiansund will always be home for Ole Gunnar, where he began (and would love to end) his days, while in Molde he is the adopted prodigal son. Manchester, though, is a second home, the centre of a life's drama. He may have been a Liverpool fan as a boy, but as a man he is an honorary Mancunian, his accent now a mix of Manchester and Molde, the defining episodes of his career all tied to Manchester United, a club as central to the fabric of the city as its era-defining bands: New Order, Stone Roses, Happy Mondays, Oasis. A city that has, now, two of the world's defining clubs in Manchester United and Manchester City.

From the moment he landed in summer 1996 to sign for the team draped in red, Ole Gunnar loved what he found. 'I came at the same time and we lived in the same area,' says Raimond van der Gouw. 'He was in his early twenties when he arrived, normal, down-to-earth, and to go from Norway to Man United, it's a big step. A few of us players lived near each other – Jordi Cruyff, Peter Schmeichel, Henning Berg, who is also from Norway, and with Ole Gunnar, we would often drive in together. We had a good team spirit.'

Ole Gunnar was teased, not always taking this gentle humour well. 'He has a baby face,' Van der Gouw says. 'So he was always looking young – I mean, sometimes he didn't like that, but I wish they would say that to me!'

The Manchester Solskjær found in 1996 was one at the centre of the Britpop explosion, due to a band from Burnage in the city's south, Oasis, who were headed by the Gallagher brothers. This was a town moving on from The Haçienda, a world-famous nightclub which closed a year after Solskjær signed.

Dave Haslam, who DJed over 500 times at The Haçienda, points to the relationship between football and music. 'Manchester's football was having an effect on the wider culture in the early nineties – it was bigger than it had been any time since George Best in the 1960s,' Haslam says. 'There was a divergence in a lot of ways. A lot of people involved in Manchester music were proper football fans. The connection between football and the wider world began with the generation slightly before Solskjær. I was running clubs in town in 1992 – Lee Sharpe, Ryan Giggs, Nicky Butt [the last two

Solskjær team-mates] – they were the characters that we'd see. When Ryan Giggs was dating that girl off *The Word* – Dani Behr – he brought her to the Boardwalk.

'He didn't take her to a VIP club, he didn't take her to some cocktail bar, wine bar. He brought her to what was then a pretty grotty underground club that played house music and disco. That was on Little Peter Street, around the corner from The Haçienda, but it was a much more local, less touristy place. So, I think it was the Giggs generation at United – coming at the beginning of the nineties – that helped broaden the appeal of what Manchester meant out there in popular culture. A lot of the stuff in the eighties was too weird. Once you had Giggs and you had Oasis, it felt like that became the ordinary world. That was the world we inhabited. It wasn't ordinary in the sense of being dull. It made the city feel cool.'

Unlike Sharpe, Giggs and Butt, Solskjær was content to eschew the music scene, nightlife and fleshpots, his intro-verted nature and long-term girlfriend, Silje, meaning he was rarely, if ever, spied out enjoying Manchester's nocturnal attractions.

Like the city, the domestic game Ole found was on a high, following England's run to the semi-finals of Euro 96, Terry Venables's side playing a brand of football that was similar to Ferguson's Manchester United. In Alan Shearer, who twice turned down Ferguson – the second occasion earlier in the summer of 1996 – there was barracking-style No. 9. Martin Edwards, the chairman, had a contract agreed with Shearer, who had visited Ferguson at his house to discuss the transfer from Blackburn Rovers. According to Edwards, Jack Walker did not want Shearer going to a (then) local rival and, as the player was close to the Rovers chairman, he was content to join Newcastle United, his hometown team.

One of the stars of Euro 96 was among Ferguson's recruits: Karel Poborský, who surely attracted the Scot's attention with the memorable lob over Portugal No. 1 Vítor Baía at Villa Park that took the Czech Republic into the semi-finals.

Soon after, Ferguson presented Ole Gunnar, Poborský, Jordi Cruyff, Raimond van der Gouw and Ronny Johnsen to the media together. When Ole actually signed the deal on his £1.5m transfer it was low-key yet memorable. To *Inside United*, OGS recalled: 'There were no media or fans. I just turned up, signed it and went home.'

Rune Edøy, a journalist at Kristiansund's local newspaper, *Tidens Krav*, and friend of Ole Gunnar, said: 'Cruyff [who joined from Barcelona] was the star. All were presented together. Nobody asked Ole a question and nobody asked Ferguson about Ole.'

Solskjær's move was also smoothed by a European Court of Justice ruling in January 1995: the Union Royale Belge des Sociétés de Football Association ASBL v Jean-Marc Bosman (1995) C-415/93. In what became known as moving 'on a Bosman', after Bosman won a case he brought against his former club RFC Liège, players were now able to sign for free for another team if their contract had ended and foreign players were allowed freedom of movement within the European Union. This ended UEFA's so-called three-plus-two rule that allowed only three non-native footballers in the XI and two 'assimilated' via a club's youth system in continental competition.

Ferguson had taken advantage of this by signing Ole and the rest of the gang of five, none of whom were British.

OGS's move became official on 29 July, yet no news organ-isation reported it. In fact, not until 11 August is there a mention of Ole in any national newspaper, Ferguson being quoted as saying: 'He's got quick, skilful feet, and he's a real centre-forward,' by Paul Wilson in *The Observer*.

This was about to change – markedly.

On 25 August, a sunny Saturday afternoon in Manchester, Blackburn Rovers were at Old Trafford and English football was about to wake up to the finishing of OGS.

His debut was a 26-minute cameo and Ole ensured this was another landmark moment in his life. United's third Premier League match of the campaign would end 2-2, Paul Warhurst opening the scoring for the visitors on 34 minutes before Jordi Cruyff replied (39 minutes), and Lars Bohinen put Rovers ahead again (51).

The Spice Girls topped the charts with 'Wannabe' and Oasis's *(What's the Story) Morning Glory?* was number four in the album rankings as Solskjær waited hopefully and impa-tiently on the bench to enter. Ferguson's starting XI had read: Schmeichel, May, Pallister, Irwin, Johnsen, Beckham, Giggs, Neville P., Cruyff, Cantona, McClair; and on 64 minutes the manager finally told Solskjær to come on in place of David May, Ole Gunnar's underwhelming profile causing many fans to ponder *why* with United losing.

On commentary, Martin Tyler says, 'This is Ole Gunnar Solskjær, the second Norwegian signing of the summer, who is a striker, and it's goals that Manchester United need.'

And so here he is – Ole Gunnar stepping onto the Old Trafford turf for the first time, alongside his hero, Eric Cantona, as he begins his journey into the consciousness of English football. Who was to know, who *could* know, what was before Solskjær? How might the 23-year-old have reacted if a teaser of all that was to come at the club flickered across his vision?

'Take the chance, show the people what you're made of,' Ole tells himself on joining the fray. United have thus far won their season opener 3-0 at Wimbledon, a game that featured David Beckham's show-stopping lob from the halfway line of Neil Sullivan in the Dons goal. Then followed this by drawing 2-2 at Everton.

Six minutes into his first experience wearing the red shirt, of performing before the Old Trafford crowd, Ole Gunnar takes charge, registering strike number one for Manchester United, a tally that will end on 126 in 366 appearances, the first and last coming against the same opposition – Blackburn Rovers, Premier League champions of two seasons before.

The finish on the shot Ole puts past Tim Flowers in the Rovers goal has its roots in his obsessive practice since he was a kid of always aiming to put the ball inside the post – Ole figuring no goalkeeper is going to reach it there. In the Manchester sunshine, after Peter Schmeichel hoofs the ball high into the air there is a clever flick-on from Jordi Cruyff, and now Solskjær bounds past Chris Coleman, smashes a shot at Flowers, and when the rebound comes this time OGS spears the ball inside the left post where the visiting keeper has no chance. The celebration is calm – serene almost, like he *knows* he belongs in this company – but he is also delighted that it is Cantona who reaches him first, a sunrise of a smile taking over Ole Gunnar's face as realisation dawns. Even Coleman a few moments later congratulates him.

'I've been asked many times what's the greatest moment of my United career. Scoring that goal in my first game and turning round to see that Eric Cantona was the first one coming towards me celebrating, that just made me realise, "I'm at Old Trafford now",' he would tell *The Independent* a decade later.

Warhurst recalls the impact Ole made that day. 'He was an intelligent player who picked little pockets and took up good positions in attacking areas and could finish,' he says.

By the final whistle it is still 2-2 and Solskjær has salvaged a point. This is not the last time he will be the closing moments' hero.

'He's got tremendously quick feet for his age,' Ferguson says afterwards. 'He's made people sit up and notice in training. He scored twice in the reserves this week and you can't hold people back when they are performing like that.'

Ferguson had previously told him: 'For the first six months, play in the reserves and get used to England, then from January we might try to get you into the first team,' Ole recalled to *FourFourTwo*. But two reserve-team strikes plus an injury to Andy Cole gave Ole Gunnar an opportunity he seized. 'I scored six minutes into my debut. I knew I'd score goals at United.'

His self-reliance, self-confidence, is evident. Despite the array of glittering talent in Ferguson's team, Ole Gunnar refused to be awed, while his ruthless ability to finish impressed.

As Jordi Cruyff told *The Times*: 'His shooting was like a computer game. Press the button, turn the joystick and it always goes into the corner. Unbelievable. Ole wasn't superfast, tall or a shielder. He just worked hard but had an amazing instinct and ability to score goals. He had a "loose" ankle – when somebody without looking knows where the goal is and can always find the corner. *Boom*. The ball was in the net.'

The refusal to be the quiet man on the periphery would become the story of Solskjær's Manchester United career. He would be discontented not to be an automatic choice – and would inform Ferguson of this – but he was always ready when called upon.

Ferguson may have billed him in a perma-cameo role as his lethal substitute, yet OGS continually forced himself into a starring role. This demotion from the first-choice XI would come after a debut season in which OGS did enjoy starting status, scoring 19 times in 45 outings in all competitions: 18 of these were in the league, which would be his best for the club as he ended as the top scorer, registering seven more than Cantona's 11, and third overall, behind Arsenal's Ian Wright and Shearer for Newcastle. As Ferguson had told him, he was hardly expected to feature, being the fourth in a quartet of strikers that also featured Cantona, Andy Cole and Brian McClair, who would turn 33 in December.

After the substitute appearance against Rovers, Ole's full debut came on 14 September, at home, in a 4-1 win over Nottingham Forest. Unsurprisingly, he scored – the opener, on 22 minutes, a second for the club.

Ole Gunnar ended 1996-97 as a title-winner, Manchester United's fourth Premier League crown in five seasons being claimed with 75 points, seven more than the second-placed Newcastle. The final outing of the campaign was a 2-0 win over West Ham United at Old Trafford, Solskjær registering the first, after 11 minutes, in what was to be Eric Cantona's swansong.

The 1997-98 season was underwhelming for Ole. Cantona had retired and was replaced by Teddy Sheringham, a £3.5m buy from Tottenham Hotspur, while Brian McClair was a waning force. Yet this would be the poorest of the six terms before his serious knee malady, managing only nine strikes in 30 appearances, six of these in the league, but there were flashes of the predator instinct, three times scoring twice. These came in starts in the 6-1 and 4-0 wins over Sheffield Wednesday and Blackburn Rovers in the league (on 1 November and 30 November, respectively), plus in the 5-1 FA Cup victory over Walsall on 24 January.

This, though, was a pivotal year in Ole's relationship with United and the fans; a special bond being forged during a match in which he did not score yet endeared himself to the Old Trafford congregation.

On 18 April, Ferguson's side drew 1-1 with Newcastle United at home, David Beckham scoring on 38 minutes to equalise Andreas Andersson's strike on 11 minutes. As the match headed for a draw, Ole Gunnar provided a late, late show of a differing kind from his usual signature goalscoring.

It was comical *and* instructive, as the fallout from this taught OGS a little about the 'United way' and his genius boss, and was a lesson for the manager he would become. On 89 minutes, when a Beckham cross from the left broke to Newcastle's Temuri Ketsbaia, the fun began. Fun that would end in Ole being sent off – having only been on 10 minutes as a sub, for Gary Neville – and given an ovation for being so. But, first . . .

Ketsbaia, a Georgian midfielder, receives the ball outside the Newcastle area with Manchester United attacking the Stretford End, as they love to do in the second half. The clock shows 89 minutes, the Premier League table this morning showed United on 67 points from 34 games, leading Arsenal by a point. The Gunners are on a late-season charge under Arsène Wenger in his first full campaign and the club's 100th in competitive football. They will overhaul a nine-point gap to United (having played two fewer games) and the 5-0 win over Wimbledon at Highbury on this day will be the sixth of a nine-match winning streak.

Rob Lee receives from Ketsbaia just over the Old Trafford centre circle in United's half with a clear run at Raimond van der Gouw's goal. And he sets off. Except what is this coming from the Newcastle half, running at Lee, seeming to gain ground? It *can't* be. Yes, it *is*.

It's Ole Gunnar trying to reach for a fifth gear that will allow him, Rio Ferdinand-style, to move sleekly alongside the England midfielder and nonchalantly take the ball off his toes and remove the danger. But fifth gear is never found – it probably doesn't exist, OGS is no speed merchant – but he is faster than Lee, markedly, and is able to make up the 20-yard start he gave him but only to enable a scything-down of the Newcastle man.

'I had to catch Rob Lee before he got into the penalty area,' OGS told *FourFourTwo*. 'I made up some ground and thought: "I'm catching him!" But I stiffened up in the last five metres and realised I wasn't catching him.' Lee suffers an illegal challenge from Ole Gunnar. Cue Uriah Rennie, the referee, showing a straight red card and Old Trafford (minus the Geordie support) applauding Ole as a near-certain goal is saved and a point subsequently salvaged.

Ferguson, surprisingly, given his street fighter's instinct, was not impressed. 'I ended up with a fine and a hairdryer,' Ole says. 'I was applauded off but I wasn't applauded by the gaffer. He laid down the law with me and said: "At

Manchester United we never win that way; we win by fair play." It was an eye-opener for me. Some managers would have said, "Well done, son," but he would not accept that way of winning, which says everything about him.'

Ole's determination to hunt Lee down and sacrifice himself to do what was right (as he thought, before Ferguson corrected him) for the team also said something about who *he* was: to the supporters and his manager, who, privately at least, was surely impressed.

United ended that season without a trophy – a virtual collector's item in the 26-and-a-half-year Ferguson era, particularly in this decade, 1994-95 the only other campaign that was pot-less.

And Ole came close to leaving – and joining Tottenham for a second time in three years. The club, led by chairman Martin Edwards, were content for him to depart, but Ferguson had a different view.

'I've still got the fax at home, signed by Martin Edwards and Alan Sugar [the Spurs chairman],' he told *Opus*. 'They send you a fax to entitle you to negotiate if the two clubs agree a fee. But it didn't feel right. There was something in my stomach. I didn't want to leave. My agent did, but I was really stubborn about staying. He's since admitted I was right. The club agreed to sell me, but what you've got to remember is that the club and the manager are two different things. The chairman was happy for me to go, but I went to the gaffer and he said: "Stay", and that's all I wanted to hear. I could have made some money from leaving, but that wasn't an issue.'

At that summer's World Cup in France, Solskjær won caps 14, 15 and 16 in two group games, against Morocco and Brazil, plus the second-round meeting with Italy. Solskjær started the 2-2 draw with Morocco, was a 73rd-minute substitute as Norway were knocked out 1-0 by Italy in the second round, but it was the final Group A match against Brazil on 23 June at Marseille's Stade Vélodrome that Ole Gunnar came to view as the high point of his international career, despite the Norway manager, Egil Olsen, deeming him not worthy of a start against the World Cup holders.

Olsen, a manager with a penchant for the long ball, preferred Tore André Flo of Chelsea to spearhead a 4-5-1 against Brazil for a Norway that included Ronny Johnsen, Henning Berg and Stig Inge Bjørnebye of Liverpool. Brazil were managed by the great Mário Zagallo, who was known as 'the Professor' to his players due to his strategic style. As a diminutive winger, he won the 1958 and 1962 World Cups alongside Pelé, then coached him, Carlos Alberto, Rivelino, Jairzinho, Tostão and the rest of the breathtaking 1970 World Cup-winners to the iconic 4-1 final triumph over Italy in Mexico, becoming the first man to win the trophy as a player and a manager.

The match featured a considerable degree of needle between Olsen and Zagallo, due to the former having masterminded a 4-2 friendly win for Norway over Brazil in Oslo the previous year and Olsen's subsequent declaration that he could do far better with the players Zagallo had if he were Brazil manager. This moved the Professor to say on the eve of the group game: 'Olsen has said a lot of things about our team, but I do not read too much into them. I feel it is a tactic from Olsen to try to unsettle us before the match in Marseille. Our necks are going to hurt so much from Olsen's high-ball tactics we're going to have to have them massaged.'

Zagallo sends out an XI studded with superstars: Cláudio

Taffarel, Cafu, Gonçalves, Júnior Baiano, Roberto Carlos, Dunga, Rivaldo, Leonardo, Denílson, Bebeto, Ronaldo. On 78 minutes Bebeto scores with a header, Ole having entered for Håvard Flo 11 minutes earlier. Now came the grandstand finish as Tore André made a mug of Baiano before powering home past Taffarel, then midfielder Kjetil Rekdal smashed home a penalty a minute from time. On the bench, Olsen jigs and when Esfandiar Baharmast, the Iranian-American referee, blows for full time the party begins.

Ole is clear about the achievement. 'Being a part of the only team to beat Brazil in the first group stage is something I'm very proud of. I didn't score and I wasn't involved in the goals, but it was still fantastic. The strange thing about the match was that before it, Kjetil, who was my room-mate, told me: "Ole, tonight I'm going to score in the last minute with a penalty." And that's exactly what happened. So, maybe there is something about inklings and destinies, but I suppose we'll never know. The 1998 World Cup was strange – I was taken off after 45 minutes against Morocco, I didn't play in the second game, and then I came on against Brazil. It was fantastic being part of that team, though, and beating Brazil must be the highlight of my international career.'

At international level, OGS's brightness of thought was in evidence. 'Ole was a very clever player who could use both feet and had many different techniques,' says Nils Johan Semb. 'He may not have been great one-v-one, but in the box he was good. He was very smart, able to find the right position, could use his left and right foot. Yes, he had a repertoire – many things that he could use. He could score from any angle.'

The story of Ole Gunnar's international career is similar to the story of his United exertions, without the dying-seconds winner to claim lifelong glory. Solskjær was never Norway's Lionel Messi or a flashy member of the squad. Dan Eggen, a defender and team-mate at the 1998 France World Cup, recalls a quiet man. 'Ole was not a dominant player in the dressing room, he was very occupied with his own preparations, but after the match and in training he relaxed, was a normal, social and humble member of the group,' Eggen says. 'He rarely spoke before the whole group without being asked.

'There was not a bunch of vivid, crazy moments connected to his participation. I would stress his character as normal, often very positive and optimistic, and enjoying the atmosphere in small groups with games, discussions and just relaxing. He was obviously suited for international football, but as a player he was not scouted as one of the best at a young age. I believe he was a late bloomer, training hard and conscious of improving all the time, and being clever on what to emphasise – developing finishing skills which were absolute top class. I also believe that certain personal skills were extremely important in his career – he was unafraid, a perfectionist and very ambitious, and of course being able to adapt and to adjust is a positive too.'

The 1998 World Cup provided the standout moment of his modest international career but the Euro 2000 championships would be of note, too – for a non-football reason: Ole Gunnar left the Norway camp for the birth of his first child, his son Noah.

The 1998-99 campaign was the highlight of Ole Gunnar's club career, one he can countlessly relive and recall in his dotage. Brian McClair had left in the summer – for Motherwell – and Dwight Yorke was bought by Ferguson from Aston Villa for £12.5m and so, with Sheringham plus Andy Cole also under consideration, Solskjær had to compete fiercely for game time as one of the lesser-rated four forwards.

'Dwight and Andy clicked, they were a combination. Me and Teddy talked about the situation. We weren't unhappy,' he recalled to *Opus*. 'I didn't play a single minute in either leg of the quarter-final or semi-final [of the European Cup] and played in just three of the group games. I hardly started a match all season apart from in the FA Cup, and yet I was the one who got to score the winning goal – funny how it works out.'

Before his Camp Nou heroics came an equally vital winner in an FA Cup fourth-round tie at Old Trafford on 24 January against Manchester United's fiercest rivals, Liverpool. If Gérard Houllier's team had knocked out United, there would have been no Treble and this was the reality they stared at following an early Michael Owen header – on three minutes – conceded in powder-puff style.

Yet what then occurred was akin to a live, in-game rehearsal of how Bayern Munich would be beaten at the Camp Nou four months later: as thrilling and visceral as the comeback in Spain. Solskjær, again, started on the bench. And as United moved towards defeat he entered on 81 minutes, saw Dwight Yorke equalise two minutes from time, then took over. After a diagonal cross hit Paul Scholes in the Liverpool area, the ball found Ole Gunnar and, after characteristically quick feet, David James, the visiting No. 1, was beaten easily with a left-foot finish.

'Solskjæeeeeeeeeeeeeeeeeeeer!' roared Martin Tyler on commentary, the Stretford End went delirious and on the bench Ferguson and his staff jigged about. The media coverage afterwards pointed to Ole Gunnar's unwanted status in the side and his disgruntlement regarding this.

'I don't want to be remembered as a super-sub, no striker wants that tag, because we all want to be playing regularly,' he said. 'It is a great feeling to come off the bench and score goals, particularly against Liverpool because of the rivalry between the two clubs. But I want to start as many games as possible. I went in for a talk with the manager about it two or three weeks ago. I reckon we were both happy with the way the discussion went – I am doing everything I can to show I deserve more games.'

Ferguson concurred and pointed to Ole's prolific scoring form. 'If I was him, then I'd be coming right out with it and asking the manager what was going on,' was his canny take. 'It's difficult, difficult – 11 goals in [only] 11 starts is some record. But he'll get his games all right, I've told him that.'

A few days later Ole Gunnar was Mr Incredible as the headlines hailed his four-goal show in an 8-1 victory at Nottingham Forest on 6 February, Dwight Yorke and Andy Cole each scoring twice, Alan Rogers registering for the humiliated home team.

'Four Blimey Ole Boy: Striker Stars in Record Breaker' roared *The People*, which reflected the general tone of the coverage of his goal glut at the City Ground.

Told by Jim Ryan, Ferguson's assistant, to take it easy as Manchester United were already 4-1 up when OGS entered (for Dwight Yorke) on 71 minutes, Solskjær decided to do the polar opposite and, in the space of 10 minutes – 80 to 90 – another page in his personal folklore was penned, his quadruple a record for a replacement that still stands two decades (and counting) later. The 8-1 result was also then the highest-ever away victory in the Premier League and Yorke, signed the previous summer from Aston Villa, was impressed by the man he was keeping out of the side. 'You would think Andy and I had done all we needed to and then Ole comes on and scores four goals in 10 minutes.'

Ole's first was a far-post tap-in supplied by Gary Neville, who was given too much space to cross. Cue the venerable Barry Davies on commentary. 'When he comes on, he usually gets a goal.' The second arrived when Dave Beasant, the Forest No. 1, parried Ole's attempted chip and he collected the rebound and slammed it home from an angle in the right-hand corner of the area. Davies: 'Oh that's brilliant.'

The third derived from some Paul Scholes trickery: the midfielder found Ole with a pass that wrong-footed the defence and Beasant was allowed zero chance. Davies: 'Wouldn't you know it? The substitute is the one who gets the hat-trick.' The fourth was forced home following a Scholes miskick. 'Oh, they're just queuing up,' Davies declared, except Solskjær's sweet knack of being head of the line ensured he scored.

'The boy's a finisher,' Ferguson gushed afterwards. 'There's no question about that. We have tried playing him out on the left, but he is better as a central striker. That is where he prefers to play.' Ferguson, again, had to answer questions about Solskjær being behind Yorke, Cole and Sheringham in the striking ranks. 'His contribution has been terrific all season, but he wants more minutes on the pitch as well as the goals,' the Scot said. 'He realises he is up against two fantastic in-form strikers and he accepts that, but he has great ability to adapt to the pace of a game as a sub.'

Solskjær left the City Ground with the match ball, having not said a word publicly about a display that had Nottingham's local radio man pleading to the referee, Paul Alcock, to please 'blow the whistle, ref, and put us out of our misery'.

When United faced Newcastle United in the FA Cup final on 22 May, Solskjær was given a rare start as Ferguson made changes ahead of the Champions League showpiece the following Wednesday. He had also been in the XI for the semi-final, a tie with Arsenal that required a replay after an initial 0-0 draw after extra time in which Ole played the first 98 minutes. He was replaced by Ryan Giggs, who was the hero of the replay at Villa Park. In this match, which also went to the additional half-hour, Ole was off the pitch – after 91 minutes, for Dwight Yorke – when Giggs, himself a 61st-minute replacement for Jesper Blomqvist, collected a loose Patrick Vieira pass inside United's half and nonchalantly and breathtakingly beat a slew of Arsenal players (including Lee Dixon twice) before hammering home for a memorable 109th-minute winner.

In the final Ole did not score but values it as particularly precious because he was in the team for a game that mattered: a tilt at the second slice of the Treble. United had secured the Premier League with a 2-1 win over Tottenham Hotspur on 16 May, the Sunday before this penultimate FA Cup final at the old Wembley. On that sun-dappled day at Old Trafford goals from David Beckham and Andy Cole answered Les Ferdinand's opener to make the place a party. Solskjær was an unused replacement, Ferguson bringing on Philip Neville, Nicky Butt and Cole.

It was OGS's first action for United for over a month, his last appearance a full 90 minutes in the 3-0 win over Sheffield Wednesday on 17 April, in which he scored the opener. There had been action for Norway in between – on 28 April – with him this time registering the third strike in a 4-1 win over Georgia at the Boris Paichadze Stadium.

'Slips it back to Paul Scholes, sets up Sheringham: one-nil,' commentated Clive Tyldesley. 'He's only just arrived in the cup final – Teddy Sheringham. Instant dividends.' The striker had come on after nine minutes due to Roy Keane's injury and scored – through Steve Harper's legs – 180 seconds later.

OGS had an integral part in United's second, laying the ball back for Paul Scholes to drill a left-foot shot past Harper from distance. 'Clear daylight for Manchester United and the Treble moves closer,' stated Tyldesley. He was correct. *The Observer's* Amy Lawrence said of Ole's performance, 'Tucked into the right side of midfield to make room for Sheringham. A selfless performance, his determination set up the second goal.'

'The FA Cup is one of the best trophies you can win, Alan,' Ole would tease Alan Shearer (who never won it) 20 years later during United's run in the competition under his interim tenure.

A glowing Alex Ferguson praised the triumph and achievement that sealed a fine half-decade of domestic success for his team. 'That's fantastic – three Doubles in five years,' he said. 'The boys were marvellous. This has been a tremendous season and once again the players produced it when it mattered. Now we can start thinking about Europe. I feel great. The spirit of these players is such that everyone is looking forward to Wednesday. The confidence is very high – it's never-say-die and they don't want to be beaten.'

A few days later came Ole's starring role at the Camp Nou, his winner against Bayern Munich the last of 18 goals in 37 appearances for the season, 12 of these in the league.

Winning Manchester United a second European Cup did everything to affect and alter his status. But, as Van der Gouw pointed out, he remained humble and hungry, a real asset to Ferguson and the side, as his next standout display showed on 4 December 1999, the 5-1 victory over Everton at Old Trafford.

Ole Gunnar's paternal grandmother, then 80, flew to watch him perform that day. 'I was with my mother,' Øyvind said. 'Ole Gunnar scored four and she had never been outside Norway and never been up in a plane, so it was a nice experience.'

Solskjær did start this match, completing a second quadruple of goals in 10 months across 29 minutes – from 29 to 58. The first derived from a neat Paul Scholes throughball, Solskjær's shot having a touch of pace taken off it by a glove of Paul Gerrard, Everton's goalkeeper, on the way in. The second was via the other foot, the ball hit into the Old Trafford turf and beyond Gerrard, drawing congratulations from Ryan Giggs and Teddy Sheringham. The third was a header as Ole completed the 'perfect' hat-trick, this strike beating the by now thoroughly disgruntled Gerrard. Ole's fourth: a slide-rule finish past the visiting No. 1.

Everton's centre-back Richard Gough, a former Scotland captain, summed Ole up in a post-game interview: 'You don't think of him as having quite the threat of Cole, because his talent is not so obvious. He does everything efficiently. There isn't the great pace of Cole, or the extravagant finishing like the overhead kicks, and that almost lulls defenders into a false sense of security. But he punishes you, because he always seems to have the knack of finding that extra yard of space, and hitting the target. He might not be flashy, but he is a truly classy finisher.'

Solskjær's blend of easy-going nature and lethal finishing is a gift for Ferguson. Four days earlier Manchester United had beaten Palmeiras 1-0 – thanks to a Roy Keane goal – to win the Intercontinental Cup in Tokyo. Ole played the first half but showed no signs of weariness following the 14-hour flight home. Valencia were next up in the Champions League and, with Ferguson having left Andy Cole and Dwight Yorke on the bench, the newly knighted Sir Alex knew the performance against Everton had given him a selection headache. 'Ole is a marvellous finisher. What he has done has put pressure on me regarding team selection against Valencia,' the manager said. The following Wednesday Ferguson did retain Ole in a strike partnership with Andy Cole. The Champions League group game ended 3-0 and Ole scored in the 47th minute. When Ferguson took off a forward, it was Cole not Ole who was switched for Dwight Yorke. While he did not score again until 4 March, this was an important goal – a 45th-minute equaliser against Liverpool in a 1-1 draw at Old Trafford, Patrik Berger having registered for Houllier's team just inside the half-hour.

From here there were seven more finishes in 12 appearances as Ole Gunnar ended the 1999-2000 campaign with 15 goals for the club and a third league title – United crowned champions by a then record 18 points from second-placed Arsenal.

Ole Gunnar was halfway to the six Premier League titles he would end with for United – the others being claimed in the campaigns of 2000-01, 2002-03 and 2006-07, alongside a second FA Cup, in May 2004.

In summer 2000 Fabien Barthez, France's World Cup-winning goalkeeper, arrived and Jordi Cruyff, who joined when Ole did, departed. Barthez was Ferguson's sole summer signing and, these being the days when transfers were allowed all year round, he remained so. This illustrated how settled the squad was – good news for Ferguson's judgement, but not for Ole Gunnar as none of Cole, Yorke or Sheringham left. Solskjær was again the fourth choice and saw Sheringham, who turned 35 in April 2001, return a stellar season. His 15 league strikes made him United's top scorer, and he was voted both the PFA Players' Player of the Year and FWA Footballer of the Year.

Yet Ole did not go quietly on to the bench. He managed double-figure league goals – 11 in 19 starts – four behind Sheringham, two better than Cole and three more than Yorke, and scored 14 in total. And this season he voiced his unhappiness to Ferguson regarding his super-sub tag, ahead of a trip to Chelsea on 10 February 2001 – the only time in his career he did.

'The manager had always said he wanted to see me play a number of matches in a row. I was in the middle of a run, so when he left me out, I said: "I thought you wanted to see me play more games." In the end I played,' Ole recalled to *Opus*. 'That was the only time I've gone against him. For me, the relationship with the manager is everything. I've never, ever felt the urge to play for myself. This is the manager's team – if he picks me, I feel I owe him a good performance. If he doesn't, fair enough. And if he sends me on with 10 minutes left, those 10 minutes are going to be the most important thing for me, not the 80 minutes I don't play.'

Generally, though, he came to terms with his status. 'I didn't mind. Obviously, I wanted to prove to the gaffer that I deserved to play more, but he had me exactly where he wanted me,' OGS told *FourFourTwo*. 'He knew that when he put me on the bench I'd be pissed off, but I'd come on and give my all. And it had an effect on the opposition, because it became a myth that I scored every time I came on. I'd rather have that role and make an impact than play 200 games and be average. At times, though, it could be frustrating.'

After playing for Blackburn against United in Ole's debut, Paul Warhust was then playing for Bolton Wanderers in the Premier League. Of his threat, Warhurst says, 'Ole was always a dangerous player coming off the bench – he seemed to be more successful doing that than starting for whatever reason but some players it suits more.'

Cole and Yorke had become fading forces, the latter's application questioned by Ferguson, while Sheringham left in the close season ahead of 2001–02 as Ferguson recruited a striker Ole Gunnar would rate second only to himself as the best marksman he played with at Manchester United: Ruud van Nistelrooy.

The Dutchman signed for a £19m fee, a knee problem having prevented him joining Manchester United the previous summer. Cole would leave in December 2001 for Blackburn Rovers, Yorke the following summer, also to Rovers. Van Nistelrooy was the main man – he ended with 23 league goals and the PFA Players' Player of the Year; Ole had registered his second highest in the competition – 17. He did not make a league start until 22 September, scoring (of course) in a 4–0 win over Ipswich Town, his last strike coming in a 3–0 win at Chelsea on 20 April.

This was a rare trophy-less season under Ferguson, United finishing third – the lowest position of the Premier League era – and 10 points behind the champions, Arsenal. The big disappointment was being knocked out on away goals by Bayer Leverkusen in the semi-finals of the Champions League. Ole started – and finished – the first leg, a 2-2 draw at Old Trafford four days after the Chelsea match, but featured only for the last half-hour of the return, a 1-1 draw in Germany.

The 2002-03 season was to be as career-defining as his famous goal of May 1999 for Ole Gunnar, though not for any similar jubilant reason. At 29 – he would turn 30 in the February – he should have been at his peak. Yet with Ferguson adhering to a single-striker system, Solskjær remained behind Van Nistelrooy (Diego Forlán had also been signed in January 2002), and the Dutchman ended with the Premier League Golden Boot award, scoring 25 times, 44 in all competitions. Ole's 78th-minute winner against West Bromwich Albion on 17 August made it a 1-0 victory in the season opener and he would end the campaign with nine goals in the league, 15 overall in 57 appearances for United and the fifth of his Premier League-winner's medals.

He was often deployed on the right-hand side, on occasion usurping David Beckham, who had fallen out with Ferguson. Ole started the Champions League quarter-final second leg against Real Madrid at Old Trafford that featured Ronaldo being applauded off by the home faithful after scoring a memorable hat-trick.

He also played nine times for Norway this season in a total of 67 outings for club and country and 17 strikes, two of these international goals. 'I also managed him in the national side,' says Åge Hareide, who was Norway manager from 2003 to 2008. 'And I used him alongside John Carew for Norway because John could take all the hard, tough physical challenges, but Ole could move around looking for spaces. That's exactly what he did at Man United. It's always difficult to come from the Norwegian league to the top of the Premier League with all the quality required, but he did it in a fantastic way. I'm very pleased for him.'

Ole Gunnar would never again enjoy a campaign not blighted by the serious knee injury he suffered at the start of the 2003–04 season.

CHAPTER 6

The Darkest Days

Old Trafford, 16 September 2003

'When I was 27, 28, I never thought I'd be a coach. Then I got my injury.'

OLE GUNNAR SOLSKJÆR

The Champions League. The glory competition. The beaming lights and shining green sward. Tuesday and Wednesday night football fever as the continent's elite swagger and bedazzle with their ballet with a ball.

At the Camp Nou four years ago, Ole Gunnar Solskjær dazzled. One memorable night in May 1999 the super-sub stuck a toe out to stab home the winner against Bayern Munich, bridging a 31-year gap to Manchester United's first and last European Cup. Then knee-surfed across the turf in celebration, into immortality.

Solskjær's strike beyond Oliver Kahn in the Bayern goal

was surely the greatest finish to any football final anywhere, anytime. A poke of the boot still seen and recounted around the sporting universe. The cinematic beauty of it; a final-reel climax of sound and sense. A life-affirming thrill akin to a fantasy: precisely because it was a fantasy. For Ole Gunnar, for the football club that is showbusiness. Their comeback on 26 May 1999 is why football fixates the imagination from childhood to old age.

But here, now, on a September night in Manchester in 2003, the mind becomes murky, the fantasy soured for OGS. This is the dark side; Hans Christian Andersen gone grim. Manchester United versus Panathinaikos, the opening Group E match of the 2003-04 Champions League. Some 66,520 are inside Old Trafford and Ole is in the XI selected by Sir Alex Ferguson to face the Greeks. Sir Alex is Ole's 'second father', and he is about to require a lot of paternal patience and love because the injury he sustained against Wolverhampton Wanderers a fortnight ago in a Premier League game will not go away.

It will be a detested, unwanted presence for the next four years. It will linger, until, finally, Ole has to quit football in August 2007 at 34 when he believed he could have played on for Manchester United for many more years.

The knee, the knee.

During international fortnight he ignored the pain and travelled to Zenica and played all of Norway's Euro 2004 qualifier against Bosnia-Herzegovina for Nils Johan Semb's team. Semb does not recall if there was any hesitation regarding whether or not Ole would start. 'Ole was ready to play. But I can't remember if there was any discussion, doubt about that.'

Twenty thousand were at the Bilino Polje Stadium to see Zlatan Bajramović's 86th-minute winner, but Ole had his own problem. At the interval he could barely walk down the stairs to the team dressing room, yet he still emerged for the second half, and when Semb made changes Ole was taken off on 87 minutes for Steffen Iversen. It is serious. He knows this now but when he suffered the injury it seemed nothing.

He wanted it to seem nothing.

The incident had been innocuous – the kind of movement Ole has done a thousand times in a match. Towards the end against Wolves, with United leading 1-0 at Old Trafford thanks to John O'Shea's 10th-minute goal, Paul Scholes threaded a pass to him along the right. What then occurred will be rewound and replayed constantly in Ole's mind as the moment when his career as a bona fide fit and flying member of Sir Alex Ferguson's team ended. For ever.

Here, now, in slow motion – and in a flaaaash! – under the gleaming lights of the Theatre of Dreams, in the 83rd minute of Manchester United's third Premier League game of their 2003-04 title defence, the Wolves left-back, Lee Naylor, advances. Ole controls the ball, moves to go inside Naylor and, as he places his right knee to the turf . . .

There!

The happening, a moment in time. Irreversible, permanent. The thought goes through Ole's head, as 67,648 look on not knowing – how can they know? – that something is wrong, very wrong. But he does not know how wrong yet, will not accept just how wrong this is, how wrong his knee is.

He has punched a hole in the articular cartilage of his right knee. His thigh muscle – the cushion all footballers, athletes, anybody and everybody relies on – has not worked and there is no protection. He still travels to Bosnia, still ignores it — tries to — and now he's on the Old Trafford turf, again — the second match since the injury Ole still wants to believe is a mere jarring of the knee. He has scored against Panathinaikos, a 33rd-minute strike that squirmed past the hapless visiting No. 1, Antonis Nikopolidis (the Greek goal-keeper will be taken off at half-time due to his horror show between the posts). And now, finally, what he has known, what has been un-ignorable, always present at the back of his mind, comes to the fore and disaster strikes — there can be no more denial — and 11 minutes after the goal Ole Gunnar is forced off, having aggravated the problem, with what is reported in the next day's newspapers to be only a minor issue, at worst.

This is one of the cruel ironies. It is a career-defining injury and yet several publications do not mention Ole's removal at all. The BBC website report of the game mentions OGS only twice — each time to remark on his goal — but he is off, and on comes David Bellion to replace him, as the Frenchman did in the Wolves game.

It will be two years and 362 days — *three days short of three years* — before Ole will score once more at Old Trafford, again in the Champions League. On 13 September 2006, just before the unwanted three-year anniversary of the goal against the Greeks, Solskjær enters on 32 minutes for Ryan Giggs and scores a 47th-minute strike in a 3–2 Champions League group game win over Celtic that is cathartic.

But after Panathinaikos, Ole is out until the following February, the 21st, when he enters as a 71st-minute replacement for Phil Neville against Leeds United. He has had the first of what will become a total of three operations on the knee. He makes 14 more appearances between 21 February and the end of May; two of these are for Norway. He does not score but claims his second FA Cup-winner's medal with the late appearance against Millwall at the Millennium Stadium. Cristiano Ronaldo caps a debut season in English football with United's 44th-minute opener before the No. 9 Solskjær rates as the finest he ever played with, Ruud van Nistelrooy, scores twice, on 65 and 81 minutes, the first of these a penalty.

This is awful; he is wrestling difficult, dark emotions. The 'comeback' has proved a failure. Ole feels as bleak as he has ever done. May 1999 at the Camp Nou was as high as this is low. Since trying to play again, Ole has been gradually sinking into a funk of desperation. Training is a trial of watching team-mates run free while he is limited. Mere everyday walking causes Ole a pain that tells him he is not how he should be. That summer of 2004, he marries Silje, his childhood sweetheart, in Florida, and they honeymoon in Barbados, but the pain is present, nagging throughout. On the opening day of United's summer tour of the US, he has to pull out as even he can't ignore the injury any more.

'Ole is still experiencing some discomfort in his right knee,' a United spokesperson says. 'He will consult a specialist about the problem.' OGS does and in August the Swedish surgeon Lars Peterson operates and another long, unwanted period of rehabilitation beckons. As he embarks upon this process, newsprint tolls the bell, the website reports blare the verdict that it may all be over for him. The *Daily Mirror*'s story is headlined 'INJURY COULD BE END FOR OLE': 'Manchester United fear Ole Gunnar Solskjær's career could be brought to a premature end by injury.'

This sums up the register of the national newspaper

coverage of Solskjær's withdrawal from the pre-season tour and his long-term future. In the *Mirror* story Ferguson precised OGS's nightmare: 'It's so unfortunate a player of Ole's calibre and desire is missing the best years of his career like this. It's a huge disappointment for him and for us. It was only in the last couple of seasons that he had established himself as a regular in the side. Until then, we had always looked upon him as a substitute. He was probably the best substitute of all time, but then he proved himself worthy of his place in the side.'

Ole is Ferguson's 'substitute from hell' and OGS is going through his own personal Hades. He has to keep on going in the hope – however distant – that he will, at some point, emerge into sunlight and honeyed days again.

Ole misses all of the 2004-05 season, with Ferguson acting in August to fill the void left by him by signing Wayne Rooney – fresh from a rampant, stellar display for England at Euro 2004 – from Everton for £25.5m, the 18-year-old ending his first season in United colours with 17 goals. OGS, though, finishes the campaign as he began: a helpless and frustrated spectator, having to watch on as United endure a rare trophy-less term under Ferguson that includes dominating Arsenal in the final of their FA Cup defence, but which ends in defeat on penalties to Arsène Wenger's team.

He remains in pain while fantasising about it finally vanishing and being able to thrill the fans again. In July 2005 Ole undergoes a third operation – again by Peterson – and he steels himself for yet more time out due to the procedure, which is to implant membrane from his shins in the articular cartilage to cover the hole. Peterson, considered the lead specialist in this area, has also injected a liquid containing up

to 10 million cells taken from Ole and from which the aim –
hope – is fresh cartilage can be grown.

He makes just five appearances and scores no goals in the
2005-06 season; the first outing a seven-minute run-out as a
substitute in a 2-2 draw at Birmingham City on 28 December,
before two FA Cup games against Burton Albion (the first
a 0-0 draw away, the second a 5-0 win at Old Trafford) on
8 and 18 January. Then, he is out again until 14 April and a
0-0 draw with Sunderland at home, before another miser-
able season ends with a 4-0 victory over Charlton Athletic,
again at home.

He is down but he is also up as only Ole can be up.
He is plotting for the future, the life beyond playing, and
he is impressing those whose trade it is to nurse players
through injury and rehabilitation. During this torrid time,
Solskjær also has to endure a cheekbone injury and ham-
string problems.

The fractured cheekbone came seven minutes into a
reserve match in a clash with Middlesbrough's Ugo Ehiogu
on 7 March 2006 that resulted in Ole needing hospital treatment and being ruled out for at least the next nine weeks.

Yet at the end of the month there was a boost as Ferguson
okayed a fresh contract – the latest indication of why Solskjær
came to view the manager as his mentor. 'I am delighted that
Ole has signed a new two-year deal,' Ferguson told the club
website. 'It reflects our hope that he would return to full play
after his recent cheek injury. It will take Ole to 35 and gives
him the opportunity to develop his coaching experience.
We also foresee him having a key role as an ambassador for
the club in the future.' OGS was more than happy. 'I have
always felt at home here and I want to repay the loyalty that

has been shown to me by the club, the fans and Sir Alex,' he said. 'Although my priority is to keep playing, I am looking forward to exploring the coaching opportunity being given to me by the club.'

Later on in his life, Ole would reflect on Ferguson's impact on him, simply saying: 'He's influenced me with everything, to be fair.'

Ole Gunnar's mental fortitude and willingness to accentuate the positives from his time on the sidelines will be drawn upon when he becomes a manager – it allows him to relate to, and empathise with, those players who also suffer serious injury. The United physio, Rob Swire, who treated Ole Gunnar through all of this, recalls how Solskjær faced the ordeal and did so in the proactive manner that marks his character.

'We often tried to get players interested in the game when injured, those who were long-term injured players,' says Swire, now a consultant. 'Just quietly along the way – you don't jump into trying this because the first thing is that they're coming to terms with being out, so you have to drop into conversation about how the time can be used. Look at the advantages – there's always advantages to situations no matter what and observing football, keeping an eye out, focusing on it can help.'

Ole was intent on doing so. Swire says, 'Some players just wanted nothing to do with it, they'd hide away until they were fit again and could go back to football. But Ole was interested in football. I don't know if we created an interest for him – he was just very interested and liked watching it, studying it, and understanding it, the tactics and everything. It's something he could think about, focus on while he was injured.'

Swire was impressed by Ole's focus on returning to full fitness, despite the prolonged time on the sidelines. 'I was always confident because of the type of person he is really – he was going to put everything into it that he could do,' he says. 'With some players you do worry whether they'll come back, because they don't seem as committed to the rehabilitation, but that was never a problem with Ole.'

Swire could harness OGS's attitude which, he states, was ideal. 'You can control recovery a little bit because I always try to put the onus really hard on the player getting fit. It's no good being told it's a six-month injury, a year, and thinking, "I'm going to sit here while people are going to do things to me – put machines on me, move my legs and then in six months, a year, I'll play football."

'It's completely the wrong attitude. Ole was one of those who was right there asking what he can do, wanting to know about it, wanting to know about the injury – some players don't want to know anything.'

This is when everything changes. It realigns him, puts him on a trajectory to management and the United dugout 12 years later. He had already been taking notes these past six years – after clicking that he was experiencing something invaluable – documenting what Ferguson does, how the Scot takes training, speaks to players, which tactics and strategies he utilises. But before the injury this was done without a definite focus on moving into management on retirement. Now, he has serious (and unwanted) time to reflect and his view of retirement from playing switches dramatically; the seemingly endless lay-off nightmare will be transformed, over time, into the dream of managing Manchester United.

Swire believes Ole to be 'a connoisseur of football', a keen watcher while being out for so long and 'very interested in coaching and tactics'. And as many players he will later manage testify, Ole's experience of being injured allows him a rare empathy. 'Very much so,' says Swire. 'You try and get a rapport with players as best you can. Your players have all sorts of different personalities. Ole's easy to get on with. Anybody can get on with Ole. He's that way. He's that sort of person. He's a nice fellow but he's no mug. He's as tough as anyone.'

Ole's cleverness, his curiosity beyond football, is a further asset. 'He's a very intelligent man, I would say,' Swire says. 'Football can be an insular profession. But Ole was very worldly. He read papers, listened to the news. You could have a conversation about anything. He's not just got football intelligence – it is certainly not like football was the only thing in his life. That's not to say he wasn't really, really committed completely to football, he loved football, but he appreciated there were things to life other than football.

'That perhaps helped him to have this overall more positive view – that it's not the end of the world if you can't play football,' says Swire. 'Some players, they define themselves as a footballer. But Ole, because he has the bigger picture, that perhaps made it easier to cope – that's very true.'

Now it is the start of the 2006–07 season, Ruud van Nistelrooy has been sold to Real Madrid in the summer, and Ole is fit for the first game, coming on after 61 minutes for Louis Saha – who was signed in January 2004 – at Old Trafford as Fulham are beaten 5-1. There is a much-required shaft of light when the first goal since the knee injury is scored – on 23 August, against Charlton Athletic in a 3-0 win at The Valley; the strike, unsurprisingly, registered after entering as an 82nd-minute replacement.

'I've waited a long, long, long, long, long time for that. I can't put into words the club's support and the fans' support,' he said. 'They've had patience with me and the gaffer's always been good with me. He just told me to take my time and in the end it's paid off. To celebrate with the fans after scoring has been one of my aims over the past few years. Maybe in my dreams it was at Old Trafford but it doesn't really matter.'

When he came on at The Valley for Ryan Giggs there had been 21 goalless games for Ole, and the thought that, yes, maybe, he would never, ever register again in the colours of his beloved Manchester United. But on a Wednesday evening in south-east London and wearing the captain's armband, there he is in the white shirt and black shorts of the club's away strip, ghosting in to the far post as Louis Saha latches on to a Cristiano Ronaldo reverse ball into the area, the finish (on 90 minutes, of course) one the now 33-year-old practised all those years ago in the playground at Dalabrekka skole and Langveien ungdomsskole: a precise shot threaded inside Scott Carson's right post. The celebration speaks of gratitude and the humility which is the mark of the man in good *and* bad times – a bowing/hailing hybrid motion to the travelling United supporters behind the goal.

Of the rest of the XI on the Valley pitch at the final whistle that evening – Edwin van der Sar, Wes Brown, Mikaël Silvestre, Patrice Evra, John O'Shea, Rio Ferdinand, Darren Fletcher, Michael Carrick, Ronaldo and Saha – only Brown was at United in 1999 for the Champions League triumph. While Gary Neville, Ryan Giggs and Paul Scholes were still at the club (though the latter was suspended for the final), OGS had outlasted fellow European Cup-winners Yorke, Cole, Sheringham, Ronny Johnsen, Jaap Stam, Denis Irwin, David Beckham, Jesper Blomqvist, Nicky Butt and Peter Schmeichel.

Moments before the goal Carson had saved a near-in attempt from OGS and he subsequently admits that his injury-enforced goal drought had caused the miss. 'I should have scored earlier but the thoughts of whether I'd ever score again were running through my mind,' Ole said. 'Thankfully it went in. That's that over and done with and I can look forward again now. That's one on the board. That was the important one for me. I have been dreaming about this day and now it has finally arrived, I just feel relief.'

Darren Fletcher said, 'It's brilliant. Ole had a hard fight with injuries but he's always kept on fighting and kept on smiling.' Yet this would prove his last season for Manchester United as a player. He would manage 33 more appearances – for the club and Norway – and 13 more strikes.

Ole, though, now knew what he would do next. 'When I was 27, 28, I thought I'd never be a coach,' he told UEFA.com. 'Because I just wanted to get away from the lime-light, but then I got my injury and I sat down and reflected and thought: "If I can't play again, I don't want to leave this game." Then all my 20 years of football madness, craziness, nerdiness, call it what you like, came in and I thought: "I'm going to go for this."

'Sir Alex said I was analytical as a player, but that was just one or two defenders you're against. I thought I knew everything about football, and then you become a coach and you need to know every single thing about every single position.'

Ole Gunnar's open-mindedness and curiosity allowed

him to soak up Ferguson's wisdom, with Ole-the-manager's touch with players, his interest in them beyond the game, also influenced by his relationship with the Scot. 'Sir Alex Ferguson was like a second dad,' he said. 'I ended up living on the same street as him and his grandkids were in the same class as my kids, so of course I had a fantastic relationship with him over the years. Whatever you asked him about, you got an answer and you sat back and you thought: "He really knows his stuff."'

The 2006-07 season ends with 35 appearances and 13 goals. Three of these games are for Norway, as are two goals – the brace against Hungary in a 4-1 win at Budapest's Ferenc Puskás Stadium, the last of his 23 in 67 matches in national colours. The bookend to his international career came in February 2007, a friendly against Croatia at Rijeka's Stadion Kantrida, which Norway lost 2-1; Ole lasted until the 64th minute, when Steffen Iversen replaced him.

His final United goal, the last of his 126 in 366 appearances, came against Blackburn Rovers on 31 March 2007. Yet again as a sub – on for Cristiano Ronaldo in the 84th minute – he beat Brad Friedel, the Rovers No. 1, on the stroke of full time, his first finish for United also having been against the Lancashire club.

Now, though, the clock is ticking – ticking down. His final appearance for United is a bitter one, losing the 2007 FA Cup final on 19 May to Chelsea. On a sun-drenched Saturday afternoon, the first cup final to be played at the new Wembley is a dour affair that drags on into extra time, Ole having to wait 112 minutes before Ferguson finally throws him on. Ahead of entering for Ryan Giggs – Ferguson also swapping John O'Shea for Michael Carrick – the manager had removed Darren Fletcher for Alan Smith on 92 minutes. Within four of Ole entering, disaster strikes as a Didier Drogba–Frank Lampard one-two undoes the United defence, leaving Rio Ferdinand flailing, and the Ivorian striker pushes past Edwin van der Sar as the keeper rushes out. 'Maybe we won't need penalties now,' says John Motson on the BBC commentary. 'Didier Drogba with his 33rd goal of the season.'

It denied United, already crowned the champions, a Double and gave José Mourinho's team a cup double, having claimed that season's League Cup. Ole's entrance barely receives a mention. The *Observer* man gave him a four out of 10 and wrote: 'Brought on with penalties in mind, the Norwegian did not get the chance after late heartbreak.'

It was a sad, downbeat way to end his playing career. He may have gone out in a final, but losing is not the Ole Gunnar Solskjær way or the Manchester United way and during his stint as interim manager he will reference this last appearance ruefully.

The cup final heartache at Wembley is followed by more a fortnight later when he has to pull out of Norway training on 3 June due to more knee trouble. He has an operation and believes it is related to a minor injury suffered in March. Ole Gunnar remains upbeat: 'Physically and mentally I'm ready to join the team at the start.'

Norway team doctor Thor Einar Andersen is confident, too. 'The surgery went fine. We found what we expected. The knee was swollen and the joint was irritated, but we treated it. Hopefully it will be better when Ole resumes his training. We hope this is not something that will return again and again.' But, it does.

On 28 August the day he hoped would still be one, two, maybe three years away arrives.

The injury has won, and the game is up. His playing career is finished. 'I'm 34 now, I'll be 35 before this season finishes and everything has to come to an end. With my knee not being 100 per cent, I'm not able to play at the level at which the manager needed me, so it was an easy decision and I feel quite relaxed about it. It has been a fantastic 11 years,' he said in a statement.

There is a rare public utterance from his father, Øyvind. 'This is sad for us, and for him, that he has to quit. He'd hoped to recover 100 per cent, but now something has happened in this knee that makes it impossible for him to continue.'

Ferguson, as he always does, sums OGS up perfectly. 'Ole has achieved everything a player could wish. He has been a great servant and has remained a model professional. Ole will hopefully go on to be a good coach. Ending your playing career is a sad day for anyone, but in the case of Ole, he has 11 fantastic years he can look back on.'

Ole finished as a Premier League champion, United's 89 points at the end of the 2006-07 title race beating José Mourinho's Chelsea into second place on 83, Solskjær scoring seven times in the competition. In all his Premier League numbers are 151 starts in 235 appearances, accumulating 13,927 minutes, scoring 91 times at a ratio of 153 minutes per goal.

He is an eternal hero to United fans, primarily due to the *Boy's Own* winner against Bayern Munich. But there are copious other reasons for the status and for him to be proud of his career as a footballer for the most storied of English clubs. The refusal to leave for Tottenham when first-team starts continued to be limited. The torturous battle with injury. The cool-eyed finishing and seemingly eternal smile. Eric Cantona, Cristiano Ronaldo, Roy Keane, David Beckham, Ruud van Nistelrooy and Wayne Rooney, and the rest of the glittering talents he played alongside, and those he played against. All the trophies and the memories and his relationship with Ferguson.

Now it is time to start his post-playing career.

Now the next adventure is about to begin.

CHAPTER 7

The Nascent Coach

The early 2000s

'I'm sure he will become a manager and a good one.'

WAYNE ROONEY

See the three figures out on the green grass of Manchester United's Carrington training base. Working in the hot June sun. Two are together, one stands apart. The two are practising finishing – the other encouraging, coaching, feeding them endless balls to try to score with. They are relentless in their quest to become better. They are Ole Gunner Solskjær and Ruud van Nistelrooy. They are being schooled by René Meulensteen, a Dutch skills coach who will one day manage Manchester United reserves and have Ole as his assistant. Then one day René will be part of Sir Alex Ferguson's inner circle, becoming first-team coach. For now, he is drilling Ole and his countryman Van Nistelrooy ahead of their coming internationals.

Ole is a natural finisher. Scoring goals is the most difficult part of football, so says the common wisdom, but he finds it oh-so-simple. Ruud van Nistelrooy is the same. They are each born to score, but still they hone their skill and talent, relentless in the quest for perfection. This is a moment in time, this practice on the fields of Carrington. One day all this will be over – the playing – and one day Ole will be in charge of Manchester United. But here, during this summer week in June, Ole works and works and works.

'Ole, overall, was tactically very astute,' says René, now assistant coach of Australia, having previously managed Anzhi Makhachkala, Fulham, Maccabi Haifa and Kerala Blasters. 'He was the kind of player that would change the game even if he came off the bench because he would read the game, he would read what opponents were doing to see what his best movements would be when he would come on, to make a difference. One hundred per cent the way he was has showed the manager he has become. When I did the reserves in 2005-06 Ole had been out of surgery for a few weeks and, when he came back, he came back through the reserves, training with us, playing with us before going back to the first team. That's how I had a lot of contact with him. And he showed even more of an investment with regards to the whole picture of the team, in terms of asking: "How did we want to play? How did we defend? Did we press high, how do we do that? If we played on a block, where would we drop into, what were the areas to hit? How?"

'Obviously, we had a good bunch of players in the reserves.

We had Jonny Evans, Gerard Piqué as the centre-backs, we had Giuseppe Rossi up front, Fraizer Campbell on the right-hand side, Lee Martin on the left. It was a good team; we played some cracking football at times.'

René admires Solskjær's work ethic – the drive to become better: this is *the* leitmotif of his playing and coaching career, a mantra when he comes to manage Manchester United, insisting that every one of his footballers must be intent each day on improvement. Meulensteen recalls how OGS went about his own betterment, keen to enhance his areas of talent.

'I think Ole's biggest attribute as a footballer was his clinical finishing and the range of finishing that he had with both feet. He was such a clean, clean striker of the ball, with both feet, left and right. It was not only the accuracy he could hit the ball with, but the pace. I did so many finishing sessions with him and Ruud van Nistelrooy. Ole sometimes also worked with Diego Forlán as well,' René says of the Uruguayan striker, who was at the club from January 2002 to August 2004.

'I can still remember that particular week in June because they were ticking over before the internationals kicked in – Ole and Ruud – and that's why we ended up by doing these training sessions. It was focused on finishing in and around the box – in and outside. About creating better shooting opportunities as well because, obviously, Ole's goals, if you analyse them, I think he scored 126 with United, most of them were two-touch, one-touch.

'To be able to do that, you need to have two things. One, you need to have the tactical awareness to be in the right place at the right time, and he has a really good eye for that. His tactical understanding about reading an opponent's movements and where to be when the attack came into the final stage, that was very good. Secondly, as soon as those chances fell for him, he was very clinical in his finishing, as I said.'

Ole has kept diaries since he was a kid and René encouraged him to take notes of sessions. 'Ole is a very strong, opinionated man. He also had a very strong desire to learn,' says René. 'He always wanted to know. He always wrote things down. He wrote plenty of our sessions down. That's what I had advised: "If you write things down, you store it on your internal hard drive. If you don't write things down, believe me, you forget it." It's true because I've lived by that rule myself. I've logged every bloody training session I've done in my career, every time. I go back to my folders and look at them to see, "How was that? How did that go?"'

On learning from Ferguson Ole told *FourFourTwo*: 'From 2000 onwards, I started to make notes of the sessions that we did. I've got all the diaries with me. I realised I was experiencing something only my team-mates could experience, because he's unique. Less was more for him. He never talked for hours but whatever he said made a difference.'

This is the importance of the Manchester United school to Ole Gunnar Solskjær. And the willingness to be open to ideas, being humble enough to want to learn, shows a self-awareness that marks out a sophisticated intelligence. Understanding what education could offer, whether as a fit player honing his skills or when in the midst of injury, OGS had, subconsciously or not, a long-term vision, a comprehension of the need, the future usefulness of soaking up any and all nuggets of information.

René believes this can be the difference in footballers. 'It's just so important – it's the same with young players,' he says.

'Young players should write things down, what they're told in terms of roles and responsibilities. A lot of players don't. Coaches get over so much information to them, yet players can tend to go through on autopilot, just go with the flow. They do what is asked of them, but it's more about awareness and understanding, and the job of the coach can be to make that link for them, make players aware of this so they can understand.'

Ferguson noted how Ole watched a match intently from the bench to ensure he could make an impact if called upon. He was the same when preparing for games in training with the first-team squad. It was the same in that hot week in June at Carrington. It was about priming himself. Which Solskjær the manager will install in his own Manchester United squad.

René says: 'That process of awareness is a process that takes place on the training pitch and on the field, but more than anything, players need to take ownership. They can only do that by going away and thinking about it. I said the same thing to Cristiano Ronaldo when working with him. "There is evidence that the people who have clear aims and targets are many times more successful in what they want to achieve than people who don't."'

Raimond van der Gouw, the reserve goalkeeper who watched the Champions League final of 1999 from the bench alongside Ole, recalls him displaying a similar instinct. 'He knows what he wants, he had a plan as a player – when he was on the bench, he was always looking at the game, analysing the game. He knew the weakest part of the opponent; at that time he was already the type of player who was tactical. This was more a plan for himself, he knew what he wanted to do. He knew which is the best way to score. We played together for six years and when he was getting older, I found out that he was already looking forward from the football.

'He's a manager now. Well, when playing he was playing the computer game *Football Manager*. So when I heard he became a manager in Norway and then he became manager of Manchester United I thought: "Yeah – I can see now the little steps he made, from a low step to a high step – in his way he is calculating the next move and is very good at that."'

If Ferguson is Ole's great guru, and Meulensteen's influence part of his schooling, the relationship he formed with Mike Phelan, who held a variety of coaching positions at United before becoming assistant manager in 2008, is also a key one.

As with Ferguson, Ole was keen to soak up the football knowledge and wisdom accrued by Phelan, who had been a player under the Scot when winning his first – and most crucial – trophy, the FA Cup in 1990, starting and finishing both the initial Wembley showpiece with Crystal Palace and subsequent triumphant replay.

In 2004 Ferguson began refusing to speak to the BBC due to a documentary on his son, Jason, who was an agent. Phelan often spoke to the corporation in his place and how he handled these duties was studied by Ole. 'I enjoy it, it's interesting, although it becomes a little bit repetitive in some ways because they're only looking for one of two things, which is controversy – and controversy,' Phelan said. 'You have to learn what the underlying question is. You can be hit by a dozen questions but it's one that they're really looking for. It's a game that you have to play but I think if you're honest, people understand that. You don't have to be controversial. You don't have to go looking for problems.'

If Ole Gunnar's handling of the media when becoming a

manager would show flashes of both Ferguson and Phelan, his admiration for the latter was illustrated when he invited him to coach at the so-called 'Solskjær Academy' (a tie-up with the Norway Football Federation and the multinational Norwegian Statoil, now called Equinor), Meulensteen also doing the same. While the academy would later prove controversial within Norway, Ole had no doubt about Phelan's worth – admiring his character as much as his football expertise.

In doing so Ole Gunnar, again, illustrated how the 'Ferguson way' had influenced him: how he'd been imbued with the Scot's vision for Manchester United, which was akin to Bayern Munich or even Liverpool during the successful Boot Room years initiated by Bill Shankly, in that it should be a family affair, promotions happening from within or by the hiring of former United players and staff so that the values and traditions – the culture – of the club could be passed from generation to generation.

In all he observed of Ole, Ferguson, with his intuition and instinctive grasp of people, saw a man who understood what being part of the club was, who thrived on this. Ferguson knew OGS was bright and curious, that he yearned to learn, that he observed games when being a substitute, and thus, while initially marking him out as an ambassador for United on retirement, the Scot made sure to kick-start OGS's coaching career by having him work with the first-team strikers during the final injury-blighted years. All of which formed part of the foundation for Ole becoming Manchester United reserve-team manager before the close of the noughties.

Of the first coaching role, which came after retirement in summer 2007, Ole told the *Daily Telegraph*: 'I promised my wife we would get back to normal when I finished playing. But the manager offered me a job after 20 seconds. I said: "I can't play any more." And he told me: "Don't worry, you were fantastic, you had a great career, why don't you join my coaching staff?" Twenty seconds after I had retired, I got a job. I thought it was a great opportunity, that it would be fantastic to come and work with him every day. I worked with Cristiano [Ronaldo], Wayne [Rooney], Danny Welbeck, [Carlos] Tevez. That was a good start for me,' he said.

Ferguson's idea of the club as a family is an underlying ethos of many vibrant and successful operations. It was a dominant factor in the supreme success under Ferguson and had Ole Gunnar likening him to a second father, pointing to the Scot's influence over him. At the end of Solskjær's testimonial, on 2 August 2008, after a Fraizer Campbell goal gave Manchester United a 1-0 win against Espanyol and Ole an apt send-off before a near-70,000 crowd at Old Trafford, he recognised and thanked Ferguson for the mentor he had become.

'I've had my highs, I've also had my lows. And he has supported me very well through that time. I can't thank him enough. I'm going into coaching. If I haven't learned from him, I can't do coaching,' Ole said.

'Throughout my life, ever since I played for Clausenengen back home, instead of listening to the teacher at school I was writing down all the chances I missed in a book thinking, "I should have done this,"' he would tell a press conference in December 2018. 'Scoring goals was all I thought about. I have a diary at home from when I met Bill Beswick [sports psychologist] when I first came to the club. He made me aware of how important it is to work on your confidence. I've got a diary of what I was thinking and how I reacted to different situations in games. It starts with me writing: "I've had enough of bad performances and bad confidence" – and that was when I was 27. I studied finishing, I studied goals, I studied movement. I worked on my mentality because that's key.'

There was also the desire to remain in a team environment, a love of the team ethic. 'I could never have been an individual athlete, like my dad, who was a Greco-Roman wrestler. I'm so happy to be part of a team, see how people gel together and work for each other and win together. That's one of the things that makes me want to go on in football after I've finished playing, as a coach or manager,' he previously told *The Independent*.

The refusal to stagnate, the focus on improvement, the desire to overcome the mental battle that defines success and eliminates failure was to drive Ole Gunnar and the first team he managed to success – Manchester United reserves.

CHAPTER 8

The First Title

'He's ruthless.'

OLLIE NORWOOD, MANCHESTER
UNITED UNDER-23 PLAYER

Retirement as a player morphed into a job as a club ambassador and, having coached United strikers for Ferguson in 2007-08, Ole Gunnar took over Manchester United reserves for the 2008-09 term, co-managing the side with Warren Joyce.

The next season was an important one in OGS's development as a coach. He took a UEFA Pro Licence course alongside fellow managers including Reading's Brian McDermott, and it also brought Solskjær's inaugural championship in management − the 2009-10 Premier League Reserve crown, a competition played by clubs' under-23 sides.

On 3 May, United beat Aston Villa 3-2 in a penalty shoot-out at Old Trafford, after the final ended 3-3, to win the championship. Ollie Norwood, now a 28-year-old midfielder at Sheffield United voted into the Championship team of 2018-19, was a member of Ole Gunnar's side, having been at United since he was six years old.

'Us playing at Old Trafford, obviously that was a big thing, and Ole managing there was a bit special for him after his playing days,' says Norwood, of victory in the final. He highlights how Solskjær tapped into his successful career to inspire his junior charges.

'I played at centre-back and thought he was brilliant, especially for the young players at Man United,' says Norwood, who won promotion to the Premier League in 2019-20 with Sheffield United. 'The history that he has with the football club means he understands what it's about. And for us as young players, to have somebody, a legend of the football club, come and help us in our careers was something you could only admire and learn from.'

Ole's influence was not only predicated on the glamour of the 1999 Champions League triumph or his six Premier League titles. It was about the example he had shown throughout his 11 years as a player under Ferguson, and about being part of an era that featured many of the club's finest ever footballers. 'I was quite fortunate in that I was part of the academy and came through the youth team and then to the reserves,' Norwood says. 'It was arguably the most successful senior team in the club's history. Ole was with others like Rio Ferdinand, Nemanja Vidić, Paul Scholes, Gary Neville, Ryan Giggs, Wayne Rooney, Cristiano Ronaldo, Carlos Tevez, Patrice Evra and Edwin van der Sar. We were fortunate to learn from these players, to stand back and watch how they worked.'

The squad being reared to be United's next successful

generation or professionals elsewhere understood what was required by Ole, citing the example of himself and former team-mates. 'The way they went about their business every day, seeing probably the top players in the world at that time, and how they treated people, the way they behaved: it's something that stood with me for my career,' Norwood says. 'Ole is humble, which was a big thing at Man United at the time – the humbleness of all the greats, because they were superstars. Like I said, it's not just about football. It's about life lessons at Manchester United. Ole being our reserve-team manager was a privilege.'

Solskjær carried on the Ferguson-instilled approach of understanding the need to mould footballers *and* human beings. Norwood says: 'The work Ole and Warren Joyce did with us at the academy was not just about being a professional, but how to live your life, how to be perceived as a Man United player and person. It was a big thing. Ole was massive in that in a way. He would say: "You're fortunate if you're lucky enough to make it at Man United. If you're not, what we do here will stand you in good stead to go and make a career away from the club."'

Joyce is glowing regarding Solskjær. 'He came with me at the start of it, we were working together in the reserves, and he had come straight from playing,' he told *The Age*. 'As a man, when you know him inside out and you know how he prepared, even though he wasn't playing [all the time, he still impressed]. What he did, coming back to training grounds and training late, to make sure he was ready for the next game, ready so he could do everything he possibly could to be right. It's not a fluke that he gets on late in the Champions League final and scores the winner.

'Forget as a coach or anything, he is exactly the right type of person. If you say there is a Man United-type of serial winner, he is that type. You see some special people, the way they conduct themselves, the way they go about things, he was one of a group like [former team-mates] Scholes, Giggs, and [Nemanja] Vidić and [Patrice] Evra, [Rio] Ferdinand, the Nevilles, they were special people.'

Solskjær also illustrated a tactical dexterity that he would display in all his management positions. 'The way he organised sessions and the way he explained the game – he was fantastic for me. I learned so much from him. He used to make me laugh – I remember telling my friends of how after training we would do finishing drills and obviously Ole is known for his finishing, but how easy he made it look, saying: "Look, lads, you're just going to do this and do that."' Norwood laughs. 'It's all right for him, but for us to try to replicate that was hard, you know?!'

'We tried many things. One was he'd make you play in different positions so I'd play at right-back – this way you'd understand what a right-back wants. It was very forward-thinking – he just knew how football worked.'

Yet despite Ole's trust in youth he was no softer on emerging talent, an attribute that suggested he would be able to manage at senior level. 'He's ruthless, just ruthless. People don't see that side,' Norwood says. 'They think he's friendly, but if there's something's not quite right, he'll tell you it's not going right. He's not going to be happy with everything irrespective.'

Ole Gunnar's management style would be to try to strike a balance that footballers, like any working person, could relate to and respect. This was to be fair and firm, driven and inspirational. 'As a young player being told at Man United that Ole Gunnar Solskjær's going to be your coach, you have nothing but admiration for him and hang on to every single word, because he knows what it takes to get to the top level,' Norwood says. 'If I did get a chance to speak to him again, I would like to say thank you for the guidance. What he taught us as young boys – now you realise how important it was.'

To have a profound effect on a footballer is a kind of holy grail for a manager. For Ole it is a recurring motif. With copious support staff and specialist coaches for every position, in an era of multimillionaire footballers, man-management of the talent is where success and failure become separated. The very best number ones are defined by the extra percentages they draw from the human beings who are the players in their charge.

Ole Gunnar illustrated he was able to turn Manchester United reserves into champions. And the achievement had a lingering effect. On his young players, sure, but also, crucially, on the club *and* his destiny. His time as reserve-team manager would be remembered nearly a decade later when Ed Woodward needed someone to come in and stabilise a club seriously listing under the management of José Mourinho.

Woodward had been a lower-ranking member of the hierarchy when Solskjær retired, having joined the club after helping to broker the Glazers' purchase of United in 2005. He was then promoted to executive vice-chairman in 2013 when David Gill, the chief executive, departed. Since then his tenure as the most powerful employee on the ground at United had been pocked by blunders. Yet when Solskjær was given the number one job – on a temporary basis – Woodward made his smartest move yet by reaching back into the club's past to try to connect it with a brighter future by employing a manager whose footballing DNA is Manchester United.

Yet before all of this, Ole Gunnar Solskjær was still to accept his first number one role. He was about to do so, deciding to end 14 years at Old Trafford and return home to Norway.

The decision OGS took was to prove prescient: in the short and the long term.

CHAPTER 9

One Man Goes Home Early

'He was like Jesus to us.'

ESPEN BUGGE PETTERSEN, MOLDE FK

In 2011 Molde FK was a hundred years old and Rosenborg BK Norwegian champions, having won for a record 22nd time in 2010.

This would be a last Tippeligaen crown for the club from Trondheim for five years. When Ole Gunnar agreed to become Molde manager, in late 2010, ahead of the new Norwegian season beginning the following March, he initiated a period of unheralded success for the club.

This began with his inaugural campaign in charge. Molde, on the south coast of Norway, had never been the champion football team of the country, yet he arrived with a firm – if privately held – belief, communicated to the players from the start of pre-season: he could change the image and history of the club.

On the day when OGS left Manchester United – 9 November 2010 – Sir Alex Ferguson, in a 22nd year as manager, said: 'Ole has had a good period with our reserve team, which has given him a foundation to start somewhere else. He feels it is time he went back to Norway, which also helps his family situation. He has been a fantastic servant to us and I am sure he will do well. He has worked with some really good young players in our reserve team and has contributed to their development.

'Once he gets experience of managing a club in its own right, who knows where it will take him? Molde is a very progressive club in Norwegian football, so this is a good start for him.'

Ole was clear working for his great mentor would be drawn upon. 'He has been amazing to watch, to look at,' he told UEFA.com. 'It's just the enthusiasm, the desire of always wanting to get the best out of you. Always that winning mentality. When you struggle as a team, you've lost a couple of games, he never pushes the panic button. He believes in his players, in the system, because he trusts his backroom staff and his own judgement. You only get that by experience. It's been a very, very good learning period. He's a fantastic motivator, he's a fantastic man-manager, I think he handles superstars so well. I learned so much from him in the last 14 and a half years.'

Ole also indicated he would be shrewd enough to draw on the knowledge gained playing for Norway under Egil Olsen, the manager who masterminded the 1998 World Cup win over Brazil.

'Egil is fantastic in motivating the players and making them believe they can do it,' Ole told UEFA.com. 'His way of coaching and managing is different to anyone else I have seen. He's very eccentric, of course, but he's very direct: "If you do this, you will be all right, but if you do that, you've got no chance." He is very specific.'

In 2009 OGS had previously rejected the chance to take over as Norway's number one – from Åge Hareide, who had signed him from Clausenengen to Molde in late 1994. Then, continuing his look to Ferguson for advice that had begun since signing for him in July 1996, he consulted the Scot: 'I did not think it was the right time for me to say yes to the offer,' Ole told the *Daily Mail*. 'But of course it was nice to be asked. I work for Manchester United and my career is going in the right direction. It would have been exciting to take on a much bigger job than my current one, but I have a job at United.'

It was a differing answer Molde received – after, of course, advice from Ferguson. 'The boss thought it was really right for me to move home to start the coaching career there,' he said. 'Those words weighed so heavily – that's why I didn't finish what I had previously said I would – that I would remain working at Manchester United as long as he is there.'

Here Ole Gunnar was, 15 years after becoming a starlet Molde striker, returning to the club as a bona fide hero and, yes, legend in Norway. And not only as a sportsman: his 1999 Champions League final heroics, the other goalscoring exploits, a silverware-bulging CV made him the country's most famous *person* – and he was about to elevate the billing further.

Becoming Molde manager meant the end of Ole's 'Solskjær Academy', the controversial talent scheme organised between the NFF and Statoil. Dynamic Solution, a player agency in which Ole and Jim Solbakken owned 30 per cent, also had as minor shareholders the former Leeds United and Norway midfielder, Eirik Bakke, and John Vik, a Norwegian who would later be a Manchester United scout.

Solskjær – and Solbakken – had faced criticism in Norway for overseeing a talent camp that, the perception ran, recruited the country's best youth footballers and allowed Solbakken, as an agent, to cherry-pick from these to become clients.

In 2007 Egil Østenstad, the former Southampton and Blackburn Rovers striker, was Viking FK sports director and offered one complaint. 'It is completely untenable that NFF and an agent company co-operate on a talent collection,' he said. 'This is a very unfortunate link with NFF and Solskjær's role. The academy has developed into a [potential talent source] for the big clubs – under the auspices of NFF. The association contributes to something they oppose.'

Østenstad was keen to underline that he criticised how the academy might be utilised rather than its actual existence, and while Solbakken acknowledged the scrutiny was understandable, he said: 'We started this academy with Statoil, so it is natural that we must have control. Keep in mind that we have had 250 players in five years and there are only two players [represented by] Solution. There are examples of agents who have far more than that. We live in a world where everyone is fighting for the best players. I have never invited English clubs to the academy [to scout], but they still come. I know scouts from the other clubs and talk to them when we meet. Yes, Ole Gunnar is there and he brings some coaches from Manchester United.'

Østenstad was insistent. 'Call all of the country's sports directors. Everyone is critical of this,' he claimed. 'The elite clubs have also raised the issue with NFF and we expect something to be done.'

The following year Ole relinquished his share in Dynamic Solution and in 2010 the Solskjær Academy had its final year in Kristiansund – the Molde co-proprietor, Kjell Inge Røkke, was owner of Aker Solutions, a Statoil competitor.

During this period Solbakken was involved in the 2006 transfer of Brede Hangeland, a defender, from Viking to FC Copenhagen and then when the same player moved to Fulham in 2008. Four years later FIFA were to fine him for irregularities.

'In 2012 the players' agent Jim Solbakken was pronounced guilty of failing to comply with the FIFA Players' Agents Regulations,' a FIFA spokesperson said. 'According to the decision passed by the FIFA Disciplinary Committee, Mr. Solbakken was ordered to pay a fine to the amount of CHF 10,000.'

Just before the 2011 season started, Ole offered a public warning to his new squad. Speaking on 2 March he said, 'Every day is a test. You can take a beer one evening, but if you take three or four, then your name is out of the squad. It's me who decides how the players will behave – and, in a small town like Molde, I get to know everything. Don't you worry.'

Despite this being Ole Gunnar's maiden management post this showed the authority he felt he possessed, as going public like this was a show of power that came freighted with the prospect of his new players taking no notice. This was also again reminiscent of Ferguson, who apparently operated a network of informants that would have impressed those recruiting for the Stasi, 'ears and eyes' who ensured the Scot knew precisely what his players were doing, when and where, 365 days a year.

'Those whose performances are inconsistent are often out in the city, taking a hamburger, not looking after themselves,' said Ole, citing how lifestyle and discipline were vital, the onus being to self-police: more shades of Ferguson, who believed in a strong and self-governing dressing room filled with players who were akin to quasi-managers. 'If they are to become top football players, then they must live accordingly – 24 hours a day,' Ole added.

The message he gave privately to his squad inspired them. Espen Bugge Pettersen, OGS's goalkeeper at Molde, says: 'It's important to remember that when Ole Gunnar was presented as the manager, when he came in – to the club, the fans, the players – he was like Jesus to us in a way. He used that standing he has in Norwegian football, especially locally in Molde too, to make us believe that we could walk on water almost.'

Despite 2011 being Solskjær's first term, and the barren 99-year history of the club, he displayed zero doubt. While Mark Dempsey, who would follow him to Cardiff City and Manchester United, was more hands-on in training, and Richard Hartis, who worked under Ferguson when Ole had been there, was goalkeeping coach, OGS now began a convincing psychology act on his charges.

Ever shrewd and pragmatic, his storied experience was drawn on to make Molde's players *believe*. 'He started really, really early,' says Pettersen. 'From the first day, Ole Gunnar and his coaching team began the process of settling in the belief that we were in a position to challenge Rosenborg, the biggest club in Norway. I remember we had several meetings and also individual talks where, when I look back on it, the main plan was to settle in belief to the squad, the players.

'He made us believe it in the way he presented the challenge and the way his coaching team did so, too. It was so easy to believe and it gave us so much energy and optimism, and enthusiasm to work hard every day to achieve it. It wasn't one specific thing he did but he kept reminding us that we are good enough, we have the possibility. For sure we took up the challenge from then until the end of the season in autumn.'

Two days before Molde's opening match of the 2011 season, their 35th in the top flight, Ole Gunnar's side lost 1-0 to Bolton Wanderers in a final warm-up game behind closed doors after the scheduled opposition for the friendly – Manchester United – pulled out.

This had followed Ole taking the side to play at the Copa de Sol tournament in late January and early February when pre-season began. There was a penalty shootout defeat to Ukraine's Karpaty Lviv in Elche, a 5-1 trouncing at the hands of Tromsø, before finally winning a game, 2-0, against Poland's Wisła Kraków.

Solskjær had made seven signings in two months. In January the forward Davy Claude Angan came from Hønefoss of Norway, followed by the midfielders Joshua Gatt (Austria's SC Rheindorf Altach) and Magnus Wolff Eikrem, whose agent was Jim Solbakken, having first impressed Ole at his soccer school, signing four years later on his 16th birthday in August 2008 for Manchester United. The other three signings in the month were defenders: Børre Steenslid (Viking), Torjus Aaland (Stranda) and Sean Cunningham (Michigan's Derby County Wolves). In the second week of February, Pål

Erik Ulvestad of Norway's Herd was Ole's final acquisition ahead of the season.

Molde had finished 11th the previous term, though this did not (apparently) stop expectations of where Ole could take them this year. The title had been mentioned when Solskjær's appointment was announced the previous autumn, and he was on a lucrative bonus should he manage to deliver it.

Kjetil Rekdal, his former Norway team- and room-mate, who was then Aalesunds FK coach, told Norwegian media, 'Expectations are very important in football. But it seems that Molde city has lost its sense completely. The only one who has his feet on the ground is Ole Gunnar himself. He knows that this will not be as easy as people there seem to believe. But I think he will succeed because he is talented.' Then in a comment that was particularly perceptive about his friend, Rekdal added: 'Some succeed more often than others – Ole Gunnar is such a person.'

Yet Rekdal's stance caused derision in Molde, as the mayor indicated. 'It's nice that he is worried about us,' said Jan Petter Hammerø, who was also a season ticket holder. 'We see the challenges [for Ole Gunnar] – so if Molde becomes one of the six best teams, we will be happy. I see that some think we are going to take a medal, and maybe gold – the championship – but we in Molde are not among them.'

Eva-Brit Mauseth of the Molde FK supporters' club, Tornekrattet, was equally dismissive. 'It must have been a while since Kjetil has been in Molde,' she told Norwegian media. 'We are not getting carried away.'

On Friday 18 March Ole Gunnar's competitive debut as a first-team manager came in Molde's Tippeligaen curtain-raiser meeting with Sarpsborg (away). If Ole Gunnar was secretly confident of being successful, fans' wariness may have been a shrewd take – given the club's start. Molde lost 3-0 at Sarpsborg, then drew the next two matches 2-2. At home to Tromsø – Pape Paté Diouf scoring the inaugural goal of Ole's reign at Molde's Aker Stadion before 8,782 fans – then away at Viking FK.

A first win came in the following outing, 3-2 against Stabæk at Molde's ground, Davy Claude Angan N'Guessan, Paté Diouf and Makhtar Thioune scoring for OGS's team. The victory kick-started what was a memorable campaign for Molde and one of personal satisfaction and vindication for Ole Gunnar Solskjær. Brann were defeated in the next outing – 3-1 away, on 25 April – before a 2-0 home loss to Rosenborg was followed by two more consecutive wins, over Lillestrøm and Fredrikstad.

Thus the pattern of Molde's title win was set. Ole's team lost only four more times in the league, never going down two games on the bounce, and winning five in a row at one stage (between late June and early August). The next match was a second defeat to Rosenborg, in the return fixture, 3-1 in Trondheim, but from that day – 7 August – Molde went unbeaten in ten until the final match of the term, on 27 November, which was a dead rubber.

It was meaningless because the champagne had already been uncorked earlier in the month, two matches before the close of the season, following a 2-2 draw with Strømsgodset on 30 October 2011: after Ole Gunnar and his side believed they had blown the chance of the championship that day.

Espen Bugge Pettersen says, 'We were ahead both 1-0 and 2-1 but in the 90th minute we conceded a goal to make it

2-2 and the disappointment was massive. The feeling was terrible. Our biggest competitor – Rosenborg – started their game just minutes after we finished playing.

'We had the opportunity to watch live in our locker room. By the time several of us players came back to the locker room they were already 1-0 down, and after 20 minutes 3-0. The huge disappointment we felt after our match was suddenly turned completely the other way around. I remember I looked over to our captain, club legend Daniel Berg Hestad, who played over 500 games for Molde – he just sat there, shocked, couldn't believe what he saw. Of course, this rollercoaster of feelings made this day very special for everyone who was involved and loved the club.'

Manager and players, club and fans were in dreamland. Now 38 years old, Ole had guided Molde to its inaugural championship in its centenary year. From the 30 Eliteserien matches Molde's record was 17 wins, six losses and seven draws for a total of 58 points, five better than Tromsø and nine ahead of Rosenborg – the defending champions soundly beaten into third place. Paté Diouf was Molde's top scorer with 12 in 14 appearances, a strike rate of 0.86 goals per outing (he left on loan for FC Copenhagen halfway through the season), followed by Davey Claude Angan, whose contribution was nine in 29, a strike rate of 0.31.

To claim a title in a debut term is candy-cane fantasyland for any manager. Ole was jubilant, as were his devoted players and the adoring fans. 'The club has waited 100 years for this,' he told Norwegian journalists. 'We have been close several times before, so this was well deserved. It was a good atmosphere in the dressing room and we will enjoy ourselves tonight.'

Molde had been second in Norway's top flight seven times – 1974, 1987, 1995 (the year of Ole's 20 goals), 1998, 1999, 2002 and 2009 – but not until 2011 and Ole's arrival did they become the champion team of Norway, managed by the prodigal son whose return was storybook, fantastical and all other overblown adjectives that can be used to hype but that sometimes, as in this case, are apt. For this was an achievement that tapped into sport's inherent romance, its ability to make the senses dance.

Ferguson contacted Ole. 'I texted him on Saturday thinking he had won the league but he was playing on Sunday,' the Scot told a media conference. 'It is a great achievement considering this is his first year. He had a great spell with our reserve team so he wasn't coming into the job blind but it is fantastic news. My knowledge of Ole as a student of the game is quite clear – every game he played and every training session he took part in, he always wrote it all down. That gives him a great start because you need dedication and sacrifice to go into management these days. He was a great player and a very nice person.'

As usual, Ferguson had some advice for Ole Gunnar and his next move. 'I don't think he should rush into returning to England because experience is good and the experience he has got at Molde is a very good one. He comes from the area. His wife and family are all back home there. He has won the championship and there is no need to hurry. The time will come and the timing will be important, but he is easily capable of coming into English football.'

Magnus Stamnestrø, then an 18-year-old midfielder, was part of OGS's triumphant squad. 'It was a massive achievement, a great year. OGS came home to Norway and Molde,' he says, 'and Molde took the league title, it was almost like a fairytale. He did it with his type of football – what he believed in. Slightly characterised by United's playing style, but with his own touch, like what one sees of his Manchester United today. A lot of possession, dangerous on the counter-attack, a lot of forward passes and forward runs and always try to express yourself. It was offensive football and freedom to use your skills.

'In pre-season he had given players and the club belief that it was possible. I especially remember a meeting from the training camp before the season. When we went out of that meeting room, I think all of us believed that this was going to be a wonderful season.'

So it proved: Ole Gunnar's belief that the title could be claimed proved visionary. Yet almost immediately he targeted the retention of the championship. Stamnestrø says, 'One man went home early from the celebration – Ole. He had already started thinking of the next season, when we did, in fact, win the league again.'

It was a feat straight from the Ferguson playbook: begin focusing on a repeat almost as soon as success is achieved. The toughest ask in sport after reaching the top is remaining the ascendant force by winning again and Ole Gunnar did this, just as his mentor had so many times. And this was achieved during a 2012 season in which, at the halfway point, Molde embarked on their debut Champions League campaign.

Pettersen recalls how Ole again focused on players' mind-sets. 'For sure, the first title showed hunger and then what was required changed a little bit in 2012. It's another thing to do it a second year in a row and so the belief that he sold to the squad, to the club, to the fans, was crucial. He just kept on building and that is the biggest reason that we won the title again.'

Ole prepared for the championship defence by making five new signings. These were three defenders – Kongsvinger's Martin Linnes, Vålerenga's Victor Johansen, and Sogndal's Even Hovland; the goalkeeper Ola Hermann Opheim from Steinkjer; and midfielder Emmanuel Ekpo of Colombus Crew.

A pre-season of 13 matches against various opposition – which again took in the Copa del Sol – ended with a 3-2 victory over Aalesunds on 16 March. Seven days later Ole Gunnar oversaw a 2-1 win over Strømsgodset at the Aker Stadion, Davy Claude Angan and Joshua Gatt scoring Molde's goals. Now followed a run of defeat, win, defeat, win, defeat before a 2-1 victory over Aalesunds initiated five straight victories, a draw and another victory. Then came a loss to Rosenborg, 1-0, on 8 July, ahead of the Champions League campaign, which commenced 10 days later.

Pettersen says, 'Two thousand and twelve was like two parallel runs. Yes, we had the league but then we also wanted to see what we can do in Europe. In my opinion, chasing the breakthrough in Europe gave us a great challenge to maintain and even increase our level in the Norwegian league.'

Molde entered the Champions League in the second qual-ifying round, the opening leg with Latvia's Ventspils taking place on 18 July at the Aker. This was won 3-0 and the return was a 1-1 draw, OGS taking his side through 4-1 on aggre-gate. In the next round, though, they were eliminated – 2-1 on aggregate by Basel – and entered the Europa League play-off, the two legs taking place in the third and fourth weeks of August. Dutch side Heerenveen were dispatched 4-1 on aggregate and Molde were in the group stage. Yet in a phase with Steaua Bucharest, FC Copenhagen and Stuttgart, Ole's side finished bottom with six points from six games, only beating Stuttgart – twice (home, 2-0, away, 1-0).

By now Molde were flying in the Tippeligaen. All three of August's matches were victories, and after a 4-1 reverse at Brann they went unbeaten until the season end: a sequence of nine, of which six were wins.

On 11 November the champagne again popped and flowed following a 1-0 win at home over Hønefoss in the penulti-mate match, the Nigerian Daniel Chima Chukwu scoring the Tippeligaen-clinching goal.

'The feelings during and after our second league title-[winning] game were, in many ways, completely different,' Espen Bugge Pettersen says. 'This year we were the favour-ites, not the underdogs of the year before. Relief is maybe the best word to describe it.

'In that match – we didn't deliver a good performance and were struggling to create enough chances. Still, 1-0 was enough to win the league, but the atmosphere, celebration could not be compared with the year before.'

On retaining the championship, afterwards Ole told Norwegian media: 'It's amazing. The boys have been con-centrating on repeating the title from last year, and we have shown that more than one team in Norway can do it more than once.' This was a reference to Rosenborg. 'We have good football players who have the belief that this can happen.' Despite the goalless score at half-time, he had been calm and told his side how to approach the rest of the match. 'It was just to play with a little more pace, and utilising the space.'

Rosenborg are again dominant in Norwegian football as title-winners four years in a row from 2015 to 2018. Pettersen adds: 'It was not easy to conquer them in the first place. I remember Ole said that his plan when he came to Molde was to win the league in 2013. And then he managed to do it on the first attempt – he has some abilities, as a person, that are really natural, that are not found in every manager.'

By the close of the 30-match campaign Molde had 62 points, Strømsgodet 58 and Rosenborg 55, while Davy Claude Angan's 13 strikes from 26 outings (at a rate of 0.5 per game) made him the third highest scorer.

This second title was evidence of Ole's Ferguson-esque managerial credentials, the Manchester United DNA he possesses of wanting to win and then to go again and win again. OGS comprehended that rivals would strengthen and all teams would want to beat the champions, and he was able to meet and overcome these challenges.

Jan Jönsson, the Rosenborg manager, signed Peter Ankersen, Steffen Iversen, Daniel Berntsen and Stefan Strandberg ahead of the 2012 campaign and added four more signings halfway through, but still Ole's Molde were too good and Jönsson departed.

Stamnestrø offers three words to sum up why Ole Gunnar's particular style of management was so effective. 'Positive, kind and caring,' he says. 'One time in training I blocked a shot on the line in the last second and got hurt on the ankle. I sat on the grass after the session finished, frustrated and with a bag of ice on my ankle, and was almost annoyed that I blocked that shot. I remember talking to Ole Gunnar – about how important it was to win and about mentality. I didn't train for a few days after this, but he was still happy with what I did.

'That's typical of OGS – it's all about mentality, offensive football, express yourself and of course win. In games and in training as well. I was quite young and at the start of my career then. He boosted my confidence by having faith in me. And he taught a lot of fine details – especially about offensive play. When we were practising different shooting drills, for example, usually Ole Gunnar showed us how he meant we should do it. And no matter what type of finishing it was – leg, head, volley, whatever – he put the ball into the net. Easy as you like. He taught me a lot that I still have with me and have great use of for today.'

Stamnestrø echoes Norwood regarding Ole Gunnar's hard edge. 'He can be strict if needed, like Sir Alex and his "hairdryer",' he says of the Scot's infamous temper. 'I only remember he used it once – at a game we played in which the football was dull, there were too few forward passes and runs. And he rushed into the dressing room and told us if we were going to play in this club we had to be more offensive and play forward.'

Ole wanted for his squad to enjoy themselves while also pursuing excellence. 'At United, we came to Carrington and worked our bollocks off,' he once said. 'But we never felt like we went to work. The gaffer always wanted us to express ourselves. He'd created an environment with inner justice. Giggsy, Pally [Gary Pallister], Keano [Roy Keane], Brian McClair, Cantona, Schmeichel – we demanded 100 per cent of ourselves.'

Stamnestrø adds: 'He is concerned with possession, and to play forward – run forward. And, of course, as he always says: express yourself. He is very clear on how he wants to play, and good on the strengths both you as a player and the team should make use of to punish the opponents. He is a manager who's very good at giving players freedom within certain limits.'

The despair Ole suffered from the knee injury that ended his career meant he could relate to, and have empathy with, his players when they suffered similarly. Børre Steenslid endured every footballer's nightmare after joining Molde in 2011 as a 26-year-old, and OGS was there for the defender.

'I was his first signing,' says Steenslid, who was a Norway international. 'When I decided to go to Molde it was because Ole Gunnar convinced me, as I wasn't sure if I should – I played for Viking at that time but he talked me into it and, yes, convinced me to join as he believed in me, talked about how he was going to use me.

'But then I got injured, a serious injury in my knee after only 18 days at the club. What I learned about Ole then was how fantastic he was with me, with all the players. When a player gets a long-term injury, yes, managers forget them a little bit. He always included me in things despite [me] being injured – the same as with other players. He was caring. He had empathy, tried to understand your situation because he himself has been injured.

'He knew what it was like and showed affection and that helped a lot. When I came back, I then got a fresh injury in the same knee. I had a real hard time but he was always there for me, showing he was a fantastic leader.'

By 2013 Steenslid's career was, sadly, over. 'In the end I got three injuries in the same knee,' he says. 'After that, I had to put my boots on the shelf. That was the end of me. Ole Gunnar sent me away for a couple of weeks just to not think about football and stuff like that. And when I came back, he offered me a position as a physical coach. Because, I think, of how I am as a person and was as a footballer – that was the reason he offered me the role.'

The move was a surprise. 'It was unexpected because, at the

time, we had a physical coach in our team but he was in his last season and was not going to sign a new contract with us,' says Børre. 'He offered me that role in August of 2013 and, by 2014, I was the overall person in charge. I'm still grateful for that opportunity, have now been around the team for some years and learned a lot. I've evolved.'

Pettersen also experienced Solskjær's pastoral side. The goalkeeper, who featured in 28 of the 30 games in 2011 and 23 the following year, says: 'He was fantastic in so many ways. For sure, he got the big results for the club and for many of the players he also influenced careers. He was great at creating belief and optimism and an energy that the players could bring to the pitch. To me he is a manager who is really good at man-management, who has great values – demanding on one side but on the other is easy to talk to. He is interested in his players' well-being.

'It could be all sorts of stuff, from being interested in myself and how my family are doing, and how my kids are. The best example in my case is when I got an injury. I broke my leg, had several months left on my contract with the club, and this injury was going to keep me out after my contract ended. I remember that when I was in the hospital bed, he was a big influence on having the club re-sign me, although I wasn't able to play for a while.'

Solskjær visited Pettersen. 'We had a lot of good talks because I was concerned that this might be it for me career-wise and that the future was really insecure,' he says. 'Ole Gunnar was fantastic. He was in the same situation at Man United.'

In two years Ole had transformed how Molde perceived themselves and how Norwegian football perceived the club.

Åge Hareide says, 'He is absolutely a hero there – first as a striker for one and a half seasons – and they finished second in his only full campaign. And when he came back from United as manager, he raised the profile of the club because Molde is a small town.

'You know how the media operates, with Molde being a local, provincial club: they just look at Molde like, "Okay. They're good, but they're not good enough." Then Ole came and changed the attitude completely because he brought in young, talented players and coached them to play entertaining football and they were really good. He raised the mood. When Molde play now, everybody raises the flag of Molde. It's blue all over the town when the game is on.'

Two seasons as the manager and two championships: a formidable start to OGS's managerial career. As he tilted at a third title in a row the squad began to break up for various reasons. The challenge of making it a hat-trick was close to impossible, but this was Ole's ambition. Out went the highest scorer of the 2011 triumph, the on-loan Pape Paté Diouf in August 2013 after only one league goal (for a further temporary deal to Denmark's Esbjerg), and Davy Claude Angan, the 2012 chart-topper, to Hangzhou Greentown. The sale of the latter appeared solely finance-driven. Tarje Nordstrand Jacobsen, Molde managing director, told Romsdal's *Bidstikke*: 'The finance is so good for us that we have accepted the bid'; while Angan told *VG*: 'I've had a good time and don't really want to leave.' Vegard Forren, a defensive mainstay of both championship wins, was sold to Southampton (though he was re-signed that July), and squad players Krister Wemberg and Simon Markeng also left the club.

Ole made five signings to cover these pre-season

departures. The defender Aliou Coly and forward Ben Spencer, who would make little impression, as too striker Lauri Dalla Valle. Joona Toivio, a Finland international, bought as Forren's replacement, would make 16 Tippeligaen appearances, scoring four goals. There was also a season-long loan deal for Agnaldo, a Brazilian midfielder, though he, also, did not establish himself.

The loss of strike power previously provided by Paté Diouf and Angan proved telling. Molde lost the first four league games, managing only three goals. They would not win for nearly two months, until game-day eight – a 4-1 victory over Aalesunds at the Aker, which meant five points from a possible 24.

Ole could not lift the side into the top 10 until 10 August and game-day 19, following a 2-1 win at Sogndal; Toivio and Tommy Høiland the Molde scorers. By the end of the final day of the Tippeligaen campaign Molde were sixth, a good recovery, with 44 points.

A fortnight later, though, Ole ensured Molde claimed a trophy – the Norwegian Cup, and this time Rosenborg, their opponents, were defeated: 4-2 at Oslo's Ullevaal Stadion.

This meant silverware in each of his three seasons at Molde. This was a fine return and a fine managerial calling card and did not go unnoticed in the English Premier League. As OGS plotted to try to reclaim the title in his fourth season with Molde, he was not to know that Cardiff City would come calling only five weeks later, in January 2014.

Ole's dream to manage in the Premier League was about to become a reality.

CHAPTER 10

The Times They Are a-Testing

4 May 2014

'After relegation Ole tried to pick everybody
up. That's the guy he is.'

ANDREW TAYLOR, EX-CARDIFF CITY

The Bluebirds are down. Norwich City's 0–0 draw at Chelsea
puts them three points ahead of Cardiff City with a better goal
difference of eight. There is a next-to-zero chance of them
overturning this when Chelsea visit on the final day, and they
do not – losing 2–1 – and so fall into the Championship after
one season in the Premier League as the bottom-placed side
with 30 points. OGS has overseen Cardiff City's instant plunge
through the trapdoor. He took over on 2 January, following
Malky Mackay's sacking, and had an 18-match audition as a
Premier League manager.

He fails. This will haunt him. Will cause soul-seeking and

solitude when home in Kristiansund. He took the position as he wanted to manage in the Premier League as a first step towards the ultimate ambition of taking charge of Manchester United one day. He had turned down Aston Villa but decided Cardiff was the correct choice – Ferguson had always told him to choose the right executive as well as club. Here he makes a mistake. Vincent Tan, the Malaysian businessman, was reputed to be an overzealous owner . . .

Ole had been approached after Mackay's removal by Mehmet Dalman, the Cardiff chairman, who was an admirer of OGS as a player, his style of football, and his vision of the game. Ole was approached on New Year's Eve – a Tuesday – and by the Thursday – 2 January – he was being unveiled.

'Absolute nonsense,' he said at his first media conference when asked if Sir Alex Ferguson, now in the final months of his 26-and-a-half-year-long Manchester United tenure, had advised against taking the position due to Tan's reputation. 'He has wished me the best and given me some good advice as he always does. I had a good conversation with him,' Ole said.

Yet he did admit some of his friends in football had sent him texts warning him not to work at the club due to rumours that Tan had meddled in team matters when Mackay was in charge. 'Everything isn't exactly what it seems from the out-side,' Ole said. 'I am really looking forward to the challenge. Whenever the manager put me on the bench [at Manchester United], I wanted to prove to him he is wrong. And if there are any doubts, don't worry, I'm coming into this with clear and open eyes, I know what I'm going into and I'm so look-ing forward to it. I'm going to bring my energy, enthusiasm, football knowledge. I want my team to play exciting football, we want the fans to come here and be proud of us.'

When Ferguson's statement that the manager is the most important person at a club was put to him, OGS said, 'I agree. I am very confident that football matters, that is my matter'; he then stressed the importance of creating a 'good dialogue' with Tan and Dalman, adding that he had held a 'great meeting' with the owner at the Emirates Stadium on New Year's Day, Cardiff losing 2-0 to Arsenal that day. 'He's willing to help this club progress and develop into the Premier League club that we want it to be.'

To have a single discussion with Tan at the Emirates during a match and agree instantly to accept the job ahead of being unveiled 24 hours later suggests haste. Here was a lesson. Jim Solbakken was also present in north London. He would source signings for Ole – his 'closest friend in a private sense' – during the January window that would be criticised regarding OGS's ability to assess what his new and struggling team required.

Despite having no Premier League experience, Dalman was '100 per cent convinced' by OGS. 'We will see much more attacking football from Ole,' the chairman said. 'Also, I like the way he communicates – that, for me, is crucial in the role I play, communicating with the manager and the rest of the hierarchy all the way up to the owner. Ole ticks all those boxes.'

There was more context to Ole being offered the job. He knew Tan's sacking of Mackay had come after the latter refused a 'resign or else' ultimatum. His departure followed the suspension, then removal, of the director of football, Iain Moody, for a rumoured £15m overspend on transfers, Mackay having recruited Moody after they worked together at Watford. Moody, though, denied the story, saying he was £4 million within budget. Tan's replacement for Moody had been left-field, even for the football vaudeville: Alisher Apsalyamovby, a 23-year-old Kazakh who was a friend of Tan's son and was at the club on work experience. Apsalyamovby was appointed on 9 October 2013 and lasted until 21 December, having to leave after only two months due to a visa issue. His remit had focused 'on gathering data on individual players', a Cardiff statement said, and was as controversial a Tan decision as his move to change the Bluebirds' blue-coloured shirts to red the previous summer.

Those recruited by Ole in the January window were the midfielders Magnus Wolff Eikrem and Mats Dæhli, plus striker Jo Inge Berget – all Solbakken clients and all players of Ole's from Molde, the others being Kenwyne Jones, Fábio Da Silva (who Ole also knew from Manchester United), and Juan Cala. There were question marks about the suitability of the six for the relegation fight Cardiff were in, particularly in Norway regarding Eikrem, Dæhli and Berget. This recruitment would be used against Ole later.

Solskjær was also joined by Mark Dempsey and Richard Hartis from Molde as he again tried to manage and man-manage his way. 'When he first came in, I was injured and he was great with me then, speaking with me. He tried to help – him and his assistant, Mark Dempsey,' says Andrew Taylor, who was a left-sided defender and midfielder for OGS at Cardiff. 'Solskjær was really good. He always had a lot of time to try to develop individuals. All of his coaches, Richard Hartis as well – the goalie coach. It was never to make you feel bad or to belittle you – Ole would show you clips from your previous games. Things that you maybe didn't do so well that you could have done better. I think that was certainly something as a management group that they were good at.'

Ole Gunnar's first league match as the Cardiff number one ended as the last one would: in defeat. A 2-0 home loss to West Ham United, the first of 13 in 20 matches in all competitions until the season end. In the Premier League, Solskjær enjoyed victory only three times. Yet Taylor, who retired in summer 2019 at Bolton Wanderers, speaks glowingly of his time under Solskjær.

'It was difficult, obviously,' Taylor says. 'The circumstances when he took over – we were in a sticky position anyway.' Cardiff were 17th with only 18 points, which put them a point and a place above the drop zone, with 18 matches left and a goal difference of minus 17. 'Given more time he certainly would have been successful there. He has the right views on football, the right visions of where he wants to go. In the time I spent with him, he made a good impression on me. He is first and foremost a fantastic person. I don't think anybody could have a bad word to say about him, but behind his smile and nice demeanour, he's got, how can you call it, a very focused personality. He knows what he wants, he knows how to get it. I think that's what you need, especially to be a manager at the top level. He's certainly got it.

'As time goes on the modern player is different to what he was 10 years ago or 15, 20 years ago. Ole knows how to speak with young players. He obviously did it with the young lads at United before he became a manager. One of the things that he used to try to instil into us was confidence. We were at the bottom and low on confidence. But he wants his players to go and play with freedom, and go play with a smile on their faces.'

OGS would come to feel he had tried to change too much

too soon at Cardiff. And the style of football he chose – attacking – was not apt for the relegation fight-fest. Taylor agrees this may have been an error. 'Well, again, he inherited somebody else's team and somebody else's philosophy, if you like,' he says. 'It was difficult for him to try to turn it round so quickly, but again he wanted us to play expansive football, with freedom, to go and express ourselves.'

Given the perilous position of the team, this illustrated Ole's inexperience. When in charge of Molde they never came close to facing the drop, so OGS was not versed in what was needed to save Cardiff.

'Sometimes when you are low on confidence anyway as individuals and as a team, it does become difficult, especially a team like Cardiff at the time,' says Taylor of Solskjær's gung-ho approach. 'He brought in a lot of players to try to help us, but that brings its own problems, because you've got no chemistry as a team. Like I say, I think if he had been given more time he certainly would have been a lot more successful.'

Solskjær was more concerned with what his team did than with the opposition. 'He was clear on the opposition and what they were doing. But then also focused on what he wanted us to do.'

Solskjær's standing in the game was acknowledged by the squad, despite this being a first Premier League post. And it is notable that, despite Cardiff being relegated, he retained this respect. 'Initially, if you're a manager with a big reputation as a player, you have respect for him because of what he's done,' Taylor says. 'But I think then, you've got to keep that respect. You've got to show them what you can do as a manager and he earned it at Cardiff.'

In an echo of the questions Ole Gunnar had to field on being appointed, Ben Turner, one of his defenders, claims that OGS was not always able to select the team on merit. Having started his career at Coventry City, Cardiff was Turner's fourth club when he joined in August 2011, having previously had loan spells at Peterborough United and Oldham Athletic. Turner was a mainstay of the Cardiff side that won promotion as Championship champions the season before Ole took over.

Yet Solskjær had some disturbing news when informing him he had been dropped after playing in a 0-0 home draw with Aston Villa on 11 February 2014, a Tuesday. The next league game was also at Cardiff City Stadium, against Hull City on Saturday 22 February, and ended – with no Turner in the XI – in a 4-0 hiding from Steve Bruce's side.

'I know he wasn't given the full sort of trust to manage the club in his own way without any interference,' says Turner. 'There were boys, including myself, who were called in and told we weren't playing and it really wasn't his decision – that it was coming from above.

'Obviously that wasn't helping anyone. If there was anyone at the whole club who was not understanding football, it was the people who weren't involved in the football. Unfortunately, there were people being picked or dropped, or both, based on what was being told from above – certain players were being dropped on that basis.

'At the time, it was bothering me on a personal level. As an example, we were in a relegation dogfight, and had Aston Villa at home midweek, I think it was a BT Sport game, and we drew 0-0. So we got a clean sheet and I honestly wouldn't be exaggerating if I said it's probably the best I've ever played in a game in my whole entire life. Then on Saturday we played Hull at home and three of the back four that started against Villa and got the clean sheet were dropped.'

These were Turner, Gary Medel and Kévin Théophile-Catherine, with only Declan John, a wing-back, making the bench for Hull's visit. Solskjær, true to type, was straight with Turner. 'I was told I was dropped for Juan Cala because he – Ole – was told from above that he had to play and that's why he was leaving me out. Ole told me this to my face – I was told that I was being dropped through no fault of my own – it was coming from above,' Turner recalls. 'And Hull beat us 4-0.'

This is a fresh perspective on the mistakes OGS says he made at Cardiff. The chief one may have been actually accepting the post. Turner continues: 'Ole said: "I know we got a clean sheet against Villa, but I've been told that I have to play Juan Cala."

'Cala was a signing that was brought in, a Spanish centre-back. No one really knew who brought him in. It didn't appear that it was from the football staff, as it were. He was brought in and it was kind of like, this is the player we brought in for you through agents and whatnot.

'I was told I wasn't playing because we wanted to try and pass the ball out more from the back. They told him – Ole – that on that basis Juan had to play, because he's a Spanish centre-back and that was one of the reasons he was brought in. Well, it was a disaster on the Saturday because Juan and Steven Caulker didn't get on, one single bit, and they were the centre-backs. It was a concern because it was new to me and what player wants to hear they're dropped because it's coming from the owner? The way I looked at it was this:

the owner's got all the money in the world. He's running a football club essentially as a side hobby and he's got new toys and the new toy that week was Juan Cala. This isn't me and sour grapes: I've been dropped as much as the next. But you want to be dropped for the right reasons.

'I had no reason to doubt what the gaffer was saying to me, that it'd come from above. He was an honest, genuine guy as far as I was concerned. Fair enough, we got relegated but he always had integrity. He was always straight with people in that respect and how straight can you be with a player just to tell him that you've been dropped because of what's coming from above.'

If a manager does not always have full control of team matters then he is seriously hamstrung and cannot, truly, be held wholly responsible for results. Turner believes Cardiff was a bad fit for Solskjær. 'You couldn't say he was anything but a gentleman, a nice person, a passionate football man and about how it should be played,' he says. 'And, being brutally honest, it was probably the wrong club for him at the time.

'At Cardiff, with everything that was going on and the fact that we were in deep trouble when he actually got there, it was probably the wrong place. But I'm sure he learned a lot from being there. The club was not harmonious – between the fans, players and owners. It was more than just trying to manage a football team.'

Nils Johan Semb, who managed Solskjær at Norway Under-21 and senior level, believes Ole Gunnar's experience in South Wales was invaluable. 'He had a tough period in Cardiff and of course he was not happy with that – but I think that maybe was the best experience for him, ahead of going into Manchester United,' Semb says. 'You can say that he made some mistakes in Cardiff, because he was very inexperienced.'

Even after the despair of relegation to the Championship Solskjær remained bubbly. 'I missed that game when we went down – I was injured for it – but I remember after that he was never really negative. He tried to pick everybody up and stay positive,' Taylor says. 'That's the guy that he is. He's not one for dwelling on things. Obviously, everybody was disappointed, but he was looking towards next season, looking for the positives.'

On 18 September 2014 Ole Gunnar was gone from Cardiff, eight and a half months after being appointed. Ole's team had played eight matches of the new season, six in the Championship, of which he'd won two and drawn two for eight points, Cardiff sitting in 15th place.

Really, he should have walked in the summer. Whatever the level of Tan's involvement in Cardiff, for OGS and the club to part only six weeks into the term suggests deep-rooted fissures in the relationship, which were surely evident in the close season. This, again, showed misjudgement from him.

His departure was publicly amicable and characterised as Ole stepping down rather than being sacked – until Vincent Tan suggested otherwise. OGS said, 'I want to thank Vincent for giving me the opportunity to manage Cardiff City FC. He has my full respect and I really wish him all the best in his pursuit of making this football club successful. However, our difference in philosophy on how to manage the club made me decide to step aside and allow the club to move forward in the direction Vincent wants.'

Tan picked up on these words, choosing to deny them to Sky Sports: 'I was quite disappointed with his statement after he left. He said we had a difference in philosophies. What philosophy? The philosophy for a football manager is to win matches, stay in the league, be promoted? What are the different philosophies you are talking about? It gives the impression that a different philosophy [is that] maybe I interfere with him, maybe I do this or do that.'

Yet Tan's take was: 'Ole was hired by Cardiff City on our understanding and belief that he would help us fight relegation from the Premier League. After the club was relegated, many people advised me to let him go, but I decided to keep Ole on for the Championship season. Regrettably our recent results do not justify Ole's continued role as manager at Cardiff.'

That sounds like a sacking. On appointment, Ole Gunnar had insisted he would not suffer any interference from the club, with Dalman going on the record in support. 'We changed the structure,' he had said. 'Until I arrived, the board had never met. That was number one. The manager will say what he wants, A, B and C. I will go to the board and say, "Do we have that money?" It gets authorised. It gets signed off. The manager goes and does his thing. Everybody is on the same page. Before, that did not exist. We have got transparency between the football side and the business side.'

Not according to Ben Turner. And not if Ole's departing words are reread and analysed – these in particular: 'Our difference in philosophy on how to manage the club made me decide to step aside and allow the club to move forward in the direction Vincent wants.'

It may have scarred Ole – certainly for a while. His father, Øyvind, said: 'He did not talk much about it. It was a bad experience with the owner.' His mother, Brita, added: 'I do not think that was a particularly good experience for him.'

Ole, though, would come to view this as a crucial lesson. Despite the first Premier League management position not working out, he now had experience of the wrong end of the division for the first time in his career. He might also have remembered that Ferguson had also been sacked years before being made Manchester United manager: by St Mirren, in 1978.

Yet for the moment, the move, though brave in terms of leaving the comfort of Molde FK for the challenge of the Premier League, had backfired. And 'my ultimate dream' to one day manage Manchester United – as he would tell a media conference in March 2019 – harboured since taking up coaching at the club when retiring in 2007, was surely over after this. This was what Ole Gunnar believed, deciding within himself that to take charge of United or, indeed, any other Premier League team, no longer drove him.

Now Ole Gunnar was to do something he'd not done since before his debut for Clausenengen in 1990.

He took a break from football.

CHAPTER 11

Soul Searching

'Ole Gunnar says everything is about timing.'

CHRISTIAN MICHELSEN,
KRISTIANSUND BK COACH

September 2015 – a windblown Kristiansund Stadion, side-ways rain driving in from the Atlantic. The tiny ground in Karihola can hold no more than 4,444 souls, though today is not a match day. It is a Friday, a training day, and Ole Gunnar is taking the second of his twice-weekly sessions as a guest coach, drilling the players of Kristiansund BK, the club that merged with his first club, Clausenengen FK, in 2003.

After the session he tells Christian Michelsen's squad they have promotion from Norway's 1. divisjon – the second tier – to the Tippeligaen in their grasp. 'Six games left – six cup finals. You're in a great position. Good luck,' he said.

A year after leaving Cardiff City due to the 'difference in philosophy' with Vincent Tan, Ole was back home and answered a call from Christian, his childhood friend and former Clausenengen team-mate.

The Kristiansund manager recalls why Ole was invited. 'It was natural, because I know if you're a player, you give something extra to have a coach like Ole Gunnar,' Christian says. 'It was a win-win situation. It was a very good experience for me as a coach. It was great for the players to have a great coach/manager in some of the training.

'I have always looked up to him as a human being, when a youngster, as a football player, and lately as a coach/manager. He has achieved so much. And being from the same town, the same street, being three years younger, it's natural to try and follow his example.

'Ole Gunnar was a Clausenengen youngster. Me, I played in another club, a neighbouring club. When I was 16, 17 years old, I moved to Clausenengen. I played there the last year with him before he went off. Then, I was playing at the top level in Norway. My biggest achievement was when I scored the goal in the Europa Cup against Anderlecht from Belgium – for Stabæk in September 2002. We won 1-0 away – that's my highlight.'

Michelsen's assistant at Kristiansund, who he took into the top flight in 2017, is Ole Olsen, OGS's first coach at Clausenengen. 'It was natural for us to ask Ole Gunnar if he had some extra time to come,' Christian says. 'And there were some great sessions we had together.'

Despite Ole's guest coaching and encouraging words, Kristiansund did not claim promotion in 2015, being knocked out in the play-offs. Magnus Stamnestrø, now 23, had moved from Molde. Of his former manager's coaching sessions, he says: 'They were very good, he gave energy and confidence to us. They were with all of the team – sometimes defence, midfield, and of course offensive players the most. He worked on details in different parts of the game.'

When Ole Gunnar left Cardiff City on 18 September 2014, he headed to Kristiansund to recharge. There, at his house on the edge of the Atlantic on the south of Innlandet, the smallest of his hometown's four islands, he could finally truly relax with his family. Now 41, he needed to assess his next move.

OGS and his wife had lived – or retained a home – in Kristiansund, at various addresses, since their younger days together and had a holiday retreat in Grip, a tiny fishing village a few miles north of Kristiansund where Silje's mother, Grete Lyngvær, was born. 'He likes to take the family there, where they have a cabin,' said Brita, Ole's mother. 'A perfect day for him is to be with the family and if the weather is good take the trip out to Grip,' Øyvind said.

At this crossroads in his football career OGS could not know that just over four years later he would be Manchester United interim manager. And that two days after his appointment the burghers of Kristiansund would display a '20LEGEND' in Hollywood-sign style above the town to herald his appointment (20LEGEND deriving from the banner that is hung in his honour by fans at Old Trafford).

This would be merely the latest tribute to a man who had become a national treasure. In 2009 Ole had been awarded the Peer Gynt Prize, the award named after the famous play by Henrik Ibsen, considered Norway's greatest playwright and poet, which features the eponymous 'hero', who is a slave trader and general miscreant. Those awarded the prize are considered to have the precise opposite values and character. So it was on 29 July he travelled to Vinstra in the Gudbrandsdalen valley – where the real-life person who inspired the play is thought to have lived during the 18th century – in central Norway for the Peer Gynt Festival to receive the honour. 'I am proud to get this prize,' said OGS, whose work as a UNICEF ambassador was also being recognised. Marit Breivik, head of the nomination committee, said: 'Ole Gunnar is a worthy and great prize-winner. I have followed him for many years and he is a wonderful sports ambassador. He cares about more than purely the sporting part of life. He works great in every way and will fit well into the Peer Gynt club.'

In 2008, when 35, Solskjær had also become the youngest Knight of the First Class, appointed by the Royal Norwegian Order of St Olav: again for being a role model. 'This award is the result of the work of all those around me, both family and coaches,' he said. 'I have just tried to do my best as a footballer.'

In 2011 and 2012, he won the Kniksen Award for coach of the year, having previously claimed a Kniksen in 1996 when voted the Norwegian player of the year, plus an honorary one in 2008. In typically deflective style, on receiving the award, Ole Gunnar said Mark Dempsey should have received it because he was 'head coach and I the manager of Molde'; Dempsey having become a key assistant of Ole's after first meeting him when Dempsey started to coach at Manchester United in 1999. Dempsey takes the more hands-on part in sessions, Ole preferring to stand back and observe.

OGS's extra-curricular role as a UNICEF ambassador since 2003 had him auctioning a custom-made watch given to him by Manchester United sponsor Tag Heuer at the club's Gala Dinner in January 2019, raising £35,000. He said, 'I remember the first association I had with UNICEF as a player in Beijing in 1999 and I'm honoured to now be the goodwill ambassador back home in Norway.'

For the moment he was content to take a break, revive energy levels by living again in his own country, allowing his children to attend the nearby school and nursery, and to enjoy a life in which friends could drop by. 'The kids get a different upbringing here than they would have had in Manchester or Cardiff,' Ole said.

Ole also coached Noah, his eldest son, and by October 2015 plans which been worked on since February of that year were approved for the family home to be demolished and rebuilt in a modern style. Bought in 2010 for a then record for a house in Kristiansund of 11.5m Norwegian kroner (around £1m), it had an outdoor swimming pool, was metres away from the scenic Skjerva beach, and was now to have a 400 square-metre ground-floor area and five bedrooms – windows and light a prevailing theme.

The scheme for Bryggekanten 2, drawn up by architect Sunniva Neuenkirchen Rosenberg, was also to sink the house a metre lower, and to feature an expansive 510-metre area across two floors and a larger utility space of 100 metres. Earlier in 2015, Ole also had plans approved for a floating dock on the water outside the stone-walled house, this to be removed in winter. The vision for the rebuild was to fully realise the stunning vistas around the home – the hills of Kristiansund and the sea.

Michelsen described how being home benefited his friend. 'There is no doubt that he thrives here – Ole Gunnar is always in a relaxed mood,' he said. Ole's immersion in local life extended to Kristiansund's Tahiti Festival, which was on Innlandet and where he presented the Tahiti Prize – awarded to a person who, goes the citation, adds to Norway's understanding of the world – having been on the jury with Norwegian musician Frode Alnæs and Harald Stanghelle, editor of *Aftenposten*, the country's largest newspaper.

Michelsen offered a gauge of OGS's mindset when talking about when he might return to management. 'Ole says that it's all a matter of timing. Local residents give him the peace he enjoys in Kristiansund and don't nag him about his future,' he said. 'I think most people want to have a chat with him, he's a big celebrity here and everyone cares about him. But we're very conscious of not bothering him.'

Michelsen, inevitably, was asked whether, should he move on as Kristiansund manager, Ole could ever take charge. If this was a way of suggesting Ole might be a threat to him, Christian was unmoved. 'You should never say never in football. But a man like Ole Gunnar is sought-after,' he said, offering a cute response. 'There are big clubs that want such a manager. As long as he lives at home, he is always welcome here to contribute as much as he wants.'

Events were moving down the road at his former club. In July 2015, the Molde manager Tor Ole Skullerud announced he would not serve the third year of his contract (for family reasons) and so would leave at the end of the season. Michelsen said, 'It will surprise me if Molde does not contact him, but I have not talked to Ole Gunnar about what he is thinking about the time ahead. Ole Gunnar himself says that everything is about timing.'

Given OGS's elevation of Molde during his three years there, it was inevitable a clamour would arise for his return. Jan Fuglset, a goalscoring hero for his two spells at the club, from 1963 to 1967 and 1973 to 1982, believed he should do so. 'Ole Gunnar Solskjær will be a good choice. He is a great guy and he has done a good job here earlier,' Fuglset said. At Molde the chief executive, Øystein Neerland, was vague. 'We haven't discussed so far – we'll look at this over the autumn. Now we are concentrating on the 16 games remaining, there is a lot left of the season,' he said.

In April 2015, when OGS had begun his sessions at Kristiansund after staying under the radar on returning home the previous year, he spoke of his joy at again being involved in football. 'It's just fun to be able to contribute a bit,' Ole said. He'd been coaching Clausenengen FK's boys' team, again accompanied by Mark Dempsey, with his son Noah one of his players. Jan Trygve Pedersen, the Clausenengen general manager, was delighted with his new coach. 'It's just a scoop. We are incredibly grateful that Ole Gunnar will contribute to our club,' he said. 'At the same time, we are aware that he can quickly disappear. Of course, CFK should not put obstacles in the way if Ole wants to go elsewhere.'

Jan Trygve offered a comparison of Ole to Noah. 'It is not so easy – Noah is at a bit of a higher level than Solskjær was at that time,' he said.

And then what felt inevitable did indeed occur: Ole became the Molde manager for a second time. On 21 October 2015 Manchester United tweeted: 'Congratulations to Ole Gunnar Solskjær, who's returned to management with @Molde_FK in Norway. #mufc.' The link between OGS and United remained firm.

OGS's relationship with Molde's owners, Kjell Inge Røkke and Bjørn Rune Gjelsten, ensured he was welcomed to the club for what was a third time in total. It meant this: the year 'off' was over. After discussing the move with Silje and the rest of his family he was again before the media as the Molde FK number one, close to five years since accepting the job on the first occasion.

Under Tor Ole Skullerud, Molde had been the champions of 2014, but he was not allowed to step away at the end of 2015 as he wished. Instead, Skullerud was sacked in August and Erling Moe, part of the coaching staff, was made caretaker manager. (Three years later he would take up the same role – when Ole Gunnar left for United – before becoming the permanent incumbent.)

When Ole took over from Moe, Molde were seventh, the side having won their last two Eliteserien matches, 4-0 against Tromsø and 3-1 against Mjøndalen, each at home. There were only three league matches left plus the Europa League campaign. Ole said, 'There are major changes since the last time I was here. I've had a year off, a vacation. I promised the family that. But I started to fancy coming back at a high level again.'

The pull of the game on OGS was irresistible. There was nothing as precious as his family yet even during the prolonged break he vowed to enjoy he still coached Noah, took sessions for Christian Michelsen at Kristiansund, and now was back in the sport full-time.

After signing a three-and-a-half-year contract, his first match in charge was the following day – Thursday – against Celtic in the Europa League, a group fixture. 'It was a shorter stay in Cardiff than I expected and hoped for,' he told a press conference. 'I felt like I was leaving Molde for Cardiff in very good condition. And it is great that I was wanted back. The club is much better off. Both mentally, in player numbers and in facilities. There have been five trophies in the last four years. This year's season has been a little disappointing, so I have to wake the hunger again.

'I know it myself: am I hungry enough to come back and give what it takes to reach the top again? The players must also think about that. We have to reverse the trend that has been there this year. It has been a bit in and out.'

On the second day of the second stint he was triumphant, Molde beating Celtic in the Europa League, in what was an impressive win against the former European champions and 46-time Scottish champions. The strategy was to retain the side chosen by Erling Moe and, in dreadful conditions at the Aker Stadion, Celtic struggled on the artificial pitch, going down 3-1. Ola Kamara, Vegard Forren and Mohamed Elyounoussi scored for Ole's new Molde, Kris Commons registering the consolation for Celtic, managed by Ronny Deila, a countryman of Ole's who previously guided Strømsgodset to the 2013 Norwegian title.

VG, Norway's biggest tabloid, headlined the result: 'DRØMMESTART FOR SOLSKJÆR: – ET FANTASTISK RESULTAT' – Dream start for Solskjær, a fantastic result. The subdeck stated: 'Ronny Deila under press etter 1-3-tapet' – Ronny Delia under pressure after 1-3 loss.

Ole said, 'Of course, it became difficult for both teams with these conditions, but my boys were incredible.' Then, he seemed to close off the notion of ever leaving Norwegian football for the big league again. 'When I came to Molde last time, I had a much bigger dream about the Premier League,' Ole Gunnar said. 'Now this is where I want to live and be a coach. It was tough enough to be away from the family last time.'

There was detail on how the second tenure came about.

'Kjell Inge and I have met once,' Ole Gunnar said of the co-owner. 'That was when I presented how I would drive the club forward and how I would bring the experience of [being at] Manchester United to make Molde a better and more professional club.'

Molde director Tarje Nordstrand Jacobsen said, 'We contacted him this summer, when it became clear that we had to have a new coach. The agreement has the same framework as his previous one.'

Ole Gunnar's first contract at Molde was worth 4.4m kroner (£390k), with 2.4m of this paid by Aker, Røkke's company, plus a 1m bonus for winning the title, which he did – twice. While Aker were not this time part-remunerating Ole Gunnar, the local bank, Sparebanken Møre, was.

Ahead of the Celtic game Ole had said, 'It's business as usual. I enter a club that is very well structured and has a clear framework. We will continue the work that started before I arrived.'

The first contract with Molde had a release term should Manchester United have come calling. This one did not. 'No,' Ole says, in what suggests a further admission that the dream of United, if not completely over, has become distant. 'Clauses have not been so important. What is important is to get back to the training field, develop myself as a manager and develop the team further. Now I am employed at Molde football club, I find it incredible to have the opportunity.

'It's a completely different starting point now than last time – then there were players who weren't used to winning. Now, players are used to winning. They have won five trophies in four years, and that does something with people.'

There were three matches left of the domestic season and

Ole Gunnar won them all, Molde finishing sixth with 52 points. He guided Molde to the head of a Europa League group that also featured Celtic, Ajax and Fenerbahçe, but they were then eliminated in the opening knockout round by Sevilla, who went on to claim the 2015-16 competition. His first complete season back – 2016 – ended in a fifth-place finish. The following year Molde were second, seven points behind champions Rosenborg. In 2018, Molde again challenged for the title, going ten matches unbeaten in what was now known as the Eliteserien from the end of August but, once more, were second, this time five points behind Rosenborg.

In 2017 and 2018, Ole's Molde played against Kristiansund and so met up once more with friends Christian Michelsen, the manager, and Kjetil Neergaard, the chief executive. 'It was tremendous for us to have a visit from Molde and Ole Gunnar in the top league,' Kjetil says. 'We played Molde two times in each season. In 2017, in the opening league game, they beat us 1-0 at home, and in the away game, we beat Molde 1-0 in Molde. The next year it was the opposite, we beat them 1-0 here and we lost 3-2 in Molde. So, two wins for each team.'

If Ole Gunnar's reputation after the Cardiff debacle was being rebuilt, his ambition of a third title for Molde since his return had not yet been fulfilled. 'We started each of those seasons pretty poorly – we weren't really close at any point, I'd say, so the two bad starts made us unable to really give it a run,' says Joona Toivio, the Finnish defender Ole signed during his first tenure, in 2013, and who left the club in 2018.

He cites OGS's management style as good on a personal

level with players while, as per his approach, instructing Mark Dempsey to be the more hands-on coach. 'He's close to the players, likes to be close to them,' Toivio says. 'Ole wants to see a lot of smiles. He's really positive in everything he does. Everybody who knows Ole knows that he smiles a lot. Mark Dempsey was an important piece of what Ole does, too. He's really involved in training – was usually the one who took most of the training. He's also a positive guy and really enthusiastic about football – I really liked him.'

Ole, along with Dempsey, wanted Toivio to be more forward-operating despite his position. 'As a defender, they both helped my game,' he says. 'They like attacking football, and stress ball use a lot – when you have the ball, look forward. Also, when defending be aware of what is around you, so that when you get the ball you can play it forward right away. Know where your strikers are and try to counterattack with it.'

Toivio, now with Swedish club Häcken, was wrong-footed by Solskjær. 'This actually surprised me a little when I got to Molde – he was really open to if players had any special requests concerning their family, this kind of thing. Really open to giving free days for, let's say, weddings, things like this,' he says. 'He really wanted players to be happy outside of football, so that they can then do their work properly on the pitch.'

OGS developed tactically, becoming more agile, as was illustrated by wanting Molde to have a fluid shape. 'We did change it quite a bit the last couple of years compared to the first year when I got there,' he says. 'Then we played a 4-2-3-1. He has developed flexibility and is able to change tactics during games. I think he's gone forward as a manager and really loves doing the job.'

Nice guy Ole could lose his cool if required. 'Yes, a couple of times. He would lose his temper only if he saw that the players weren't giving 100 per cent,' says Toivio. 'If players were giving 100 per cent, then he wouldn't really get mad because then the guys are trying, doing their best. But if people were 90 per cent and doing badly, then he could sometimes lose his temper – but it wasn't often.'

On 24 November 2018 Molde closed their season by winning at Sandefjord 3-1, their goals coming from Kristoffer Haugen, Magnus Wolff Eikrem and Leke James. They were second and Ole Gunnar was determined they would not be again in 2019.

Yet events at Manchester United were about to take control of his destiny. Just over three weeks later he was to replace José Mourinho, on a caretaker basis. 'When he got the temporary job, I was actually thinking that he will do well there because that's how he is. It was a good time for him because he was experienced and his aim was for players to be happy. You could see from the outside, from tweets or whatever, that they were not happy with the last coach – Mourinho,' says Toivio.

'That's obviously never a good thing, but I thought he had a chance of doing well because of how he is and how he wants there to be a good atmosphere in the group.'

It is a fundamental ask of any manager that players – the entities on which performances, results and *his* livelihood depend – should be content, and yet it seemed a secondary priority for Mourinho when in charge. It was certainly, as Toivio relates it, the first priority for Solskjær at Molde, and also when he replaced the Portuguese at Manchester United. 'He manages people,' says Børre Steenslid. 'He's extremely good at that.'

Yet Ole Gunnar had failed at Cardiff. In addition to Ben Turner's claims about team selection being forced on him, there were counter-contentions from those at Cardiff whose view was that Ole was simply not up to the job. Specific criticisms here include him being 'too defensive' – a strange charge for a striker of Ferguson's swashbuckling teams and a student of his managerial school – and that his players were not fit enough, which, again, is at odds with the man who, on taking over at United, decided his players were not in optimum shape and addressed this in summer 2019.

The chastening experience in South Wales had moved him to state publicly that the bright lights of elite management no longer burned for him. Being away from the family when in charge of Cardiff during those ill-starred nine months proved a dispiriting experience. When he was a United player and then reserve-team coach, the family were based near Manchester. As Nils Johan Semb says: 'Of course, he was not happy with that period, but maybe it was the best for him. You can say that he did make some mistakes in Cardiff, because he was very inexperienced. The expectations at Molde and in Norwegian football are lesser and you cannot compare to Manchester United, exactly. But, more or less, it's the same thing: there are expectations at both. He learned to manage them and also had the difficult period at Cardiff City.'

As Semb states, the experience in South Wales was vital to Ole's growth and toughened him to the travails of management. It was part of the process that led to this moment, now. The deep love for a sport that can be cruel plus the narcotic found in the pursuit of excellence meant that when Manchester United came calling there was only going to be one answer from Ole Gunnar.

United's executive vice-chairman, Ed Woodward, and owners, the Glazers, were impressed by how he had responded to the Cardiff failure, by the second-place finishes with Molde and the accomplished Europa League showing. Tenacity and resilience had been added to a reputation rebuilt and, when Manchester United required a temporary fix to right the downward spiral under José Mourinho, he became the obvious candidate.

PART THREE

The Dream Job

CHAPTER 12

Death by 10,000 Cuts

'Do you want him to be happy with the
players around him?'

JOSÉ MOURINHO ON ALEXIS SÁNCHEZ,
JULY 2018

José Mourinho is finding it all so frustrating. A frustration
managing Manchester United that will precipitate his sacking
in five months' time.

A frustration that will clear the way for Ole Gunnar's arrival.

Right now, it is midsummer 2018 and the sun dazzles
and life in Los Angeles is trying for Mourinho. As is the
vivid LA light, the south California vibe, Hollywood being
around the corner, Santa Monica and Malibu a drive away,
the beaches of golden sand, the attractions of Echo Park and
Griffith Observatory and Grauman's Chinese Theatre, and
the vibrant sense of being in a town that is movie-star rich
and silent-screen storied.

So very trying.

UCLA's state-of-the-art training facilities used by Mourinho and his Manchester United squad. The smell of pre-season and the sound of the first *thwacks* of ball on boot and the promise of the new campaign to come: virgin and fecund with hope. Life being here, right now.

It is all so trying.

It boils down to this: José Mourinho is missing 13 players from a summer tour that starts here on the West Coast before hitting Michigan and Miami. This is the crux of the matter; the bottom line regarding his rising dudgeon. Well, this and other things. Primarily, that the club are not going to back him in the transfer market how he wishes, how he believes they should.

He may have a point. He is the manager, after all. He wants a centre-back. Harry Maguire is one. He wants the Leicester City player but will not be allowed him. Twelve months later Ole Gunnar will want him and be given him for a world record sum of £80m. When the deal goes through you can understand José's frustrations – why no Maguire for him but for OGS??

But, for now, it's the 13 absent frontline footballers who are eating away at José. Of the Mourinho Thirteen one case is a minor farrago that confuses: why would a club of the scale and operation of Manchester United allow this to occur? Alexis Sánchez was not involved at Russia 2018 as Chile did not qualify for a World Cup that finished earlier in this month of July. Yet a visa issue means the forward did not land in LA with the rest of the squad. If the club should have sorted this out long before jetting to the US (Sánchez will arrive when United fly to San Jose up the coast in a few days), then how about the other missing 12?

Paul Pogba, Romelu Lukaku, Marouane Fellaini, Marcus Rashford, Jesse Lingard, Marcos Rojo, Victor Lindelöf, Ashley Young, David De Gea, Nemanja Matić, Fred and Phil Jones are all not here. Why: because they are on post-World Cup breaks or injured. And this, for Mourinho, is a near-crisis, as he puts it, 'very bad'. Yes, when he appears in the media conference room on the UCLA campus in Westwood, the fact that a large proportion of his players are having a rest after Russia 2018 has Mourinho downbeat. Strangely downbeat.

'Everything is really bad and then we go to the UK and have to play the Premier League,' he said. 'The broadcasters were not nice to us with the Friday match, against Leicester City on 10 August, which complicates more things.'

Hmm: Ole Gunnar Solskjær would surely *never* do this. It is just not his style or modus operandi to complain about what is, really, a fait accompli. As managerial moves go this may be straight out of the Mourinho playbook and yet: the self-anointed Special One is actually, really, complaining about a position United's rivals – Manchester City, Liverpool, Chelsea and Tottenham Hotspur – are all also in: missing personnel due to the World Cup tournament. Mourinho has stated he wishes to manage United for the long term and that his so-called third season syndrome, which features him and whichever club he is at falling out, is a media confection, yet here he is kicking proceedings off on his third campaign at Manchester United and getting his excuses in (very) early.

He is not even the worst off when it comes to absentees. Pep Guardiola at Manchester City, the champions of the previous season, has 16 players not with him on their tour of the US. And, although Mourinho does say his absent footballers means it is 'fantastic' for the young players to have come to the US instead, this feels a throwaway line. And, yes, he shows this to be so when, less than two weeks later in Michigan Manchester United play Liverpool, he uses Sánchez to make the point that there are *too* many of the club's emerging talents on the trip.

Where Ole Gunnar's default positon is optimism, José Mourinho's seems to have become weariness.

At Manchester City Guardiola's spin on his situation is to state his club should be proud of having so many players involved at the World Cup, as it illustrates their profile and status. 'I learned when a little boy in Barcelona, don't find excuses. We are happy to have 16 players out – the most – that's a good sign. We are going to adapt, it's as simple as that,' the Catalan said.

And, contrast Mourinho's limp take on his predicament with Solskjær's 'nothing is mission impossible', which he declares the following March ahead of the Champions League last-16 second leg at PSG when Manchester United are 2–0 down and Paul Pogba is suspended, one of the 10 players the interim manager is without for the game.

The fantasy-world mansions of Bel Air to the north, the Beverly Hills domiciles lying east and the affluence of Brentwood due west may surround the bucolic UCLA campus, with Sunset Boulevard due south, but Mourinho is displaying precisely zero strut and swagger. This is B-list stuff from the Portuguese as he starts principal shooting of a B-movie of a campaign that will bomb at the box office and by mid-December will have him as its fallen star, his stock having plunged like John Travolta pre-*Pulp Fiction*.

Plunge: this is José Mourinho and this is Manchester

United under him before he is sacked. When Ole Gunnar takes over there is a chasm of 11 points between the three-time European champions and fourth place with its berth for next year's Champions League. Mourinho's opening 24 matches of 2018-19 – which will prove his last in charge – read: WLLWWWDDLDWDLWWWLDWDDWLL. Ten wins, seven defeats and seven draws.

He is bugged at UCLA and remains bugged until Ed Woodward, the executive vice-chairman, axes him on 18 December. And what is bugging him beyond the 13 absentees at the start of the tour of the US does not stop bugging him until then. The Centre-back Question. The failure of the club to allow the Portuguese to sign Maguire or another of his choice, which he views as a symptom of the club's reluctance to allow him sovereignty over the millions of pounds required to strengthen his squad.

Mourinho has a case. His Manchester United finished second last season with 81 points. This is still 19 behind Guardiola's champions and Mourinho, a career title-winner, believes he knows best regarding how to close the gap. This is his job as manager, after all: to be the football expert. To try to bag Manchester United a 21st championship.

He is not happy or at ease. His perception is that Woodward and the Glazers are not allowing him to manage how he wishes. The near-open warfare between the two sides is crystallised in a briefing by a source close to Mourinho that he wants Anthony Martial to leave (he and the French forward are not on the best terms), while Ed Woodward does not. This occurs after the tour game against San Jose Earthquakes – a 0-0 draw – at Levi's Stadium in Santa Clara. Mourinho's preference is said to be for Martial to go to a club outside of the Premier League. Woodward does not want Martial gone at all, as he is viewed as precisely the type of footballer United need.

Whichever way this standoff is sliced it is a mess and not good for Manchester United moving forward.

Ditto the thorny issue of Maguire, or indeed A. N. Other centre-back target that Mourinho identified and the hierarchy rejected. The spat over this will cause smoke signals from the club which say, in essence, that Maguire or A. N. Other target is no better than those central defenders already at the club – Victor Lindelöf, Phil Jones, Chris Smalling, Eric Bailly and Marcos Rojo.

Another Mourinho target for the position is the Colombian Yerry Mina, a 23-year-old Barcelona player who scored three times for Colombia at the World Cup, but who is vetoed by United's recruitment department because of his injury record and the view that he will not improve the squad. When Mina moves to Everton his record with maladies suggests the recruitment department did their job well by standing up to José.

This only compounds Mourinho's frustration. This is understandable and his predecessor, Louis van Gaal, underlines the level of vexation managers can have at the club. His time at Manchester United, which ran from July 2014 to May 2016, took in two summer transfer windows. 'I get not always the players that I want. That's the problem. There is Woodward and his right hand is Matt Judge,' the Dutchman said of the head of corporate affairs, who is responsible for getting transfers over the line. 'I met Judge once in a while but not too much. And then there was the head of scouting – that was the structure, but you are always dependable on

Woodward and Judge. I thought always Manchester United can buy every player because they have a lot of money. A few players were not reachable for Manchester United. I cannot understand but it was like that. So, when I want – ask for – a player then, I don't get.'

In Van Gaal's experience, it is not the owners who have the ultimate say regarding who United can buy, but the executive vice-chairman. 'I think that the Glazers were not deciding about it,' he says. 'Woodward is the one who talks with the Glazers. I only talked with the Glazers when they were attending a game.'

Whatever the precise dynamic, José Mourinho does not receive who he desires and the US tour is farcical. Sánchez's late arrival is followed by Martial going home for the birth of his son, but the manager then has a problem with him not returning. After losing 4-1 on 28 July to Liverpool at Michigan Stadium, Mourinho says, 'He has the baby and after the baby is born – beautiful baby, full of health, thank God – he should be here and he is not here.'

Now comes Mourinho's slating of the youngsters in the tour squad who are in the US because, yes, of the absentees (not all are on post-World Cup breaks, some are injured, like Nemanja Matić and Antonio Valencia). Sánchez has looked dejected in the Liverpool game and Mourinho offers a classic Mourinho barb to explain why: 'Do you want me to be very happy with the players he has around him?'

It is a great quote *and* an odd entry in the man-management annals – how to alienate every constituent part of the club: the young players on tour, the fans who love seeing young players, the hierarchy who want to see young players come through, and any of the senior players who were young players once and know how difficult building confidence can be when a young player.

Here is the XI Mourinho was 'forced' to select against Liverpool. It is not so young; instead actually relatively experienced, especially for a side on a pre-season tour when for all kinds of regulation reasons – World Cup cry-offs, injuries, a wish to see potential new first-team squad members – there will always be a sprinkling of youth.

Lee Grant, Matteo Darmian, Timothy Fosu-Mensah, Eric Bailly, Axel Tuanzebe, Demi Mitchell, Scott McTominay, Ander Herrera, Andreas Pereira, Juan Mata, Alexis Sánchez. In Grant, Darmian, Fosu-Mensah, Bailly, McTominay, Herrera, Pereira, Mata and Sánchez there are nine – *nine* – experienced professionals; there are only two youngsters: Tuanzebe and Mitchell, each of whom has played senior football for the club. The point, here, really is that Mourinho is moaning about a scenario that is no one's fault. Those missing due to post-World Cup breaks and injury cannot be helped, so Mourinho's complaint seems to be a function of his own disquiet at the club and unhappiness in his job.

He also said: 'The atmosphere is good but if I was them, I wouldn't come, I wouldn't spend my money to see these teams.' None of this pleases Woodward or the Glazers. How can it? The club's pre-season tours are money-making PR exercises and Mourinho's words are firmly and starkly anti-money-making and anti-PR.

Mourinho's concerns about how this is affecting preparation for the 2018-19 campaign actually prove sagacious. Manchester United lose 3-2 at Brighton & Hove Albion and 3-0 at home to Tottenham Hotspur in their second and third games of the new season, yet here he may have proved the high priest of the self-fulfilling prophecy. By mid-December, Mourinho is gone. An appointment that always seemed doomed to end as it does, does.

United had been reluctant to appoint the Portuguese. He had always seemed the wrong fit for the club. As long ago as 2012 Sir Bobby Charlton, who as a director was the driving force behind Ferguson's arrival, had questioned his candidacy, pointing to some of his antics as not befitting a Manchester United manager. Later, after his sacking, the logic behind United finally deciding to hire Mourinho emerges. Prime here was how Mourinho was wanted to re-establish a title-winning mentality. If this seems obvious, there was a disconnect between the Mourinho methodology and that of the club. It is a strategic thought process Ed Woodward and his executives will come to regret. Mourinho may be a winner but he has no deep love for the club, no instinctive bond with Old Trafford and the fans and the history and culture of Manchester United.

Yet the hierarchy had still been sure of him as late as June 2018 – a month before the Sánchez outburst. Privately, some players were complaining about Mourinho's style during his second season, though the moans were not as bad as under Louis van Gaal. But, then, came the comments about Sánchez, and the bell began to toll loud and clear regarding his future. From here, Mourinho's demise became a kind of death by 10,000 cuts. This despite United having handed him a contract extension in January 2018: more evidence of the muddled thinking at the club.

In Mourinho – and Van Gaal – United went for serial winners. In Ole Gunnar Solskjær the first priority was to have a manager who could make the club – particularly the players and fans – happy again. In this he would be successful, certainly in the opening period of his caretaker tenure. The joy of playing for Manchester United was rediscovered under Ole, as was the joy of following the club for fans.

But, before this occurred, some of the cuts that killed Mourinho were to show more than others . . .

CHAPTER 13

Three Fingers, Four Words

'Respect, respect, respect, man.'

JOSÉ MOURINHO, 28 AUGUST 2018

In 2004, José Mourinho took over Chelsea and there he was like a mirage, larger than life and English football, appearing as if from a puff of smoke, Brian Clough-with-looks – packing a super-sharp mind, flashing eyes and Johnny Depp hair, a prince with a strut, making the cognoscenti swoon. Here was a football manager who lived in his own sphere and took the English game on a ride of his magic carpet through José Mourinho World. Two consecutive titles were landed for Chelsea, in May 2005 and 2006 (to then match a feat achieved only by Sir Alex Ferguson's Manchester United in the Premier League era). But midnight and pumpkin-time arrived in September 2007 and Mourinho left the club, departing west London like the ugly sister he had morphed into.

Factor in a tetchy time at Real Madrid, a tetchy end to

his time after returning to Chelsea ahead of his sacking in December 2015: if the Portuguese was hired as Manchester United manager in summer 2016 as the antidote to Pep Guardiola at Manchester City, Ed Woodward and his executives also knew he was high maintenance. That Mourinho's modus operandi can cause division and turf wars *within* the club that employs him.

Comprehensively *not* Ole Gunnar's style, Mourinho's discontent first became visible in the summer of 2018 and ratcheted up via a peak sulky display at a press conference on 28 August in the Old Trafford media room, following United's 3-0 loss to Tottenham. This was the moment when José Mourinho was *out*, and Ole Gunnar *in*. From this juncture the Portuguese's fate – the exit door – felt inevitable.

A fate that was crystallised by a furious sentence, issued as Mourinho rose to his feet at the end of the press conference, which he addressed to a national newspaper journalist: 'Respect, respect, respect, *man.*'

Four words, the last italicised here to emphasise how out of character the outburst was, certainly in the context of his career in English football. Sure, Mourinho had been recalcitrant, one-eyed, temperamental. But, on these shores: to actually lose control – lose his temper? No, certainly never while in the Premier League, when in charge of Chelsea each time, 2004-07 and 2013-15, and then Manchester United, from 2016 up to this juncture, when a journalist from *The Guardian* gave him a rather light cross-examination.

As Mourinho had claimed that the United fans, having applauded at the end of the 3-0 defeat to Spurs, were the best barometer of how well his team performed despite the result (they had been okay-ish before the break, poor afterwards), the *Guardian* scribe wondered, then, what it said of his side that large swathes of supporters had departed well before the 90 minutes were over. Mourinho's response gave the questioner and everyone else present in the media room a slightly surreal sense that the Special One had become the Losing It One.

Here was a remarkable blow-up. 'I would do the same, losing 3-0, taking two hours from here to the centre of Manchester, because it's where I live and I know that after matches it takes two hours, so I would do the same, so keep trying, keep trying, keep trying,' Mourinho said, though 20 minutes is probably the time required to reach the city centre, on foot, from Old Trafford. 'We lost last season here against Sevilla – last season in the Champions League last 16 – and we were booed, because we deserved, because we were not good, because we were not dangerous enough, because Sevilla deserved to win the match. Today the players left the pitch after losing at home and they were applauded, because they deserved it, so keep trying, and trying, and trying, and keep trying.'

Instead, though, Mourinho keeps trying as he raises three fingers. 'Just to finish, do you know what was the result?' – indicating his digits – 'Three-nil, 3-0. Do you know what this is? Three-nil. But it also means three Premierships and I won more Premierships alone than the other 19 managers together. Three for me and two for them two [Pep Guardiola and Manuel Pellegrini]. So respect, man, respect, respect, respect, man.'

Four more months were needed before Mourinho was finally sacked. This, though, was the hari-kari moment. Professional suicide. In public. All frustration popped: the issues with Anthony Martial, the lack of support in the market for his preferred centre-back, his on-tour dudgeon regarding the squad he had with him. The sense that the muddled state of the club meant he would never catch Pep Guardiola and Manchester City. The mask slipped and here was the portent of a sacking-to-come.

A sacking that would be executed a few days before Christmas. That would prove to be glad tidings for Ole Gunnar. And what Ed Woodward and his football brains trust saw in Ole was the anti-José Mourinho. The breezy persona, the tanker always being half if not totally full and spilling over. How he bounced back from the Cardiff disappointment. His love of the club and the 1999 goal and the track record as a successful manager of United reserves a decade before.

And, also, there was something else. Something crucial that Manchester United needed immediately. Were desperate for. That the kind of human touch OGS possesses so naturally might be able to fix. This was a serious financial concern that Woodward and the Glazers believed Ole Gunnar could help them with. Because if they were not careful a particularly dismal piece of business would be overseen. And one thing anathema to the executive vice-chairman and the owners is below-par hustling: having to write off millions of earnings that could easily have filled the coffers but for duff practice.

This problem was impossible to solve while Mourinho was still in place so was a key factor in his removal. The problem was this: under the Portuguese, Paul Pogba, Anthony Martial and David De Gea all wanted out. De Gea may not have been unhappy playing for Mourinho – he was considering his future due to career ambitions – but the other two certainly were.

Pogba was under contract until 2021 with an option of an extra 12 months, so the club held the aces and a sizeable fee would be secured if he was sold. But there was dismay in the hierarchy that a footballer who was 'pure' Manchester United would want out due to a personality clash with the manager.

Football reasons alone are enough of a minefield when trying to keep star talent happy (the prospect of no Champions League next season for the World Cup-winner that is Pogba, for example) without the man in charge failing in the fundamental demand of ensuring good relations between him and them. Yet Pogba and Mourinho were close to enemies. When Ole arrived, the Frenchman had been dropped from the side and stripped of the vice-captaincy. (A footnote here is that the story of Mourinho taking the vice-captaincy from Pogba was leaked by the Portuguese's camp and came on the day of a game – the 8-7 League Cup penalty shootout defeat to Derby County on 25 September: an interesting ploy.)

As the only A-list outfield player in a paper-thin squad, this had to be man-management gone awry from Mourinho. Disaffecting £89m of prime player quality that can help the side and you, as the man who relies on results for success, to avoid the sack, is close to the dictionary definition of how not to do the job.

Financially, business-wise, the cases of Martial and De Gea were even more dire than Pogba's. In talent and style, they too can be considered pure United. But the alarm bells clanged when Martial became seriously disillusioned under Mourinho – culminating in the summer fallout on the US tour – and De Gea prevaricated about signing a new contract.

Martial, fully contracted-up, is worth around £100m on the open market. De Gea, as one of the world's best goalkeepers, maybe more. If the Liverpool No. 1, Alisson Becker, cost the Merseysiders £67m, and Chelsea paid £71.6m for Kepa Arrizabalaga – two goalkeepers who were unproved in English football – then De Gea, an eight-year Manchester United veteran with a Premier League-winner's medal, would surely break the £100m barrier.

Except De Gea's original contract expired in summer 2019 and Martial's the same. Under Mourinho's management, each refused to sign on again, forcing United into triggering each of their respective one-year options on their terms to ensure the protection of two prime assets – until the summer of 2020.

Woodward did the sums and the total he came up with that was in danger of being lost was frightening. If neither agreed another contract (the preference at United is now five years plus the option of an extra one), then around £200m of footballer would walk out of the door for zero and cost whichever (happy) club snapped them up a signing fee and salary only.

Mourinho's dislike of Martial had been strong enough for the briefing by a source close to him who offered the opposite stance to Ed Woodward and the club regarding the Frenchman during the US tour. Mourinho's reasoning was said to be that since *Martial* wanted to depart, why try to keep him? The Portuguese's preference being that the forward should be sold outside of the Premier League to disallow a competitor benefiting from his services and potentially giving the club a black eye.

Yet missing here was why Martial wanted out: again, because of a sour manager–player dynamic.

By December 2018 it was not the Frenchman that would have left. And why following Mourinho's sacking the call

Ole Gunnar's beloved Kristiansund, where he was born, raised, and intends to retire to.

nullet-sporting young Ole was a prolific rksman – as the number of digits raised ply.

In 1994 Ole with lifelong mentor and friend Ole Olsen during his days at Clausenengen, the club he made his professional debut for.

OGS and Øyvind Leonardsen, a Molde and
Norway team-mate who played for United's
fierce rivals, Liverpool, have a joke with Ole
Olsen in 1997.

In action for Molde, where after only
a season and a half Manchester United
came calling.

Ole was looked up to by Christian Michelsen when they were street footballers and the
Kristiansund BK manager remains a good friend.

What a moment: Ole scores the European Cup-winning goal in the dying seconds of the greatest end to a final in the competition.

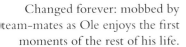

Changed forever: mobbed by team-mates as Ole enjoys the first moments of the rest of his life.

With Sir Alex Ferguson – a manager, friend and mentor.

Ole who? In a gang of five Ferguson signings in summer 1996, Karel Poborský, Jordi Cruyff, Raimond van der Gouw and Ronny Johnsen were more heralded than the unknown 23-year-old.

Ole had long been mentally filing tips accrued from Ferguson and here, at the club's Carrington training base in 2007, he moved into coaching.

2003 and a four-year, career-ending injury nightmare is about to start as Ole takes on Panathinaikos's Panagiotis Fyssas in a Champions League group game.

...e as co-manager of United reserves with Warren Joyce (his arm on OGS) after winning the 2009–10 title in the final at Old Trafford. A young Paul Pogba is centre.

Norwegian glory: Ole claimed Molde a very first championship in his very first season as a manager in 2011 and then, as pictured, retained it the following season.

South Wales blues: Ole had a difficult yet invaluable few months managing Vincent Tan's Cardiff City – seen here at Arsenal on 1 January 2014 before accepting the post.

A natural: in his first press conference as Manchester United manager in December 2018 Ole was surprisingly at ease.

With sons, Noah and Elijah ahead of the former's debut Kristiansund BK in summer 2019's tour game against Ol Manchester United.

22 December 2018 and Ole plots during his first match in charge of United – a 5–1 triumph at Cardiff City.

Anthony Martial's agreement of a new contract was a sure sign of Ole's man-management.

Bruno Fernandes: an inspired signing by Ole in January 2019, who quickly became the most significant acquisition of United's post-Ferguson era.

Ed Woodward, the executive vice-chairman whose refusal to sack Ole during some dark times was vindicated.

Under Ole Marcus Rashford blossomed to return a career best 22 goals for the club in 2019–20.

March 2019: a memorable night as Paris Saint-Germa are knocked out of the Champions League by Marcus Rashford's dying moments penalty.

In 2019–20 Ole's United beat crosstown rival Manchester City three times, including a league double.

Ole at Old Trafford: his home from home.

went into Ole Gunnar to offer him the job as the temporary manager.

He did not have to think twice before giving his answer.
His status at the club would draw the instant respect of senior
players, but this would soon need to be replaced by evidence
that this biggest of jobs could be handled.

CHAPTER 14

Moyes, Van Gaal, Mourinho: Now Ole Gunnar

'Ince rages at Solskjær "madness".'

THE SUN, *19 DECEMBER 2018*

The glitter of being Manchester United manager comes with a demand to persuade and perform, coax and convince, whether the man in the hot seat wants to or not. It is a confidence trick, a high-end barker act. Perception is all.

Come and buy my wares, come listen to me declaim on the opposition, tactics and transfer targets, how our rivals all want to pull us down, merely for being Man Utd, see how they think we – Man United – get all the decisions at Old Trafford because we are Man United. See how I understand this, how I AM the ideal and best candidate to be the manager; the magic football man who has ultimate mastery of the always changing, always challenging entity that is this fine and maddening club in the fine and maddening universe of football. Come walk with me, players. Come walk with me, fourth estate. Believe.

He also has to deal with the white noise of criticism and negativity. And for Ole Gunnar it has already begun. This was Friday, his opening media conference. On the day of his appointment, Wednesday, he had been given several barrels from Paul Ince, the former United midfielder who left in 1995, the summer before OGS arrived. Ince pointed to Ole's failure at Cardiff and said: 'Solskjær might be good for the fans but in Steve Bruce and Mark Hughes there are two experienced former players who know the club and are out of work.'

The sense from those sceptical can be summed up thus: what the hell was going on appointing a man whose only experience of Premier League management was in the half-season from January 2014, when he took down Cardiff City, and was removed in September of the following term? What was Ed Woodward doing? Why did the executive vice-chairman hire this man, a man on loan, who will be in charge on a temporary basis only, returning to Molde in May 2019?

To find the club at the juncture where José Mourinho had gone so wrong that he was sacked in mid-December in the same calendar year as he signed a fresh contract tying him to the club until summer 2020, with an extra option to 2021, was to find the latest of the post-Sir Alex Ferguson wrong turns Manchester United have taken. A sorry catalogue that can be counted out as five long years of wrong turns, muddled thinking, false starts and dawns, since the last of a record 20 league titles. Five long, *long* years: perhaps there is a deeper flaw in the structure. Perhaps what was needed was blue-sky thinking, the joined-up, holistic stuff that makes Manchester City the powerhouse across town.

Perhaps what is required is what City have in Txiki Begiristain, a person in an overarching position of sporting director/technical director/director of football: the description does not matter, the role does. Bring in a person responsible for the values and tradition and long-term vision of United and then proceed to hire managers and players who are in concert with this rather than the hodge-podge routine that has plagued the club since Ferguson stepped down.

But, no. Not yet, anyway. On 11 August 2018, *The Guardian* had reported that United were, indeed, ready to create their first director of football role: 'The move will allow United a continuity of football style and ethos as well as a more streamlined transfer policy,' it wrote.

Yet Mourinho, when still in the job, was not happy at the development and the position had still not been filled by the time he was sacked: another puzzling occurrence in a catalogue of puzzlers in a sequence post-Ferguson, another to prompt the poser that has become perennial: what was occurring at the world's biggest football club? An operation that boasts nearly three-quarters of a billion fans worldwide. An operation with copious partners and sponsors, a blue-chip entity worth around £3bn and that one day will be worth £10bn-plus.

This is the club that began in the Three Crowns public house in north Manchester; the club of legends. Of Duncan Edwards, Sir Bobby Charlton, Sir Matt Busby, Sir Alex Ferguson, and Cristiano Ronaldo. Of the 1968 European Cup triumph and the 1958 Munich Disaster. Of famous nights and days, glory, trophies, and memories and more memories.

And, in recent times, of wrong turns. Ole Gunnar's own

hiring as an interim manager seemed a glaring one. Hiring a caretaker manager on a timeshare from another club. Surely not. In David Moyes, Louis van Gaal and José Mourinho, Ed Woodward took the club up three managerial dead ends, roads to nowhere in the land of faltering form and flagging confidence, where the halcyon Ferguson days seemed a foreign country. Having to replace a genius like Ferguson is a thankless task and at the time each appointment had an internal logic to it, which illustrates the fickle nature of football.

There was applause when Moyes got the gig. He was the British, 11-year time-served Everton manager who came with the seal of being Ferguson's Chosen One. The logic, this: *how refreshing and wise a decision.* Rather than going for a stardust name, United were retaining the 'United way' by going for Moyes – a Scot like Ferguson – who would be down-to-earth and provide the requisite counter-balance to the club's insatiable hunger for the next dollar, the next deal. Like Ferguson, Moyes was hard-working, had a modest playing career, developed youth players, was steeped in the Premier League, and had husbanded Everton's modest resources impressively.

There is an acceptance now within the hierarchy that the six-year contract given to Moyes in summer 2013 was an error. That the terms of this were not cute enough. You do not have to be related to Einstein to deduce this. When Moyes bombed and was sacked, the prospect of Louis van Gaal intrigued and made as much sense as Moyes. The Dutchman was a promoter of youth in line with the United way. The 20-time English champions' long-running tradition of hothousing its talent, including the Busby Babes, the Class of 92, Adnan Januzaj – who was blooded by Van Gaal – and the current young hopes, Marcus Rashford, Scott McTominay and Brandon Williams.

Van Gaal's young guns tradition was founded in 1995 when his fledgling Ajax team beat AC Milan to win the Champions League, the only goal scored by Patrick Kluivert, who was 18. Just as good, Van Gaal was a bull of a man: brash and forceful and harbouring zero inferiority complex about United. He was employed to steady the side and allow the club time to overhaul areas of its back-of-house operation, and in May 2016 Van Gaal went and won a first FA Cup for United since 2004.

Unfortunately, LVG's football was anti-football – pedestrian and plodding. He argued that this was because the players he had 'could not perform the system to attack' (and he had a point), yet when the results became just as pedestrian he was out – days after winning the cup (a first trophy of the post-Ferguson era) – and Woodward made his third permanent appointment in three years, José Mourinho.

Woodward and the Glazers had been reluctant to hire him and tried first to land Atlético Madrid's Diego Simeone but could not and so, in the end, plumped for Mourinho, and how he fared has led to this moment, now, for Ole Gunnar.

The announcement of his appointment as the Portuguese's temporary replacement was presaged by a somewhat *Fawlty Towers*-ish moment, a page being posted on United's website 12 hours before which described OGS as 'our interim manager'. When this was hastily taken down and Ole's hiring eventually made official, a mix of takes and slants from former team-mates followed.

Ince had his say and Robbie Savage, a former Manchester

United youth player, was as unconvinced. Ole being the interim boss was a 'shambles' and Savage asked: 'Is this where United are really at? Solskjær is a legend and the fans still sing his name, but, really, the biggest club in the world appointing an interim boss who manages Molde?'

Ole moved quickly in having Mike Phelan join him, asking him to be his assistant manager, Mark Dempsey again also being part of his coaching staff, along with Michael Carrick, Kieran McKenna and Emilio Álvarez.

Ole had worked under Phelan when he was Ferguson's assistant, from the Treble year of 1999 to 2001. Phelan was a former player of the Scot's, a member of the 1990 FA Cup-winning side that ignited Ferguson's 23-year run of trophy-laden success. Phelan had also been reserve-team and first-team coach when OGS became a member of Ferguson's football staff. And having managed Hull City in the Premier League, 2016-17, was an ideal brain and sounding board for United's new temporary number one.

'Mick's absolutely brilliant, with his experience, his knowledge and personality around the place. Not just for the players and coaches, but the rest of the staff as well,' Ole Gunnar would explain a month later at a media conference. 'We've been here so many years that we know people. We talk about a family and, when you've known people for 25 years, it's easier to create a good atmosphere. Mick's tough but he's kind. He's got everything I would want in an assistant.

'We respect each other so much, and I really value Mick's, Kieran's and Michael's opinions on team selection, on training. That's what it's about. It's a team. We achieve so much more than if I have one way and they disagree with it.'

Ed Woodward hinted at the discord under Mourinho that

he wanted eradicated in his welcome to the new manager. 'Ole is a club legend with huge experience, both on the pitch and in coaching roles,' he said. 'His history at Manchester United means he lives and breathes the culture here and everyone at the club is delighted to have him and Mike Phelan back. We are confident they will unite the players and the fans as we head into the second half of the season.'

All of football fixed a gaze on Ole Gunnar. This was the spotlight OGS was under as he embarked on the role that is a Renaissance man act. Of being all things to all men, women and children. The chosen one, given the gilded position, has to be a sage and raconteur, a showman and cabaret artist – a movie star, a name-in-lights draw. The A-list attraction, the alpha and omega male, *nonpareil*.

Sir Alex Ferguson had it and *was* it: all of these components; the Scot oozed charisma, wit. Arc lights lit him; he was the biggest draw in every room – wherever he went his own personal spotlight followed and bounced off him. It buffed and sheened, projected the great man as the 10,000-foot gargantuan he was. Try to compete with this: that's the challenge, the demand of being the Manchester United manager.

In this glare David Moyes, Ferguson's first successor, wilted. He lacked chutzpah, X factor, devilry, his own kind of cool. He was a solid man and solidity is for Stoke City, not Manchester United.

Louis van Gaal packed a natural Manchester United charisma – a cocktail of arrogance and humour. He had the persona but not the product.

José Mourinho arrived an enigma and left an enigma. Where was the pop-star likeability? Where were the glitzy results of his first Chelsea incarnation of 2004-07? That incarnation was a quasi-deity, the same one who claimed Internazionale a first-ever Treble in Italy of Scudetto/Coppa Italia/Champions League in 2009-10.

The Manchester United job is the leveller, the great test. A beauty parade and a war – only the best-looking, the quickest brain, the man with the heavy artillery and Napoleon-style acumen, the impressionist touch and Mozart-like ear for the mood music: only a football genius, the finest complete managerial package, will win enough battles to go down as having belonged at the club. As being a natural.

Van Gaal and Mourinho won trophies, so did not bomb like Moyes, but they didn't land the prize of the championship. Do this and they would join the lineage of Ferguson, Sir Matt Busby and Ernest Mangnall as a great United manager – Ferguson, Busby and Mangnall, the only three men to claim the league title. Magnall in 1908 and 1911. Busby in 1952, '56, '57, '65 and '67. Ferguson in 1993, '94, '96, '97, '99, 2000, '01, '03, '07, '08, '09, '11 and '13.

This is what Manchester United is about. This is the history all new managers step into, become part of. Have to impact.

Except: when Ole Gunnar walks into the Aon Training Complex's Jimmy Murphy Centre on 21 December 2018 for his first media conference as interim manager, he does not have to make Manchester United champions.

No. He is the stopgap, the firefighter. The caretaker. He has to take care of the club because, well, it needs taking care of.

The team are in near-freefall and OGS has to try to pull an *Avengers* act: rescue them as they plunge towards the ground. A challenge to test any manager. Manchester United are in sixth place with 26 points from 17 games, 22 points behind the leaders, Liverpool. TWENTY-TWO POINTS.

To be deemed successful in this context Ole has to turn around the dismal results and points tally. Regain United some respect.

And now here he is, facing the media for the first time. It is two days since he was appointed as Mourinho's temporary replacement and a day before the Norwegian takes Manchester United to Cardiff City for his first match, his debut as the interim number one. He steps through the main room of the Jimmy Murphy Centre and takes his seat. He is in the limelight; time to put on a performance, the barker act. Charm and schmooze. Fix a 10,000-watt smile on, present a perma-charming self. It is a near-impossible ask, given the media exist in constant judge-and-assess mode. A misspoken word, an unguarded reaction, and the game is up: *now the real man behind the façade is seen.*

Whatever the vagaries of the media, this is it now: showtime. And, he does not disappoint. His eyes are lit up, have a Christmas Day sparkle. He is tuned in, relishing this. Like this is Ole Gunnar Solskjær's destiny.

Take these lines from him, riffing on the label given to Sir Alex Ferguson's famous temper. 'Maybe I should get the hairdryer out of my pocket because I've got a hairdryer. When my hair needs lifting, I use it on myself, but I am also not afraid of, if you like, laying down the law. You know with your kids when they disappoint you: you tell them off, you don't give them some chocolate, do you? So you treat players similar to how you treat your kids really, because you want the best for them, you want to guide them, you want to help them, but if I get disappointed . . . ?'

Neat. The reference to the hairdryer is the first of many to quote or cite Ferguson. When Ole's United are winning – as they do in his opening eight matches – this is judged as wise and prescient. When they are not, it becomes a weakness, a mini Sir Alex affectation, a man who shrinks to a manager stuck in the past, still in awe of a sepia age that is *long* gone. Do not blame the media and pundit class, this is the force of winning or losing in football.

The bottom line. The only way to control the message is victory.

Ole will look for the first of these in South Wales at Cardiff City in 24 hours' time. Next to the media centre are the first-team training pitches and beyond is Manchester and the watching world of football.

It must be strange for him – how quickly he has changed from Molde FK manager to Manchester United saviour. Even in football's dislocating universe this is a shift, an unheard-of transformation of profile and expectation. He has barely been back in a city in which he lived and worked from 1996 until 2010, yet in the nine years that have passed the football culture of the place has changed.

This can be summed up in two words: Manchester City. They are no longer the joke they were in Ole's playing and reserve-team days at United. The boys in sky blue have become pre-eminent.

Dave Haslam is the author of *Manchester, England*, a chronicler of the city and a DJ who for many years played at the now-defunct, world-famous Haçienda nightclub. Now the mob from across the city are four Premier League titles in – since their first in May 2012 – and have an ever-growing reach and profile.

He says: 'I travel as a DJ and when I go to a city like Lima in Peru, or Geneva, everyone from barbers to club promoters asks: "Where are you from?" You say: "Manchester." And then it used to be: "Manchester United." It's not like that now. Now the barbers and club promoters when I travel to a city say: "Where are you from?" You say, "Manchester." And it's, "United or City?" That trend is interesting.'

It reflects where Manchester United are. The club Ole Gunnar now leads has flatlined since Ferguson left in 2013; the change, when compared to the United he joined as a player under the Scot, is stark.

Ole's opening meet-and-greet is peppered with references to Ferguson. Take this soundbite: 'When I got the call of course I texted the boss and I have been in touch with him. I am going to enjoy a nice cup of tea back at his house to sit down and enjoy and discuss a few ideas.'

And Ole Gunnar points to his vision of how Manchester United should be led as being the same as Ferguson's. 'The way he's dealt with people, the way he was the manager of the club, how he kept 25 international players happy, hungry and wanting to improve. But also the way he dealt with staff in and around the place. He's been my mentor. From my injury in 2003 at least, I was making all the notes, what he did in different, certain situations. Of course I've already been in touch with him, because there's no one better to get some advice from.

'If you play at Man United, you play without fear and you play with courage. You go out there and express your skills. I've had the best manager. He [Sir Alex] just said, "Go out and express yourselves, take risks."'

Ole is experiencing a whirlwind. It has happened so swiftly. Molde were contacted by Ed Woodward two days ago, given permission to speak with OGS and, now, here he is discussing the plans for his new team. 'We're not used to being sixth. We are used to challenging for the league. Of course, that's maybe a step too far now, too many points, but that's where we have to aim and to look forward,' he said.

When being pulled up on a comment that his job is to ensure United's players enjoy their football 'again', an apparent reference to the dog days under Mourinho, Ole neatly dampens the prospect of any headlines citing him as being critical of his predecessor. '"Again" – that's just maybe my English,' he said and smiles. 'My job is to make them enjoy football and play their best football because when you are a kid you love playing football.'

An impressive first performance before the cameras and scribes is summed up via a warning about who is in control that Ole combines with another winning epigram about the Manchester United way and 'walls'. 'I'm not sure about you saying the power has gone to the dressing room,' he said. 'The power is with the manager. He picks the team, the tactics, the strategy. The philosophy is in these walls. That legacy is more important than any player power.'

The first media conference is over. Solskjær bowls away and out of the Jimmy Murphy Centre. The surprise has been how easy it was for him. How he emanated aplomb. How natural this seems. That even those who are doubting him may be in for a surprise.

CHAPTER 15

The First Game

'There was a discernible strut and swagger.'

THE GUARDIAN

There is a surreal feeling at Cardiff City Stadium on a dank and cold pre-Christmas Saturday. Ole Gunnar Solskjær is the caretaker manager of Manchester United. *Ole Gunnar Solskjær is caretaker manager.* Yes, it is true. This is happening. Ole Gunnar can hardly believe it. He has been in the job only four days and it is still difficult to comprehend what is happening. The *why* of this.

The *why* him of all the former Ferguson players who know the club: why is HE in charge now?

Take a pick: Steve Bruce, Ryan Giggs, Nicky Butt, Paul Scholes, Gary and Phil Neville, David Beckham, Peter Schmeichel, Eric Cantona – yes, Eric: King Eric, how the faithful continue to dote on Eric C. Yet instead it is Ole. He has dreamed of this for a long time, the dream fading after the failure at the very club before him now as his first opposition in charge of United – Cardiff City. The dream faded then, but never died.

And, yet. This is still close to surreal for him, and the football world feels the same. Even Darren Fletcher, the former Manchester United midfielder now at Stoke City who is usually so measured, in the build-up to this first game, said of having a caretaker manager in charge of England's record 20-time champions, its most garlanded club: 'Manchester United should never be in this position. They're almost writing off this season and next because if they appoint a new manager in the summer, he's not going to have much time to look for new players. There is a real concern that you could have two seasons of rebuilding again.'

Fletcher is not the only one who is sceptical. And others, as Paul Ince was on Wednesday, are being more scathing, even rude. What better way to answer the jokes and doubt about him as the temporary boss loaned from Molde until the end of this season than with a 5-1 win in your opening match, as Ole does here and now against Cardiff City. This is the first time since Sir Alex Ferguson's last game five years ago (5-5 with West Bromwich Albion on 19 May 2013) that United have scored a quintet – Ole's connection with the Scot seems always to hover in the ether – and the only survivor from that outing is Phil Jones. There is, actually, another survivor from five years ago: Michael Oliver, the referee who officiated at the Hawthorns is in place in South Wales.

At 5.30pm Ole's reign begins. He watches from the bench, Mike Phelan doing much of the technical-area prowling, ahead of the match being won by the proverbial mile. Ahead of his new team showing what OGS hopes will be the way forward from this point on.

The first Manchester United XI he sends out is a 4-3-3 shape that reads: David De Gea, Ashley Young, Victor Lindelöf, Jones, Luke Shaw, Paul Pogba, Ander Herrera, Nemanja Matić, Jesse Lingard, Marcus Rashford, Anthony Martial. This is who he entrusts to start turning the club's fortunes around.

The results – like the club – had gone south under Mourinho. One win in the last five, two losses, the last of which was a terrible 3-1 reverse at Liverpool. Jürgen Klopp's outfit are serious contenders for the title, Mourinho's men were enduring a living nightmare. Paul Pogba is the emblem of the rot under the Portuguese. The World Cup-winner who scored in the final against Croatia and walked into the FIFA team of the tournament cannot get a game. His last league start was the 2-2 draw at Southampton on 1 December, three weeks ago.

Today, Pogba is back and will remain in Solskjær's first-choice XI until the end of the season, though towards the end his future, again, will become a soap opera. For now, the start of a mesmeric, magical run of results under OGS begins. Marcus Rashford, the 21-year-old striker who was (yet another) in and out of the side under Mourinho, scores three minutes in against the Bluebirds. Ander Herrera, a Mourinho outcast, on 29 minutes. Mourinho wanted Anthony Martial sold in the summer: he nets four minutes before the break. Jesse Lingard – Mourinho *kind* of fancied him in that lukewarm way of his – scores twice, a 57th-minute penalty and right at the close of the match. Víctor Camarasa's 38th-minute strike is as distant a memory as the morose and sluggish days of Mourinho already seem.

Pogba operates behind the (at this juncture, anyway) fans' dream front trio of Jesse Lingard, Marcus Rashford and

Anthony Martial. Romelu Lukaku is absent due to leave granted by the club but it is doubtful if he would have started, given how Ole wishes to play: fast, slick, fleet-footed. With Ander Herrera as minister for muck and bullets in midfield, Matić as Pogba's head footman, and the De Gea–Young–Lindelöf–Jones–Shaw back five close to what will become Ole's favoured defensive alignment (Jones or Chris Smalling becomes a selection vagary), this will prove, injuries and form's fickleness aside, OGS's preferred XI during these early days, with Scott McTominay to later force his way in, and Andreas Pereira convincing Ole Gunnar to be given opportunities to impress. When the final whistle is blown and victory confirmed, that this is against Cardiff makes this day all the sweeter, ensuring a party for Manchester United, the fans and the new manager. Afterwards he said: 'They, the players, grasped some of the ideas very quickly.'

From here, United go on to complete a run of eight consecutive victories in total, a record for the club. The roll of honour will read: 3-1 v Huddersfield Town and 4-1 v Bournemouth (home); 2-0 at Newcastle United, 2-0 v Reading (h, FA Cup), 1-0 at Tottenham Hotspur, 2-1 v Brighton & Hove Albion (h), and 3-1 at Arsenal (FA Cup). After a 2-2 draw with Burnley (h), Leicester City and Fulham are beaten 1-0 and 3-0 at their grounds before the first loss under OGS: a disappointing 2-0 defeat to Paris Saint-Germain at Old Trafford on 12 February in the Champions League last-16 first leg.

After victory number eight at Arsenal, on 25 January 2019, there is a perfect storm of admiration around OGS. How he has achieved this impresses – everyone.

Beating the Bluebirds 5-1 was emphatic, but it is only the start . . .

CHAPTER 16

The Magnificent Eight

'United's speed of passing and thought dominated.'

THE GUARDIAN

This is a cause célèbre. This is a *happening*. This *cannot* be happening. Surely, surely not.

Manchester United are winning and winning and winning. It has to be an illusion. David Copperfield take note. Ole Gunnar Solskjær is breaking all records. This is like waking up and finding George Best, Bobby Charlton, Eric Cantona, Wayne Rooney and Cristiano Ronaldo playing five-a-side (no goalkeeper required) on the kitchen table if you're a Manchester United fanatic. Fantasy football made real by Ole Gunnar.

This is the team that is supposed to struggle. This is the team that *did* struggle under Mourinho. It wheezed and creaked and ended as a moribund rabble who forgot the boys they once were who loved the game and why they ever wished to play elite-level professional football. Forgot the sheer lightning-bolt thrill that went through them when signing for Manchester United.

Not any more. No more forgetting; the players are now remembering. And winning. They cannot stop winning. And Manchester United are doing so in style. In the style of their perma-grinning manager: with fun, bounce, devilry and chutzpah. Ole Gunnar has lifted the mood. No, he has transformed the mood and the club and the outside perception of Manchester United.

This is a Magnificent Eight of victories. The start to Ole Gunnar Solskjær's interim tenure as Manchester United manager is a fantasy beyond anything the board of directors – who include in their number Sir Alex Ferguson, Sir Bobby Charlton, former chief executive David Gill, plus the actual power-base of Ed Woodward, the executive vice-chairman, and owners, the Glazers – could ever have hoped for. Ole was hired as a caretaker boss who may have 'an outside hope' of the main job but who represents a classic holding-pattern appointment, allowing United to pause and shrewdly go 'back to basics'.

This is what Ole Gunnar begins to oversee during his temporary tenure. A reconnection of Manchester United to Manchester United. A reset of the culture of a place that has drifted since Ferguson retired in 2013. A return of discipline, smartening up the players again, ensuring they wear club suits, button shirts to the top, have ties on, and encourage all of them to be keen and happy to sign programmes and any other paraphernalia for adoring fans.

All of this occurs as the victories pile up, and at this juncture the conclusion is that Ed Woodward has played a blinder in appointing him. The derision has faded, praise has taken over. Ole Gunnar simply understands what Manchester United is. Gets the place and how to manage the team and the expectations and the media glare. This is what the opening eight wins blare. He gets that his natural destiny is to be here and what he has to do: starting with making everyone smile again. And after this start everyone *is* smiling and laughing and jigging again.

The bare statistics of the Magnificent Eight read: six league wins, two in the FA Cup, 22 goals, five conceded. It is done through bravery, through flair, taking the game to opponents, by the shot to the arm that is the injection of the Solskjær Factor.

After victory number one at Cardiff it is on to his home-coming – the Boxing Day meeting with Huddersfield Town at Old Trafford, a first as temporary manager before the adoring home support.

Post-Cardiff Ole said, 'Nothing is history quicker than a football game.' And nothing delights fans more than history of this kind repeating itself via a second consecutive victory at their stadium.

A surprise as jolting as OGS's actual appointment are the breezy one-liners. Ahead of Huddersfield's visit he offers: 'Confidence is not something you store in the fridge and pick out.' Then he talks about the prospect of occupy-ing the same seat at Old Trafford once graced by Busby and Ferguson – referencing the 2009–10 Premier League reserve-team final win he oversaw. 'I was sat next to René Meulensteen in a reserve-team game once as a coach, and I was there [Old Trafford] with Cardiff. But, of course, it will be special.'

As it proves for Ole and the United congregation, the Theatre of Dreams a 74,523 sell-out to see him stride out after the stadium announcer, Alan Keegan, declares: 'Will you please welcome back the legend: Ole Gunnar Solskjær.' To which 'Ole! Ole! Ole!' is the response as he is serenaded to his seat. What follows is more of the free-and-flowing stuff seen against Cardiff and which does for David Wagner's side. This is not perfect from United – there is a second-half stutter until Pogba nets on 64 and 78 minutes to follow Nemanja Matić's 28th-minute opener, Mathias Jørgensen's 88th-minute strike proving immaterial.

The maligned Fred starts in midfield and is pulled off after 53 minutes, but this is a footnote. The feel-good factor is back, mainlined into the club in front of an Old Trafford that is left delirious. This is football: high emotion. But it cannot last, can it . . . ?

Four days later Bournemouth are dispatched 4-1, again at home, and *The Guardian* writes: 'Solskjær, so far, has been as faultless in front of the media as his team has been on the field. There is an excitement and authority when speaking that stems from his bona fide hero status at United. The trick now is for him to reach May with the same billing. Do this and Solskjær may yet be a serious contender for the permanent role.'

The festive season is becoming rather jolly for Manchester United and 48 hours before New Year's Day this match only increases the Yuletide cheer in and around the club. This is another goal glut – the four put past Eddie Howe's hapless patsies taking the tally under Ole to 12 in this third outing. This was the Paul Pogba show and Old Trafford, which can have a hush akin to a church prayer service, was at raucous house-party volume by the close, belting out the '20 times' song about the club's record number of English league championships. Marcus Rashford and Romelu Lukaku – who began as a substitute in a big call from the manager and an indicator of how he wishes to proceed – score as well, and no one of a red persuasion gives a hoot about Eric Bailly's red card towards the end.

Pogba is cutting about the difference between playing for Ole and Mourinho. 'Maybe we have just realised that we are Manchester United and we need to be at the top of the league,' he said. 'You've seen the reaction of the players. Everyone is enjoying themselves and that's what we need. We need to enjoy playing football, work for each other. We are more offensive, we create more chances, play higher. So this is how we want to play. We want to attack. The manager wants to attack. And that's what we are doing.'

Another way of summing this up is that Mourinho built his side around Romelu Lukaku at centre-forward rather than the central midfield force of Pogba. The Portuguese didn't trust Pogba, which caused mutual bad feeling and fallouts. In this, Mourinho's ego may have been the barrier to fully realising the Frenchman's talent.

To Ole, Pogba is 100 per cent his kind of player – 'go out and enjoy yourself, Paul'; be the man in essence. *Mourinho* wanted to be the man as much as any non-player can be. He did not want footballers who go off-piste, who are off-the-cuff. Just like Lukaku, Mourinho's most important footballers during his career – Frank Lampard, Didier Drogba, Diego Milito – might be characterised as machine-like, easy for José to programme and then to watch as they carry out orders. Pogba is a complete opposite to Milito et al. As is Ole to José.

If Mourinho is Super- Ego, Ole has ego like Carlo Ancelotti has ego – subservient to the players, keen to see his footballers shine and dazzle.

Whether Pogba feels *he* is a United player – and so an Ole player – is yet to be seen.

On 2 January OGS takes his team to Newcastle United for what ends as a 2-0 win. The magic touch continues. Romelu Lukaku is supposed to be a bit-part man under Solskjær: the off-the-pace, anti-Marcus Rashford. Yet, again, he springs off the bench for a second successive game to score with a first touch just after the hour. This trip was billed as the trickiest outing yet for the manager and team, the man who took Cardiff City down versus Rafael Benítez, the man who masterminded Liverpool's Miracle of Istanbul 2005 Champions League triumph.

But, no. Rashford's third in four matches for OGS means United cruise to a four-out-of-four record and Solskjær joins Sir Matt Busby, in 1946, as the only United manager to win his first four games. 'I don't want to,' OGS says when asked, post-game, if he will end his tenure in May. At this rate he will not have to do so.

Next up a Juan Mata penalty and a Lukaku goal knock Reading out of the FA Cup third round on 5 January at Old Trafford. Ole Gunner has now equalled Busby's non-wartime club record of five consecutive victories at the start of a tenure, as Manchester United continue to progress. He makes nine changes and swats away the notion that the quintet of victories has been simple. 'It's never easy,' OGS says, then flags up the coming opposition. 'Spurs away, Wembley, that's a proper test.'

For the team – and for him. And what is seen for a first

clear time is Ole Gunnar's ability to be tactically smart – on Sunday, 13 January 2019. After beating Cardiff City, Huddersfield Town, Bournemouth and Newcastle United, the subtext of the trip to Wembley was that Ole was about to be exposed as the greenhorn/imposter many suspected him to be. A schooling was incoming from opposite number Mauricio Pochettino, the favourite at this juncture to take the United job full-time in the summer, and whose 10 years in charge of Espanyol, Southampton and now Spurs was a pedigree and track record that illuminated Solskjær's relative managerial naivety.

Except Ole Gunnar did have one thing on his CV that his critics forgot about and Pochettino continued to dream of – actual trophy-winning success: the two league titles and a cup in Norway. The Argentinean's best result was taking Tottenham to the runners-up berth in the 2015 League Cup. Surprise, surprise, then: OGS had a plan that wrong-footed Spurs, showed an imagination and a willingness to listen to his coaching circle of Mike Phelan, Mark Dempsey, Michael Carrick and Kieran McKenna. He also had a goalkeeper in David De Gea who produced 11 vital saves, as Manchester United claimed their sixth consecutive victory under OGS, five in the league to equal Sir Matt Busby's all-time mark for the club.

How Ole did it was to choose Jesse Lingard at centre-forward – a first. The move had Spurs scrambling, Solskjær eschewing Romelu Lukaku (the No. 9 was on the bench) and positioning the pacy Marcus Rashford and Anthony Martial either side of Lingard. The ploy worked, as did the overall strategy of a front-foot-first mode that was maximum United of yore, the kind of bold approach away from home, against a direct rival, that David Moyes, Louis van Gaal and José Mourinho often ignored for a safety-first strategy.

United's winner came when a smooth Paul Pogba pass found Rashford, who beat Hugo Lloris expertly on 44 minutes. Rashford roved in from an inside-right channel where usually Lingard is positioned to score.

When the final whistle was blown the interim manager had sent the first notice to Ed Woodward that the executive vice-chairman and the owners should start considering him seriously for the full-time job. Afterwards Solskjær said, 'You expect to win every single game at Manchester United. You won't, but you must think that. That's the mentality of this group.'

The result, and the way OGS plotted it, started to make naysayers consider converting to yaysayers.

Pogba is at the copious-enthusiasm-for-Ole game – *again*. 'It's a pleasure to be reunited with him,' he said. 'I knew him from the academy and the reserves, when his nickname was "Super-sub". He is doing a really good job. Before the coach arrived back, I was in the shadows, on the bench, and I accepted that. It is a pleasure to play again. That's normal. Now I am always smiling. I am playing a bit further forward. I have more security behind me, it gives me the freedom to go forwards to try to get into the box and support the strikers.'

Paul Ince is at the won't-be-fooled-by-Ole game – *again*. 'We can't get too sucked in with what Ole's done. I could have gone in and done the same thing, so could Steve Bruce,' he said. 'Anyone could have gone in and done what he has done. What the club need to do is bring in a manager who can get United competing with City and Liverpool – and Mauricio Pochettino is the man.'

Ince is being honest, not playing the United Old Boys bit, which is refreshing. Unfortunately for him, he draws derision for this and Ed Woodward, for one, is not listening. And though the view has some plausibility, it should not be underestimated what Ole Gunnar is doing. United had become shambolic under José Mourinho and the club had slipped into negative morale. The wrong personality – say, an abrasive one like Paul Ince can be – might have further alienated the players and plunged United into a deeper morass. What Ole is performing is a tight-rope act, showing a deft touch that marks out the classier managers. He is also starting to convince that he may – just may – have the all-round package required for the job. This includes the ability to think differently from game to game *and* the *cojones* to execute this, as his deployment of Lingard as the centre-forward proved.

It is 19 January and victory number seven is about to be enjoyed, over Brighton & Hove Albion, a 2-1 win via goals from Paul Pogba – his resurgence continues to be remarkable – and Marcus Rashford. The latter ensured appearance 150 for the club was memorable courtesy of a superb curled effort, strike number 41 in United livery for him. The month anniversary of OGS's appointment as the temporary gaffer is one to celebrate. The 11-point gap to the fourth-place team, Chelsea, has been slashed to just three and only one more separates United from Tottenham Hotspur in third. Under José Mourinho the goal difference plummeted to minus one: a negative value in this column is virtually unheard of for the Reds. Now, it is 13 as 17 league goals have been scored and only three conceded in Ole's six matches in charge.

Rashford is performing like the genuine A-lister he can be. 'Can' being the operative word. At this point in his career he can also play like a chump and make seasoned watchers wonder how they could ever have rated the forward. Under Mourinho, everything Rashford tried could go off wrongly, casting him as a classless imposter, lacking the touch of arrogance that executes tricks and runs and passes, the psychological bullishness to boss opponents and the game. This was his fifth goal in six appearances for Ole, who replaced him near full time. 'He was tired towards the end because his work rate is unbelievable,' OGS said. 'I have to be fair to the boys. I do demand a lot of sprinting and high press because we are Manchester United. Maybe after the last two games it has caught up with a few, but we have got another week to be ready for Arsenal, so we will be ready for Arsenal.' The point about fitness is intriguing and it's his belief that Mourinho did not have the players fit enough. Of Rashford, Ole added: 'Harry Kane is injured so maybe that gives him the chance to be the best at the moment.' Is there a hotter manager at the moment?

A month into Ole Gunnar's tenure and he took the team to Arsenal in the FA Cup fourth round on 25 January. The result was a convincing 3-1 victory. The transformation was so dramatic that this felt no surprise. Here was the measure of the world OGS was creating for the team. Winning had become an expectation among those watching and following the fortunes of this new Manchester United. Football's hypnotic ability to change sense and meaning via the elixir of a string of wins means Ole Gunnar's candidacy ever being questioned seemed odd and foolish to those who did. And that was only four weeks ago.

He is the miracle worker of the Premier League, of management. Of *man*-management. In north London even the out-of-form Alexis Sánchez scores, at his former club, along with Jesse Lingard and Anthony Martial, the Emirates Stadium quietened as the Ole Gunnar Solskjær juggernaut rolls on.

'After 8 – Why wait?' asks the *Mirror*'s John Cross, the paper's chief football correspondent heralding the record-setting run as a way of posing the reasonable question of what more do Ed Woodward and the Glazers need to see in order to give Solskjær the position full-time. The fans sing Ole's name throughout the win – as they have since he walked back through the door. He is, understandably, elated. 'A massive step forward for us performance-wise,' Ole said. 'The structure was much better compared to Tottenham, where we hung in there and David De Gea saved us. We've been working on that. We need to dig in and defend properly against big teams.' He plays Romelu Lukaku on the right and gets a performance from him, with Jesse Lingard the de facto No. 9 – each selection showing a dexterous, strategic football mind. 'It's a tactic we can use and we know how strong he is,' OGS commented of Lukaku. 'He held the ball, ran the channel and brought other players in. It was a great finish by Alexis. For every player, the more confident you get, the more you want to get out on the pitch and train and you trust yourself. He has been injured so it's good he got 70 minutes and he can only improve. Jesse is a big-game player. We never hesitate to put him in the Man United team. He knows the history. He knows all the counterattack goals we have scored against Arsenal.'

This, though, is it. The Magnificent Eight fails to become Nine because the next result is a draw, and it is a gauge of how Ole has raised expectations that there is a definite sense of deflation when his team only manage a 2-2 with Burnley on 29 January at Old Trafford. Yet there is a further indication of the spirit he has created, the togetherness missing under Mourinho. United are 2-0 down with nine minutes left before a Paul Pogba penalty on 87 minutes and Victor Lindelöf's equaliser 180 seconds into added time maintains Solskjær's unbeaten start. 'The way they came back was fantastic,' he said. The late, late show screams Fergie Time; the way in which the Scot's vintage sides piled forward at the death to turn contests their way.

What it also sealed was an honour for Ole Gunnar that has not been claimed by a Manchester United number one since Ferguson's time, despite the club holding the record for the highest number: the Premier League manager of the month award, the latest bookending the inaugural one that was handed out in August 1993. That was the first of 27 for Alex Ferguson, his last being handed him for October 2012 in his final season as he guided United to the last of their 13 Premier Leagues.

Six years and three managers came and went before Ole Gunnar Solskjær claimed the club a 28th monthly prize. He said, 'I'm a little bit against individual team awards for a team sport. But it means we've been the team of the month, so this is both for the staff and the players.

'We complement each other really well – the hours and hours that Kieran McKenna and Michael Carrick spend on planning the sessions, doing the sessions, working with individuals. The more you know the culture of the club, the culture of the players and the way that we have been successful, that has helped me. Emilio Álvarez's working with the best goalkeeper in the world and to bring Micky

Phelan in with me is very reassuring because he's so calm and experienced with players, so ultimately it's how they respond to what we tell them and they've been fantastic, so all credit to them.

'We're a good group. We bounce off each other. Opinions are being thrown about in that office and in the end, I'm the "lucky one" that has to make a decision on who to leave out or to play. We want to be winning games. We want to move up the table and this is the start of it.'

Marcus Rashford matches his manager by winning the player of the month gong for a January in which he scored three times. 'It's always good to pick up individual awards but I think the way we've performed as a team has been very good over the last few weeks,' he said. 'The aim for us now is to just continue it, but we have to take it game by game and one step at a time.

'The consistency is what's most pleasing – I've always said that's the difference between the best players in the world and good players. In football, the fact that you can repeat it time and time again, season upon season, is the big difference between the two categories of players. Consistency is something you always want to improve and, for a young player, it can be difficult but I think over the last two months we've got it right.'

Rashford is the first United player since Zlatan Ibrahimović two years before to win the award, for December 2016, and only the third since Ferguson retired, Anthony Martial being the other, for September 2015.

After the Burnley draw Ole Gunnar's next two results are wins. A 1-0 victory at Leicester City, Rashford with a sixth goal for OGS in what is a deeply purple patch for a player who operates in patches. Then, away once more, Fulham are beaten 3-0, two of these from the still resurgent Paul Pogba – a seventh and eighth under Ole – and one from Anthony Martial.

Now, though, comes the first defeat of Ole's stewardship when Paris Saint-Germain come to Old Trafford for the Champions League last-16 first leg on 12 February. It is four days short of two months since Manchester United lost a game of football, and tonight is the night. Ole Gunnar's impressive start ends at 10 wins and a draw and Pogba is sent off on 89 minutes so is suspended for the return leg in the French capital.

Presnel Kimpembe on 53 minutes and Kylian Mbappé on the hour score the goals against a United XI that loses Anthony Martial on 45 minutes and Jesse Lingard on 49 to injury. OGS struggles to get his side to match a team that are champions of France and, when two of his three key attackers are forced off leaving only one on the field (Marcus Rashford), the lack of depth of quality in his squad is exposed. He turns to Juan Mata and Alexis Sánchez when Martial and Lingard limp out. One – Mata – is too slow and lacks presence. The other – Sánchez – is a busted flush who was a statement signing in January 2018, who makes the wrong statement virtually every time he takes to the field.

Ángel Di María, once United and British football's record £59.7m signing, shines, and is the ghost of another failed Manchester United transfer – Louis van Gaal's. The Dutchman maintained the Argentinean just was not good enough after trying him in every position, the Iron Tulip maintaining, even five years later, that Di María was never a first-choice target of his. Here, again, the muddled recruit-ment policy overseen by Ed Woodward is highlighted.

Afterwards Ole Gunnar is as scathing as he can be about Di María's fellow South American, Sánchez. 'He needs to find himself,' he said. 'Because we know there's a quality player there.' Ole is equally dismissive of any players who don't respond the correct way. 'They are not to be sorry for themselves. Anyone who feels sorry for themselves probably won't play against Chelsea in the next game. Today is a reality check for us. Mountains are there to be climbed, you can't lay down and say this is over. We will go there, play our game and improve from today.

'They had the momentum after the first goal and con-trolled the game. You could see we hadn't played at this level for a while and we will have to learn. It was an experience that can go either way; it's not going to be a season-defining one, it's one we have to learn from.'

Ander Herrera sings the same song. 'We have good exam-ples. We won away against Tottenham, we won against Arsenal. They are teams that are as good as PSG, so we will go there to try and make it difficult for them.'

The starting XI tonight has been: David De Gea, Ashley Young, Victor Lindelöf, Eric Bailly, Luke Shaw, Paul Pogba, Jesse Lingard, Ander Herrera, Nemanja Matić, Marcus Rashford, Anthony Martial. This team was the most telling illustration yet of the difference between Solskjær's way and José Mourinho's. In what is Manchester United's biggest night of the season, Romelu Lukaku is left out and Marcus Rashford is trusted. Mourinho would and did have the oppo-site view of the abilities of Lukaku and Rashford. A lack of pace was an issue throughout the XI when Mourinho was in charge: quick feet that shred defences, and the quick thinking that makes mugs of the opposition and casts those doing the mugging as operating in a differing sphere. Pace is something Ole Gunnar will address in the summer transfer window. Pace plus youth plus talent is the equation that sums up the player template he wants.

When Solskjær arrived at Manchester United he had to firefight two towering infernos. There was a clearly visible on-field one that smouldered, but also a less obvious yet as serious financial concern that a cash mountain of £200m could be burned if Anthony Martial and David De Gea saw out their contracts and walked away for free in 2021.

This all changed when Solskjær took over and what was also a corollary of the run of fine results under Ole was the happiness of Martial and De Gea – and the whole squad – as well as that of Pogba. 'He is one of the best people I have ever met in football,' Ander Herrera would say in May. 'Everyone loves him in the dressing room. Everyone wants to fight for him. When you have the players behind you and wanting to fight for you, part of the job is done. I believe in karma and if you are a good person, if you are honest and sincere with the players and the fans, sooner or later it will work.'

Clanging bells had sounded when Martial became as unhappy as Pogba under Mourinho, and De Gea prevaricated over signing a new deal. Yet with Ole Gunnar in place, on the final day of the January 2019 transfer window the sight of the forward and interim manager photographed together as Martial signed fresh terms until 2024 (with the one-year extra clause) was the cause of celebration in Woodward's office and the Glazers', across the Atlantic in the USA. Here was another mission accomplished by OGS – secure Martial's future – to go along with Pogba's revitalisation. And, although the question mark over De Gea's future would continue into the summer, the temporary boss's man-management talents had been demonstrated; and, given how crucial this ability is in an era of multimillionaire footballers, it was another missive to Woodward and the owners that he should be seriously considered for the permanent role.

How at this juncture Pogba was turned around was a case study in cute HR handling. Ole publicly billed him as a 'no-brainer' starter and rescinded Mourinho's stripping of the midfielder as vice-captain. Instead, OGS posited that Pogba was certainly a future Manchester United captain (if he stayed) and the 26-year-old's form was close to stratospheric during the start under Ole: all-round midfield play that featured nine goals to take his season tally to a career-high 14 and would have him voted into the PFA Team of the Year, the sole United player and sole non-Manchester City/Liverpool footballer.

Ole also moved swiftly regarding Marouane Fellaini, which was a fan-pleaser. The sight of him being shipped out to Shandong Luneng at the end of the January window was greeted with close to universal applause. The Belgian began as the emblem of all that was wrong with Manchester United in the post-Ferguson era when David Moyes signed him in summer 2013. He continued this status, particularly under Mourinho, becoming a kind of on-field representative of the Portuguese's stultifying playing style. So, when Ole Gunnar finally ended Fellaini's career at the club, this became a symbol of the new United under him.

A new team that was going places. And what was about to happen one spring eve in Paris was, surely, the sealing evidence: an invigorating display that was to be the one that would all but hand Ole his dream job.

CHAPTER 17

Big in Europe

'We always believe.'

OLE GUNNAR SOLSKJÆR

Paris Saint-Germain are OUT of the Champions League. Hold, redraw, enlarge, super-size, *HYPE* (if possible) the back pages.

Manchester United have done it. Ole Gunnar Solskjær has worked the miracle. He has done it without 10 frontline players. Including Paul Pogba, who was suspended.

How??

Wednesday night in Paris. The atmosphere crackles. The Parc des Princes is a neon light-show before kick-off, febrile anticipation electrifies the stadium. This is the 17th match for the caretaker manager and it is his first daunting challenge: Ole Gunnar cannot pull this off, can he? Cannot pull off the triumph of reversing the 2-0 defeat to Thomas Tuchel's team in the Champions League last-16 opening leg at Old Trafford three weeks ago? No side has ever recovered from a 2-0 home first-leg defeat in the Champions League knockout stages. This is in 106 previous 2-0 losses: *count them.*

Statistics are statistics, sure, but this one does add to the sense that United's hopes of overturning PSG's 2-0 advantage at Parc des Princes are remote. Surely.

In the build-up OGS says, 'We can do it.' This is delivered simply, casually. In the manner of a million-and-one managers across the years who say all kinds of things about their team's chances when the chances amount to close to minus a million-and-one-to-one.

Except Ole Gunnar means it and will prove it. He has a plan going into the game and the plan works a treat. Once again OGS shows – proves – he has the guts all the best managers require to succeed by acting when it really counts: match day. Whether the plan includes knowing he will be yanking Eric Bailly off after 35 minutes due to Juan Bernat's terrorising of him along the United right is not clear. What is clear is that OGS has the tactical flexibility and bravery to do so. To *act.* And: the player OGS brings on is Diogo Dalot and it will be *his* shot that forces the tie-winning penalty Marcus Rashford converts in the 94th minute. Rashford has never taken a competitive penalty for Manchester United before. Ever.

He smashes it home. It crowns a famous European night for the club. Wembley 1968: Manchester United 4 Benfica 1. Turin 1999: Juventus 2 Manchester United 3. Camp Nou 1999: Bayern Munich 1 Manchester United 2. Moscow 2008: Manchester United 6 Chelsea 5 (penalties; 1-1 after extra time). Now this.

Two minutes – *two minutes* – is all Solskjær's band had

needed to silence (nearly) all the 44,441 inside Parc des Princes as Romelu Lukaku puts United ahead on the night, 1-0, and makes the tie 2-1 to PSG. The home faithful are stunned and the delirious travelling support buzzing. On the touchline OGS has a bib on under referee's orders – he looks like a reserve, warming up; the joke is he's readying to bring *himself* on, in classic Solskjær substitute-striker fashion, as he was thrown on by Ferguson for the club countless times.

He doesn't need to. Juan Bernat may equalise on 12 minutes but Lukaku is at it again, giving United a 2-1 lead on the night and making it 3-2 on aggregate to the French. The promised land tantalises, is near-reached. And it is happening thanks to a player who is not an Ole first choice but who the caretaker manager has kept onside enough for him to perform like this.

Another goal – *just one more* – and United have completed the mission impossible OGS billed as mission possible, via the away-goals rule. It feels like Manchester United of old. Well, not *that* old. Of, say, six or so years ago, when Sir Alex Ferguson's team could still burn opponents.

That was Ferguson's United and this is Solskjær's. Tonight. This is his movie and it is happening here in widescreen Technicolor, and when Rashford smashes his late, late penalty past Gianluigi Buffon on the pitch are the 17-year-old Mason Greenwood and 19-year-old Tahith Chong, each academy products, so too are Rashford (21) and Scott McTominay (22) – the latter born the same year – 1996 – Ole arrived at the club from Molde. The sense is of a supernova champagne moment, of exhilaration, of a future of fantastic potential.

Later, Solskjær offered a Ferguson-like verdict. 'This club, this is what we do. That's Man United.'

Rashford's penalty was awarded via VAR by the referee, Damir Skomina, after Dalot's shot hit Presnel Kimpembe on 90 minutes. First, there were two minutes of viewing the pitch-side monitor. Then, two more before Rashford could take it as PSG's players attempted to distract him. 'There were no nerves, he's fearless,' Solskjær said of the forward.

The night was too much for Neymar, PSG's injured Brazilian superstar. 'This is a disgrace,' he posted on Instagram. 'They put four people that know nothing about football in charge of looking at the replay for VAR. There is no penalty. How can it be a handball when it hits his back! Go fuck yourselves!'

And, all of this, without the suspended Paul Pogba, who is deputised for by Fred, a midfield artist previously maligned but who suddenly looks a General MacArthur in the battle lines where football is won and lost. McTominay, too, has performed as if this is his coming-out party into the senior ranks of the Manchester United squad. This is also a night when Andreas Pereira plays the most important 80 minutes of his still-nascent career, Ole's belief in him being repaid. And how much of a boost was it for the callow Greenwood, just 17, to make his debut in this arena, on an evening like this?

Gareth Southgate, the England manager, is in the crowd. He later related how Sir Alex Ferguson was impressed. 'I was talking to Alex after the game and he was saying, "That was the United DNA – never say die." You've got to say that Ole has that connection with fans, he has all those experiences. The players have a smile on their face but also tactically he changed formation a couple of times during the game,' he said.

If the Lingard move to centre-forward at Tottenham was

a first note to Woodward and the Glazers that Ole Gunnar should be viewed seriously, this is a second. Before this, OGS had stumbled in the Champions League home defeat to PSG. That was disappointing, though was down to players not carrying out his instructions. That night was the angriest his players had seen him so far.

This night, in the return game, was the happiest.

CHAPTER 18

Always Ready for his Close-up

'He is perhaps the most famous person
in Norway.'

OLE OLSEN

The perception-busting feats of the opening eight wins on
the bounce, the PSG triumph and the closing of the gap
to a Champions League qualification finishing berth were
matched away from the field by a smooth-operator performance before the cameras and notebooks of the media.

The two may have been related. If Ole Gunnar performed
brilliantly in the media glare, relations between the manager
of Manchester United and the fourth estate are always an
intriguing affair. Sir Alex Ferguson's supreme power meant
he was nearly always in charge, the (top) dog wagging the
journalistic tail. He was combative and fiery and contemp-
tuous and usually a step ahead of his inquisitors, harnessing

most media conferences to his own end, often saying only precisely what he wished to say.

Until Ole's arrival Ferguson's successors were hardly as at ease. David Moyes stated at his inaugural media meet-and-greet that 'Success is tattooed right across the club badge.' The epigram was as pithy and as Oscar Wilde-like as the doomed Scot was to be in the motorway crash of a tenure.

To be precise, Moyes delivered the line sometime around 4.20pm on 5 July 2013 and there is a case for saying that this is when he peaked as a speaker for United and himself. This is a man who was not always the politest with the media as far back as his time in charge of Preston North End, from 1998 to 2002. He is known for being uncomfortable before the cameras – preferring the print media which, while a boon for these corps, was not a great state of affairs for a man who would be thrust before a lens on a continual basis. He also had the odd behaviour of being less than enamoured with Manchester United's own in-house television channel, MUTV, and so, instead of working *with* the organ and the people who work there, he immediately back-footed them and made them wary.

After his Wildean moment Moyes became the king of the clumsy soundbite, the master of the public faux pas. He did, though, do something that Ferguson eschewed – certainly in the latter of his 26 years – as well as José Mourinho and Louis van Gaal: tried to build a relationship with journalists. This began with a dinner in Sydney on the summer tour of 2013 and ended with a Christmas get-together that December for lunch and a chat. This was appreciated and showed Moyes to be a decent man, and he did offer one memorable insight into Ross Barkley, who was then a 20-year-old playmaker Moyes had left at Everton when taking over at Old Trafford.

In precis, he claimed Barkley, now at Chelsea, did not possess the fleetest of minds. And used his star United man, Wayne Rooney, as his point of reference, suggesting the latter had a fleeter one.

Manchester United was just too big for the Scot. It swallowed him up. He shrank before the spotlight. Do this and the days of a Manchester United manager are ordeal-ridden *and* numbered. As he found out. His sacking cleared the way for Louis van Gaal and he began his media duties with a bang. 'This club is guided in a commercial way and it's not always possible to meet commercial and football expectations,' he said at his unveiling in Old Trafford's Europa Suite on 17 July 2014.

The Dutchman had the chutzpah, the humour, the alpha-male edge David Moyes lacked but made the error of not allowing his private persona to be his public one. Or, the more complex take: he did not do it enough. Or, when taking questions, his public self could be a curdled version of his private self.

Not always. The above quote was Van Gaal in classic bombastic form, right at the start of his incumbency, not giving 10,000 hoots about the club that was paying his lucrative salary by moaning about the commercial pull of Manchester United and how this might impact the team.

But it came down to (a lack of) trust. Just as David Moyes was wary, so Louis van Gaal was a man on the edge, radar primed for the next slight, the media the enemy always. Behind the scenes, though, the Iron Tulip was friendly and inclusive, inviting the press officer, Karen Shotbolt, into his inner circle for meetings. Publicly, there were no such levels of inclusion.

Next up was José Mourinho, whose relationship with the

media needs no further description apart from to point out how far removed it was from Ole Gunnar's ease so far in this sphere. OGS's relaxed demeanour matched the success of his interim tenure and made him appear the complete package.

It meant he was about to receive the ultimate reward of being offered the full-time position. As he led Manchester United to win upon win, OGS was pulling a quasi-renaissance manager act: open to any question, ready with a quip or soundbite, a refreshing proposition who made the enquirer feel as if they'd shared a chinwag over a livener in a late-night bar.

He was the Babe Ruth/Frank Sinatra of the pre-game press conference, the post-game flash-quote: Ole Gunnar smashed it out of the park, crooned those Manc-accented Norwegian tones to sweet music. He made it all enjoyable and took the questioner, the press pack, the pundit-class with him. Even the rival fan whose modus operandi is founded on the detestation of rival teams and managers could not help but cast furtive looks, flutter surreptitious eyelashes at OGS. Tweets were tweeted that began: 'I'm no Man Utd fan but Solskjær is certainly . . .'

How? How does OGS hold the lens, the room, with an aplomb akin to that of Sir Alex Ferguson? Why is he a charm-laden media performer in a way that is a few universes apart from his post-Ferguson predecessors?

A vignette came on Tuesday 26 February 2019, in a media briefing ahead of the next day's meeting with Crystal Palace. Manchester United are 14 matches into the OGS interim reign and the press pack are inside the Jimmy Murphy Centre at the AON Training Complex. The Reds are in fifth place with 52 points, one behind Arsenal in the final Champions

League berth. The Eagles have 30 points, are in 13th place, six above the relegation zone.

The 'top-line' – what print journalists call the best quote or story – from Ole's discourse for that night's 10.30pm embargo (meaning it does not go live on newspaper websites until that time) is relatively decent, though hardly Pulitzer Prize nomination fare. Solskjær says that the heightened training under him may be the cause of a spate of injuries and adds, causally, that it means sink-or-swim time for his charges: a 'survival of the fittest' for his players. Here again is a reference to player condition, which will become a leitmotif of OGS's assessment of the team's performance.

The standout, telling moment of a briefing that starts at his regular time of 9.30am is not 'news' related. It comes at the end when a journalist from a national broadsheet, who often wears prescription sunglasses, suddenly hears his name being called out by Solskjær, after Karen Shotbolt, United's media manager, calls the session to an end.

OGS, offhand, says to the room, 'Okay?' And winks as the journalist approaches to collect his recording device, saying to him: 'We've got a new sponsor, Maui sunglasses, and I've not seen you wear sunglasses and I thought, "They fit you."'

Laughter erupts as OGS presents a pair of the shades and the journalist takes them. He shakes Ole Gunnar's hand and says, 'You've made me blush which is not something I often do. I thought I was in trouble then.' Grinning, OGS says: 'You didn't have them on now so I thought it was about time you have some new ones.' More laughter follows and with a wink Ole Gunnar walks out of the room, leaving behind the sense of a man enjoying himself, at ease, indulging in light japery for light japery's sake.

Just imagine Mourinho, Van Gaal or Moyes doing this. Or Ferguson. No way. The prospect would not even have reached proposal stage. Instead, Ole was open to the joke and subsequently pulled it off with ease.

Another element in play here is a prevailing characteristic of his: an instinct to think the best of people, which is a kind of trust. Instead of seeing minefields in every face-to-face with the media, Solskjær's approach is the opposite, to have trust. Not necessarily in the media. Because who knows who might misquote, spin, do the wrong thing, at any time. No, this is the trust in himself that began with the secure childhood in Kristiansund and has been nurtured through all the highs and lows of his experiences since. Trust and a sense of self-possession, of self-ease. A rare commodity in the managerial ranks whose default is often the polar opposite: suspicion.

Solskjær does not worry about being stitched up because he does not think in this manner. He sees no minefields in questions because he sees no minefields. He does not have to switch himself 'on' when required. An illustration of this last point was found when he spoke to the press on the night of Wednesday 6 March 2019, the night of the KO of PSG from the Champions League. This is in the bowels of the Parc des Princes, in the press room of the old stadium, and he is glowing and a Norwegian journalist has just asked OGS the following: 'This is for the English media in the room,' he says. 'Put your hand up if Ole should be given the manager's job permanently after this win.'

The question brings an instant show of hands from all the English journalists apart from one, who thinks the question a little mawkish. Yet on seeing the journalist's hand remaining down and recognising him as the same man he gave the sunglasses to, Solskjær lets go an instant, tongue-in-cheek: 'OH!' Pretending he cannot believe the writer is not backing him for the job – *where is your support??* – while poking fun at himself. The outburst causes laughter and the writer, sheepish, tells Ole: 'I was just being professional – of course I want you to have the job.' Solskjær smiled and left to fly back to Manchester after overseeing one of the club's most famous European victories. Departs having charmed everyone – again.

Footnote: just before the game in Paris, OGS did an 80-minute podcast called *Fotballklubben* with two Norwegians he knows personally. During this he clarified that the new contract he had apparently signed with Molde in early December, just before he got the call from United, was not a factor, removing one less obstacle to his becoming the permanent number one. This was a newsworthy line and showed Solskjær was comfortable going off-piste by talking off-diary to non-mainstream media. Ferguson would never have done this. Except, counterintuitively, he actually did. In his latter years at United, the Scot talked to SiriusXM, a 32m-plus subscriber US radio station, whose presenter, Charlie Stillitano, is an American who organises the International Champions Cup, the go-to pre-season summer tour competition.

Just as Ferguson went his way, so too did Solskjær, despite him being only the caretaker boss, not yet in the role for two months. Another illustration came on Friday 15 March ahead of Manchester United's trip to Wolves for an FA Cup quarter-final. Two weeks or so after the sunglasses skit, OGS is previewing the game and discussing the first league loss of his caretaker tenure – a 2-0 defeat to Arsenal at the Emirates Stadium.

Now he says, 'We can't look at the performance and say we were shit – to be blunt.' This causes Karen Shotbolt, the media manager, consternation – her features say so – which Ole notices and says, gently but with total authority: 'Don't worry about that, Karen,' drawing laughter while showing who is in control. At the end of the briefing there is, as usual, a smile and bounce from his seat and away off the dais, a 'See you', and he is gone, sounding like he will *actually* be happy to see the media again.

Later this month OGS is to be, undoubtedly, extremely happy.

CHAPTER 19

Fantasyland

Thursday 28 March 2019

'The last few months have been a fantastic experience.'

OLE GUNNAR SOLSKJÆR

Here it is.

Here is the day of days of Ole Gunnar Solskjær's life. A day for the books, for the annals of OGS and his family. The day when all the days become just one day. When everything he has dreamed about does this: happen.

He has been given the job. He cannot believe it; he *can* believe it. He is manager of Manchester United. Repeat: he is the manager of Manchester United.

Manchester United manager.

Permanently. No more interim role. He is no longer only here as a caretaker on secondment from Norway's Molde FK.

He has pulled it off. He has convinced Ed Woodward and the Glazers that he is the man for this role of all roles. The job he first dreamed of since the knee injury that cut him down in his prime as a player and caused despair and soul-searching and the recalibration of his view of the future.

Ole Gunnar Solskjær. The man whose life can seem anointed. When appointed as caretaker manager, the reaction ranged from bemusement – *what the hell?* – to derision – *what the hell?* Yet how quickly perception changes, opinions are forgotten. And it is OGS who has convinced – from 19 December to 28 March: 99 days. Ninety-nine days to turn the team around and make yourself an irresistible candidate for the job. Since Ferguson left, United have drifted and meandered. They just could not find the right manager: a man who lives and breathes and *gets* United.

But, no longer.

The clamour for Ole to be given the permanent position has grown and grown. Five weeks earlier Ryan Giggs, a former team-mate and Manchester United player for 23 years, was clear he thought the club should appoint Ole. 'I do,' he said. 'We've messed around far too long. When you've got someone who knows the club, who is tactically astute, clearly has the players and fans on board, that gives you lots of momentum. There will be bumps in the road but most fans imagine what he could do with the money that's been spent the last few years.' Giggs did, however, add that 'I wouldn't be in any rush' to make it public, 'to derail the current situation'. This would prove prescient.

A week later, following a goalless draw with Liverpool at Old Trafford, another former team-mate and United captain, Gary Neville, said: 'Three months ago if it was 0-0 at home they would have been singing "Attack, attack, attack". They were singing "Ole Gunnar Solskjær" all of the second half. The mood has completely transformed.'

The draw with Jürgen Klopp's team was another display of Ole's brain for the game. After 11 victories in 13 matches a test came during the first half at Old Trafford, as all three substitutes had to be deployed when Ander Herrera (on 21 minutes, replaced by Andreas Pereira), Juan Mata (25, Jesse Lingard) and Alexis Sánchez (for Lingard himself, just before half-time) were all injured.

Liverpool knew that if they could win this game in hand a three-point gap over Manchester City would open up in their bid to end 29 years without a league title. Despite the serious disruption to the original Solskjær game plan, his team showed spirit and an unwillingness to bend. By the close, a well-earned point had been won, seriously frustrating Klopp and his side. 'Everything that could have gone wrong did go wrong, and I've never seen the like of it before,' Solskjær said. 'But we learned so much about their character. I was very encouraged by the team, with the character and with the attitude.'

Gary Neville also said after this: 'He has the crowd with him. I think at this moment in time if you're the board you are not in a position where you could give it to someone else, I think there would be a mutiny.'

A mutiny. Strong words, which Woodward and the executive have heeded and others from the cognoscenti. Now, after all the managerial wrong appointments, Woodward and the Glazers have finally cracked it – this is the hope, anyway. The hope and the dream when they decide to elevate him to the permanent job.

To be granted the honour had been OGS's hope and

dream. There had been signs it would occur. It is the March international break and Ole Gunnar had been back in Norway and Molde FK had been in lockdown. Erling Moe, the caretaker number one during OGS's loan to United, and the chief executive, Øystein Neerland, went to ground, were incommunicado – not their usual status. Then, a few minutes ahead of 9am on Thursday 28 March 2019, Manchester United sent out the notice confirming Ole's appointment as permanent manager.

The words he offered were among the sweetest of his life. 'From the first day I arrived, I felt at home at this special club. It was an honour to be a Manchester United player, and then to start my coaching career here. The last few months have been a fantastic experience and I want to thank all of the coaches, players and staff for the work we've done so far. This is the job that I always dreamed of doing and I'm beyond excited to have the chance to lead the club long term and hopefully deliver the continued success that our amazing fans deserve.'

He targets the championship. 'The Premier League title is vital for us. I know we will be successful but it's about taking it step by step.'

And he once more points to Ferguson, saying he has spoken to him. 'Yeah, I have. I'm not going to discuss what we spoke about but it's one of the first phone calls you make when things were decided,' Ole said.

Woodward said, 'More than just performances and results, Ole brings a wealth of experience, both as a player and as a coach, coupled with a desire to give young players their chance and a deep understanding of the culture of the club. This all means that he is the right person to take Manchester United forward.'

Woodward and the Glazers view Ole Gunnar as the all-round package required to be United manager. One characterisation offered from within the club is that listening to OGS is akin to a combination of 'Sir Alex Ferguson mixed with Wayne Rooney and Rio Ferdinand'. Some billing. A heady blend of the genius manager plus the club's record goalscorer (Rooney) and gilded defender (Ferdinand), who lifted the 2008 Champions League trophy for United. This would mean nothing, of course, if the results had not also been returned, and Ole Gunnar's yield of 32 points from a possible 39 was not something anyone at the club had dared to hope for when he came in at Christmas. The hierarchy knew he would promote home-reared players and was attack-minded in the United tradition, but they'd had no searing belief he would win quite so impressively as well. The idea that they have made an emotion-led decision by giving him the job, predicated on his status as a club legend and the record-breaking start, rather than a cool-eyed logic, is rejected privately by the hierarchy – of course it is.

OGS's appointment is not considered to be the same as when Roberto Di Matteo was given the Chelsea post full-time after winning the 2011-12 Champions League as caretaker boss. Appointed in June 2012, Di Matteo was sacked by Roman Abramovich, the owner, the following November, lasting only five months in the permanent role. No, instead, the stance is that a confluence of culture between United and Ole Gunnar, plus, crucially, that the players believe he and the club are a natural fit, has made the decision an easy one.

And, yet: football in the way only football can is about to make all these calculations and logic seem close to farcical. Because these same players who believe and want OGS to be their long-term boss are about to let their man down in the closing two months of the season. Big time.

Big time enough to show up the real size and scale of the challenge Solskjær has before him. Fitness will be cited, as will the psychological wear-and-tear of the season that began under José Mourinho. And before the players and the team do start to plunge, there will be auguries of this: from the moment OGS returned from Molde to be announced as the number one.

Not on this day of all days, though. Everywhere is sunshine and flowers; all has an endless summer feel. Ole Gunnar hails his appointment by striking his always light note. 'The day I walk out of the doors, I hope it is with a smile on my face. I am not going to change, I will be an optimist and we will do this together,' he said.

Øystein Neerland, Molde chief executive, said of his now former manager, 'It is first and foremost fantastic. It is impressive by Ole Gunnar to be in a situation where it is possible to get such a good offer. For us as a club it is good to get a clarification.'

This last comment referred to there being no formal arrangement for compensation between United and Molde regarding Solskjær's appointment. 'It has been speculated that there has been such an agreement, but there has not been,' Neerland added. 'I have had contact with Ed Woodward yesterday and today. Then Ole communicated this to us today. When we finish this day, I don't have to comment any more on United rumours and can concentrate 100 per cent on Molde.'

The Manchester United Supporters' Trust are enthused. 'Along with the overwhelming majority of supporters, we welcome the appointment of Ole as our permanent manager,' a MUST statement reads. 'Over just a few short months, fans have witnessed a turnaround that even the most optimistic could not have predicted. Results on the field have been delivered through the playing style and team ethos that successive managers, since Sir Alex stepped down, were unwilling or unable to create. Following that night in Paris, in the eyes of many fans, he has already given us the best night since the Ferguson era and we can be confident that more will follow.

'It is now essential that the board back him fully in providing financial resources for world-class signings to strengthen the squad further and the right expertise and infrastructure to facilitate long-term player recruitment and academy development to re-establish the "United Way". We've long advocated the appointment of a director of football, as the presence of professional football people at the most senior level to support the manager and guarantee a ring-fenced budget is important to allow us to once again compete and deliver trophies at the highest level.'

The mention of 'board backing' and 'director of football' is pointed: here are the twin concerns many supporters hold. Will Ole be given the funds and allowed to buy the players he wants? Will a director of football or technical director finally be appointed?

All of this is before him on this day of days. He is canny and will have to show it. Display a shrewdness learned from Ferguson and which his ex-manager flagged up when Ole Gunnar took his opening steps in coaching and management. Then, he was about to take over Manchester United reserves. Now, a little under 11 years later, Ole Gunnar is the new occupant of the hot seat and the real work of grappling with the always-morphing club that is Manchester United begins . . .

The opening match of his permanent incumbency is on Saturday. Watford are at Old Trafford on a sun-tinged afternoon for Premier League game number 31 of the 2018-19 season. In his programme notes OGS wrote:

'Since I came back to the club, the response around the place has been fantastic and we've had some brilliant results, but that's all history now as far as I'm concerned. This is the start of the start. Now the hard work starts for all of us. Now we focus on rebuilding and getting back to where we belong, challenging for trophies, with the same attitude as we've shown. We want smiles on faces, positive football, but we've got to make sure we defend as well.'

After walking out under blue skies to a memorable hero's welcome Solskjær watched Marcus Rashford (on 28 minutes) and Anthony Martial (72) dispatch Watford. These two players have been emblems of the OGS way: young, swaggering and inventive, carrying a goal threat.

And, afterwards, in the media conference room to the side of the bar that serves the dignitaries in the directors' box, Solskjær shows some of the steeliness he will need to become top dog among his peers and make United top dogs again. Watford had pushed United back, particularly in the second half. This causes a Norwegian journalist to ask if United should, actually, be dominating at home against a 'team like Watford'.

Solskjær eyed the questioner. 'What do you mean, a team like Watford? You're not giving them the respect they deserve. Watford are a good team, they play in the semi-final of the FA Cup, have some very good players, the possession was 50-50. Maybe they had a couple more shots than us, but I don't think you are giving them respect, seventh or eighth in the league, along with Wolves, they are one of the best sides after the top six.'

This silences the inquisitor but there is more. Dom McGuinness, talkSPORT's respected man-in-Manchester, decides to ask about a ball from the United left-back, Luke Shaw, that split Watford's defence and created Rashford's strike: 'You surprised Luke Shaw did that pass?'

OGS, again, has a steely response ready. 'What do you mean?' Now comes faux indignation. 'Luke has got so much in his locker. He is exceptional going forward and I can't wait to see him blossom. I thought he was total class today until he got his cramp.'

The Solskjær charm means the gentle upbraiding leaves no one upset. The conference is over. He leaves the press room.

The Ole Gunnar Solskjær Era has begun. The job is here, now. Upon him. The fantasy is real.

CHAPTER 20

The Naysaying
Madrigals Are Back

'Odds slashed on Solskjær's future.'

ODDSMONKEY

The supreme manager makes victory seem simple and commonplace. Part of the natural order. He has a way with players and teams and opponents and the league table. He is the kingpin, he operates on a different plane. He *knows* something the ordinary football manager will never know and never know he will never know.

Ole Gunnar breezed into the club before Christmas and for a while made Manchester United formidable again, leaving José Mourinho looking oafish and outmoded. For those eight wins from his first eight matches – a total of 14 in the opening 17 – he was the specialist in victory and his Portuguese predecessor the specialist in taking down the stock of players and staff as well as his own.

This is how OGS cast the serially decorated Mourinho; a manager supposedly a force of football nature. By the close of the season the impression was tempered, the image of Solskjær as a (seemingly) master motivator and tactician faded. The way he outthought Mauricio Pochettino to beat Spurs at Wembley with Jesse Lingard at No. 9. The way he outsmarted Thomas Tuchel and motivated players on the periphery like Romelu Lukaku and Fred to overturn PSG's 2-0 advantage on that night in Paris surprised experts and fans – including those of Cardiff, who believed he was hopeless in this department when overseeing their relegation in May 2014.

All of this began to feel unreal, a mirage. Serious questions were being asked as Ole's side slumped to only three wins in the final 13 outings. But it *was* the truth of his beginning: eight scintillating victories from the eight matches. And the best of these suggested that he did possess a tactical mind, an ability to think laterally, and was willing to take a chance when required. The in-game theatre, the 90 minutes on the green grass, between the white lines, is where all PR and chat is pushed aside and sport's universal bottom line – the win – sifts the best from the average.

Ole Gunnar had first been exposed in the last match before his appointment as full-time manager, the FA Cup fifth-round tie of Saturday 16 March 2019 that ended Wolverhampton Wanderers 2 Manchester United 1. His team enjoyed 70 per cent possession and could do little with it, suggesting United were predominantly a counterattacking proposition that found oppositions hard to breach if the onus was on them. All sides, of course, find this difficult – Pep Guardiola's supreme Manchester City team, for one.

Yet this was a stumble, a first sight of Ole Gunnar frozen and hapless on the touchline. Unable to affect his team, the score, events and the narrative. This was a second consecutive defeat, as the fairytale started to hint at demons. United had played well at Arsenal on the previous Sunday – a league game – and lost 2-0, and they came away feeling cheated. OGS believed that if chances in north London had been taken, the result would have changed. Could've-should've is the go-to of the loser, but there was credence in what he said, reason not to be too despondent in how that match went.

The reverse at Wolves was different. In a 7.45pm kick-off at Molineux Stadium, United have most of the ball and this plays into Nuno Espírito Santo's hands. The Wolves manager has a fine record against top-six teams. His side drew the league fixture at Old Trafford on 22 September, 1-1, recorded the same score at Arsenal on 11 November, beat Chelsea 2-1 on 5 December, beat Tottenham Hotspur 3-1 away on 29 December, and drew 1-1 with Chelsea at home the week before beating United, having knocked Liverpool out in the third round of the cup, 2-1, on 7 January. This evening he is again clever. The Portuguese instructed his team to allow United to hog the ball and soak up any pressure and be patient because chances would come. They did. The tie was scoreless until the 70th minute. Then, Victor Lindelöf allowed Raúl Jiménez too much room and he swivelled and shot and beat Sergio Romero: 1-0. Six minutes later it was 2-0. This time a classic counterattack has Diogo Jota tearing away from United's rearguard and Romero can do nothing again. Marcus Rashford scored on 90 minutes but this was a consolation only. Five United players are booked – Lindelöf, Diogo Dalot, Ander Herrera, Nemanja Matić and Rashford – a sure sign that the side has been given a chasing.

In minute 71, OGS brought on the error-prone Andreas Pereira, then Juan Mata and Scott McTominay (both on four minutes before time), but the truth is nothing worked for him. Ole Gunnar explained the result as a lack of 'quality' and on the eve of the return to Molineux two weeks later on 2 April – following the win over Watford on 30 March – for Premier League outing 32, Solskjær admitted that United had a problem using all the possession Wolves allowed them.

'We feel that when we have to defend, we are well-organised, say in the away PSG game,' he said. 'Our intention is that we're not going to be broken down. I think Wolverhampton are a team that enjoy playing against big sides, which their results against all the big sides have shown. It's up to the team in possession to do things quick with quality through the lines. That's the difficult part in football, to be constructive and creative.

'I don't think that's more of a challenge for us than anyone else but that's where we want to get to. We enjoy those games and putting pressure on teams. That's a work in progress.'

United again lost 2-1 to Wolves – and the question began to nag: had he been good or lucky so far? Football – like all sport – is the business of making deities of the triumphant and a laughing stock of losers, whatever occurred in the actual contest. Victory is non-negotiable, unanswerable. Lucky or not, OGS has to be victorious. This is what he has found out now.

After being made the permanent Manchester United manager, Ole Gunnar discovered that fortunes had changed.

Winning had become difficult and losing easy. Far too easy.

On Thursday 18 April, and following a run of two wins and three losses, came a first notice from the gambling industry that Ole Gunnar Solskjær was feeling the heat. Three weeks to the day – just three weeks – after he was given a three-year contract as permanent Manchester United manager, odds were being offered against him surviving until the end of next season.

His record in these three weeks: the 2-1 defeat at Wolves, and losing 1-0 to Barcelona and then 3-0, Lionel Messi's strike that made it 2-0 the result of a David De Gea error that is part of a late-season run of mistakes that costs goals and points just as Ole does not need them. The wins: 2-1 victories against both Watford and West Ham United. The Barça results meant Manchester United were out of the Champions League. There was no disgrace in losing to Lionel Messi's band, but going down 2-1 at Wolves, to follow the FA Cup KO by the same score to the same side, was a concern and left Solskjær and his team the only target of a top-four finish, qualification for the European Cup, left to fight for.

It was not the prize Manchester United should be tilting at in the business end of any season but this was the status of the club in the post-Ferguson era. And the email quoting odds on Ole's future said: 'Just weeks after being confirmed as Manchester United manager on a permanent basis, bookmakers have slashed the odds on him leaving before the end of next season.'

Three days before the trip to Everton on Sunday here was the 24/7, knee-jerk football cabaret in all its glory. It illustrated how precarious management is. The glaring truth was that a loss at Everton would make it four defeats in the last five, which, for any number one at any club, has the band tuning up to blast out the 'Executioner's Song'. Really, there was no job security for Ole, just contract security. The three years he has signed on for gives him a soft landing if he is bumped out of the role. It is a Russian roulette existence. A dicing with managerial death.

The run of bad results in full reads five defeats (including the loss at Arsenal and the Wolves cup defeat before Solskjær took over permanently) and two wins. On Sunday, it is about to extend to six defeats in very dire fashion. But, first, on the Friday, comes a departure in tone of a press conference from Ole Gunnar at the Jimmy Murphy Centre at Carrington. This was the most cutting Ole had been since walking through the door the week before Christmas. In that first briefing, Ole contemplated the trip to Cardiff and what the next few months as the interim manager might hold before he would (reluctantly) hand over to whoever would become the full-time replacement for the freshly sacked José Mourinho.

Now, as the promise of a sun-bathed Easter weekend put smiles on the faces of the assembled correspondents of the national newspapers plus those from TV, radio and websites, OGS opened up. The last game was the 3-0 defeat at Barcelona on Tuesday night at Camp Nou. The performance was pathetic. Ashley Young gave the ball away needlessly to Lionel Messi and he zipped forward and beat David De Gea from distance. This was 16 minutes in. Four minutes later De Gea was the culprit, allowing a speculative Messi shot to somehow squeeze under him, and this was 2-0 and game over well before Philippe Coutinho inflicted more misery on 61 minutes. This meant a 4-0 aggregate defeat at the Champions League quarter-final stage, United having failed to take advantage of a near-toothless Barça in the opening leg at Old Trafford the previous week, when Messi operated as a kind of Juan Riquelme-like quarterback playmaker, dropping deep, moving at half-pace, like the Argentinean did at the 2006 World Cup. Messi still managed to create Luis Suárez's winner at Old Trafford with a pivot-and-chip to the forward. The truism about the best still being the best even when not at their best being demonstrated again.

Now, Ole is not happy. 'I've learned a lot about them – the players – over the months I've been here,' he said. 'You get to know them. Most of them have really impressed me in their attitude and there are some that need to get a reality check on where they're at. I've got to create this culture that we want.'

He mentions Anthony Martial by name. 'I've spoken to individuals and they know, and Anthony's one of them. I've spoken to all of them individually what we expect from them. Anthony's got a massive talent, he's signed a new contract, he knows we believe in him, so just keep on working. I think anyone who plays for Manchester United has to deliver to stay in the squad and stay in the team.'

Ole was even-toned – and correct – though not in the way he wished and hoped for. A reality check was indeed incoming – at Goodison Park – but the actual manner of this was not how he or any United fan would wish.

'Rancid': Gary Neville's description at the end of the 4-0 shellacking Everton handed Manchester United under a blazing sun at Goodison Park. Try these adjectives, too: mystifying, wounding, embarrassing, sad, humiliating, and, underlying all of these, *what the??*

The display was a nadir not known since David Moyes's Manchester United lost 2-0 at Olympiacos on a February evening in Pireaus five years ago. Then, Manchester United were listless and redundant. Moyes's XI on the night of 25 February 2014 read: David De Gea, Chris Smalling, Nemanja Vidić, Rio Ferdinand, Patrice Evra, Tom Cleverley, Michael Carrick, Antonio Valencia, Wayne Rooney, Ashley Young and Robin van Persie.

The XI Ole sent out at Everton that attains a similar unwanted notoriety was: De Gea, Victor Lindelöf, Phil Jones, Smalling, Diogo Dalot, Paul Pogba, Fred, Nemanja Matić, Romelu Lukaku, Marcus Rashford, Anthony Martial.

In Greece Danny Welbeck and Shinji Kagawa replaced Valencia and Cleverley on 60 and 61 minutes. On Merseyside Phil Jones, who was injured, and Fred are taken off at half-time, for Young and Scott McTominay before Andreas Pereira replaced Rashford on 75 minutes.

Which of these XIs is better or worse? The one sent out at the port town near Athens or the one fielded at the venue by Stanley Park in Liverpool? Moyes's XI was made up of the English champions of the previous season. Then, Moyes's United were in sixth place with 45 points after 27 games. They were 15 points behind the leaders, Chelsea, 14 behind second-place Arsenal, 12 behind Manchester City (third), 11 behind Liverpool (fourth) and five behind Tottenham Hotspur (fifth), and ahead of Everton only by a better goal difference of two – 12 to the Toffees' 10.

When Moyes was sacked on 22 April of that year it followed a 2-0 loss at Everton two days before. United had 57 points then after 34 matches and were seventh with a goal difference of 16. They were 13 points behind the leaders, Liverpool.

On 22 April 2019, the day after the 4-0 debacle at Everton,

Ole's Manchester United were on 64 points after 34 games, 24 points behind the leaders, Liverpool, with a goal difference of 15, and three off Chelsea in the final Champions League berth. In the five years since David Moyes's tenure, United are only seven points better off, have a poorer goal difference of one and are 11 more points behind the leaders. Has the club really moved on in the five years since Olympiacos? Does Ole Gunnar now, post-Goodison Park, truly understand the scale of his task? He should.

The display at Everton was (arguably) poorer than the one at Olympiacos. The presence of Paul Pogba – dubbed the 'Mesut Özil of Manchester' by one wag due to the flatter-to-deceive tag attached to him – Romelu Lukaku, Marcus Rashford, David De Gea and Anthony Martial all make a case for this team being stronger. Wayne Rooney, Robin van Persie, Michael Carrick, Rio Ferdinand and De Gea (again) might argue otherwise, though, De Gea apart, this quintet was in the autumn of their careers – part of a band that Louis van Gaal would describe as 'over the hill'.

Not in doubt is how bad United were against Marco Silva's Everton. The defeat comes via goals from Richarlison (after 13 minutes), Gylfi Sigurdsson (28), Lucas Digne (56) and even Theo Walcott, who Everton want to sell, and who came on after 51 minutes to score the fourth on 64 minutes. By the end of the match United have had one shot on target and Anthony Martial's refusal to track back is an emblem of the team's torpor.

Ole was shell-shocked and knows this was the poorest performance under him in this, the 25th match thus far of his reign. When Paul Tierney, the referee, blew for full time Solskjær walked over to the away supporters end to greet them and apologise. They still sang his name. They sang precisely zero of the players' names.

He was sad and confused: how could this occur? From here he embarked on a plethora of 'I'm sorrys'. This was the game in hand over Chelsea, so OGS's side have spurned the chance to draw level on points with the fourth-place team. Now, with four matches left, qualification for the Champions League is further beyond their grasp, the west Londoners' greater goal difference of eight effectively making them a further point clear.

Ole said, 'We have got to apologise to the fans because they were absolutely fantastic. That performance is not good enough for a Manchester United team, from me to the players. We let the fans down. We let the club down. That performance is difficult to describe because it was so bad. They beat us on all the basics: long throw – put your head in, our corner, they counterattack and score, their corner, they score. We were beaten on all the ingredients you need, added to the talent. There is no place you can hide on the pitch. It was 85 minutes before we got a strike on target, which is not good enough.'

He has previously stressed the need for United players to be the fittest in the league – it becomes his mantra, a way of clouting José Mourinho for a lax approach to physical conditioning and of pointing the way to a brighter future. As a group they ran 8.03km less than Everton: imagine this occurring at Pep Guardiola's Manchester City. Imagine it happening at *any* club where players are paid to be full-time professionals. Asked if his squad care enough, Ole takes an age to answer. 'I don't know – you've got to ask them. I have asked them. If you want to play at this club it has to be more. I want my team to be the hardest-working team in the league. That is what we were under Sir Alex, Giggs, Becks, Gary Neville, Denis Irwin. No matter how much talent you have got, you run more than anyone. You can't change your whole squad. One step at a time. I am going to be successful here and there are players who won't be part of that.'

It is the fourth loss in five outings. Yes, one of these is the Champions League quarter-final second-leg defeat at Barcelona which can occur to any team. But this is a terrible run and, with Manchester City up next – on Wednesday at Old Trafford in the 178th derby – here is a serious examination of Ole and his managerial ability.

On the Tuesday before the derby, Ole looked the most vulnerable since taking over. The eyes appeared watery, the demeanour friendly yet somehow braced. Braced for what might come his way as the media pack are back at Carrington with the first chance to question him now he has reflected on the debacle at Everton.

The mood is classic gallows humour, hack-style. One attendee joked that Ole should be asked if he will consider resigning; another quips/wonders if Ole will last until the end of the season – *this season*. He will certainly do so – there are only four games left. There was no particular ill-will here. The opposite was true – there was a lot of goodwill towards him.

Yet, what now occurred illustrated the challenge of being Manchester United manager and the job's gargantuan size and range. Simon Stone of the BBC posed a question that might have seemed premature but this is United, this is 10,000mph elite football. He asks Ole if he was the right man to take the big decisions and OGS noticeably flinches.

'I would like to say yes, but it's not down to me to say that. I'm confident in my team and myself to take this challenge on. It's a big challenge and when I came in here, I said I'm going to enjoy every single second. I don't like losing but it's a challenge when you go through bad results.'

Pressed again on whether he can oversee a required summer cull of the deadwood in the squad, Ole responded: 'I would like to think so. I like all these boys – I love them.' Now, to business: 'But I've got to manage for the club and I am managing the club and the players – I've got to put all my effort into making sure we do what is right for the club.'

Having to defend his position was not a great look only 25 matches into his tenure, though Ole Gunnar handled it smoothly enough. Someone mentions later that giving OGS even a light grilling can be akin to 'clubbing a seal cub' – another illustration of how he is liked – and there was a definite sense that being in this position stabs at him. Yet while he is tough and big enough to absorb it, one side of being a manager is often forgotten: there is a man behind the public persona, a human being with feelings.

All of this has been said in the non-embargoed section of the media conference – quotes that go out instantly, live. When United's media manager signals it is time for the embargoed part – this stuff to be held until 10.30pm tonight – proceedings become more involved.

Ole was asked about the view that Pep Guardiola's City team commit fouls high up the pitch because – and here the questioner's sentence is finished off by OGS – 'You don't get the yellow cards there, do you? But that's just because they commit so many players forward and you can clearly see that they've got them in that mould of trying to win the ball back, and they do make fouls. It's not my decision, it's the referee's responsibility to do that.'

By 1.30pm at City's training base Guardiola was in position and asked about this. The Catalan can be guarded or can shoot from the hip. This time he is in gunslinger mode. 'I don't like it,' he said of OGS's discourse. Pep then suggested Ole was trying to pressure Andre Marriner, the referee, ahead of the derby. 'That's the reason why, of course.'

The view from inside City was that Solskjær has committed a faux pas, as the statistics show United make more fouls in the opposition half than City. Opta, the stats mogul, bears this out. United have made 195 fouls against City's 170. Yet City's domination of the ball – up to around 65-70 per cent possession – means they may well foul more given their lesser time without it.

Guardiola was not happy but the media are. This was the best tale offered up on derby eve for a few seasons. The last for seven years, to be precise, when United went down 1-0 to City at the Etihad Stadium on 1 May 2012 to a Vincent Kompany header, and Sir Alex Ferguson and Roberto Mancini had a touchline spat, engaging in man-bags following a Nigel de Jong tackle on Danny Welbeck.

This left Mancini playing the post-game bemused what-did-I-do role, and Ferguson moaning: 'He refereed the game. He was out on that touchline the whole game haranguing the referee, the fourth official and the linesmen. The minute I come off the bench for a bad tackle by De Jong on Welbeck, he was out again.' Mancini's riposte came laced with sarcasm. 'Who said this? Him, no? He doesn't talk with the referee or the fourth official? No, never.' Funny.

The bottom line of the Ole–Pep rumble is that here

was an enticing slice of head-to-head between managers who, for differing reasons, had to win. Guardiola added that playing Manchester United in their stadium is 'not scary' any more, which is correct. City have lost there only once since February 2011, a defeat that featured Wayne Rooney's spectacular overhead volley (actually shinned), while winning seven times, a sequence including 6-1 and 3-0 victories.

Ole's team are in a creative slump. As they headed into the Wednesday night encounter, the last time they scored from open play was 437 minutes ago – Scott McTominay's 13th-minute strike in the 2-1 defeat at Wolverhampton Wanderers. United's only other goals in the past three weeks and four matches were Paul Pogba's 19th- and 80th-minute penalties in the scrappy 2-1 victory over West Ham United at Old Trafford 11 days before.

The Guardian's back page – like all the nationals – features the spat: 'Guardiola hits back at Solskjær over "foul" claims'. This feels like a pre-planned ploy from Solskjær. If so, it has worked – so far. Pep Guardiola has bitten.

On derby day there is a fizz in the Manchester air. The prospect of red-shirted and blue-shirted men going against each other. The clash of creativity, force and power. Picture them: David Silva in blue weaving his patterns, Marcus Rashford in red bursting through the centre. See them all: a 22-man vision of Manchester derby number 178.

And the hot air was whirling – listen to Ole Gunnar. 'We have to be ready for their quality. There's no time for players to drop their heads now. It's about changing the mindset, changing the attitude, and whoever gets picked has to be ready. There's no hiding place on the pitch. Go out there, puff your chest out again and show that you want to be a Man United player. The result will happen.'

On this cool, late April day, Ole and United needed a result. For the Champions League place that was in their sights and for his own sense of calm and reassurance. And ahead of the fun kicking off, at 5.15pm, it started raining – hard; an attack of lightning and thunder over Old Trafford that lashed the famous stadium and offered the prospect of a sodden encounter, a slick and skiddy affair that Ole's team had to win to keep up the chase for the top four, and City had to win to keep the retention of the title in their hands with three matches left after this. No club has recorded consecutive Premier League championships since Sir Alex Ferguson's 2007–08 and 2008–09 vintages. Trying to thwart the men in sky blue in their bid to bridge the 10-year gap was an extra motivation for Solskjær but, really, he had to have a response from his team for himself and the club and supporters following the Everton defeat.

There *is* a reaction but still United go down to a seventh defeat in nine outings. Before the 2-0 loss, viewers of Sky Sports are treated to a portion of prime Roy Keane punditry. The captain of Manchester United in their 1998-99 Treble season offers a scathing analysis of the squad Ole Gunnar has to manage. 'These are the same players who threw Mourinho under the bus and they will do exactly the same to Ole. There are too many bluffers.'

This is the big debate, one that is central to football management. Is it the players or the man in charge who is to blame when results are dismal? The scenario for Ole was clear: he had overachieved with his squad and the squad now performed like the rabble of the first part of the season under Mourinho.

Next, an interview with Paul Pogba was shown in which the Frenchman – not for the first time – trotted out the routine about how the performance at Everton was awful, the team was upset with itself, and had to respond, etcetera. Keane, wholly in character, is unequivocal. 'I wouldn't believe a word he says. I hear they were throwing hair gel at each other it got so heated. He's a big problem for United. He's a talented player but you need to be more than talented. The really top players make their team play better and he doesn't do that. He plays for himself,' said the Irishman.

Now, to the game. Ole made five changes from the Everton debacle. In came Ashley Young, Luke Shaw (suspended for the past three matches), Andreas Pereira, Matteo Darmian and Jesse Lingard. Out go Phil Jones, Nemanja Matić, Diogo Dalot, Romelu Lukaku and Anthony Martial.

The two starting XIs are worth comparing.

Manchester United: David De Gea, Ashley Young, Matteo Darmian, Chris Smalling, Victor Lindelöf, Luke Shaw, Paul Pogba, Fred, Andreas Pereira, Marcus Rashford, Jesse Lingard.

Manchester City: Ederson, Kyle Walker, Vincent Kompany, Aymeric Laporte, Oleksandr Zinchenko, Fernandinho, Bernardo Silva, İlkay Gündoğan, David Silva, Raheem Sterling, Sergio Agüero.

The gulf between these XIs is so wide that only one of the United outfield players has a chance of being in City's and this is Pogba. This point was underlined when the PFA Premier League Team of the Year was announced the morning after the derby: there are four Liverpool footballers – Sadio Mané, Andy Robertson, Virgil van Dijk and

Trent Alexander-Arnold – and six of Manchester City's – Ederson, Aymeric Laporte, Raheem Sterling, Bernardo Silva, Fernandinho and Sergio Agüero. The only player from the other 18 clubs to break the Liverpool–City hegemony, the XI selected by a vote from his peers, is Pogba.

None of this matters to Solskjær. It is immaterial to the business of facing Manchester City on a night of high emotion at Old Trafford. To try to overcome the class divide, OGS fields a back five in which Darmian's inclusion is an eyebrow-raiser. He was out of favour and heading for the exit door last summer. He seems to be always leaving the club, having been poor since being signed by Louis van Gaal in July 2015. It is the Italian's first start under the Norwegian, his last being at Liverpool on 16 December, a 3–1 defeat to Liverpool that was Mourinho's final match before being sacked.

United have not kept a clean sheet in the last 11 in all competitions – their poorest run in 20 years. Liverpool, at Old Trafford on 24 February, are the last team that failed to breach their goal. That Premier League meeting, ending in a 0–0 stalemate, is a result Jürgen Klopp's men will live to rue, as they are to be pipped to the title by the City machine by a single point.

In the afternoon before the derby Ole had taken the team to The Cliff, where he'd trained as a United player until the move to Carrington in 2000. 'It has not changed a lot but it is such a great place,' Ole told MUTV. 'We just had a stretch and a jog, fitness tests on one or two players. It was just to freshen up their heads. You can stay in a hotel all day long and that is not good for you. So it was nice.'

He explained the changes. 'A couple were forced, fitness-wise. Team shape, we have analysed City and we think the way we are going is our best chance to use our strength and maybe stop their strengths,' said Ole.

His final words before kick-off are: 'Every time you lose a game of football you want a game as soon as you can. Now just let the feet do the talking on the pitch, get a good start, be bright, be focused, stick together as a team and show that you are ready for these games.'

The shape works – in the first half City are off-colour. Kyle Walker, Olesandr Zinchenko and Vincent Kompany hit aimless passes and the latter cannot handle Marcus Rashford's Usain Bolt-like speed. But United do not capitalise and after the interval the visitors take over. Even when not at their very best, City are the finest of sides. When Fernandinho is forced off with an injury after 51 minutes, on comes Leroy Sané. Fernandinho has been brilliant yet Sané will score – after Bernardo Silva slides one past a hapless David De Gea on 54 minutes – by sliding one past the (even more) hapless De Gea on 77 minutes. The first beats De Gea on the near post to his left. The second on the near post to his right. De Gea's display is a one or a two out of 10 and it may be his poorest ever for Manchester United.

Through all the travails of the team since Sir Alex Ferguson, De Gea has been a beacon of world-class excellence, and the question has to be asked whether his future still not being decided is distracting the Spaniard: an issue of prime importance for Ole Gunnar in the coming close season.

By the final whistle his side have been soundly beaten by City and OGS trudges off to face the questions. Remarkably, Arsenal have lost 3-1 at Wolverhampton Wanderers. This means that, as United next host Chelsea on Sunday, they can still qualify for the Champions League if they win all of their games and Arsenal, who are two points ahead of United, somehow manage to lose one of their last outings.

The Gunners are at Leicester City at noon on Sunday, before United take on Chelsea at 4.30 later in the day. United then travel to Huddersfield Town and host Cardiff City on the season's last two Sundays. Arsenal, who have the 'distraction' of a Europa League semi-final against Valencia, host Brighton & Hove Albion and travel to Burnley in their last two league outings.

Ole remains positive. 'We need more quality on Sunday and if we win that game, we have two more games. Of course, we want to get into the top four. I haven't been planning on playing on Thursday nights yet – for the Europa League. It's maybe taken its toll on the players. It's my job now to see who wants to sacrifice enough to be here.'

Roy Keane has had another say, following the loss to Manchester City he is proving an eager Mr Rent-a-Quote. As at Everton, Ole's men have managed close to zero efforts on goal. 'One shot on target at home,' Keane fumed. He also criticised Fred and, on being asked about the Irishman's comments, Ole chose his words carefully. 'With Roy I've always had a great relationship. And, how do you say, I value his opinion very highly and he's got his opinion. We played together for many, many years and he's a Man United guy, as well, he hurts just as much as anyone else connected to us, that we are as far behind City as we are. And that's my job, to make sure when we come back for pre-season that I have the right characters in and around the squad.'

Now the run is seven defeats from nine. For all kinds of reasons Solskjær has to start winning again. Beginning with Chelsea, on Sunday, at Old Trafford. The mood is further darkened by the glaring stat that it is 527 minutes, 26 days – seven whole matches plus 77 minutes of another game, the 2-1 defeat at Wolves – since a Manchester United strike in open play: from Scott McTominay. And if Ole's side cannot beat Chelsea, who are in fourth, then any chance of the 'promised land' of a Champions League place is surely gone.

The fallout from the derby defeat continues. United were supreme underdogs against a supreme Manchester City team – 7.5–1 to win in a two-horse race against Manchester City on their own turf. So there should have been no real surprise they lost. Yet there has been the usual feverish over-reaction by those who forget who were favourites, and not for the first time a sizeable amount of hostile feeling has coalesced around Pogba.

When United are victorious he often shines, when they lose he often still tries to but can look lost. Against City he was again the one United player trying to make things happen, which is his natural game. Ole Gunnar admires and understands Pogba's talent – it is why he builds his side around the midfielder and why there will be a glaring hole in his squad if the Frenchman departs in the summer.

After the upturn in form under Ole at the start of his interim tenure, this has become Pogba's wish and is not too difficult to comprehend. He is 26, signed three years ago for United, and the team has gone close to nowhere. He is a World Cup-winner and the one United footballer talented enough for City or Liverpool or Bayern Munich or Real Madrid or Barcelona.

Yet when United are duff it is often only about him, which is a frustration for the Frenchman – and Solskjær. The bottom line is that Pogba is surrounded by mediocre talent;

is United's one true outfield star who, despite José Mourinho berating and dropping him during the fractious first half of the season, has 16 goals in all competitions (his highest ever), 13 in the Premier League with nine assists, the best record of any midfielder in the division. Achieved in a side that is not Pep Guardiola's City or Jürgen Klopp's Liverpool.

At Friday's pre-Chelsea briefing, Ole is asked if Pogba will still be at United next season. Solskjær said, 'You can't guarantee anything in football but, yes, I think Paul's going to be here, he's very determined to succeed at Man United. Everyone looks to Paul, saying could you have done better? But he's done fantastic for us; he's a human being as well and we're all the same.'

On De Gea, and the question of whether he will be dropped for Chelsea following his run of blunders, Ole is unequivocal. 'No. Not at all. Because I trust David and he's for me been the best player United have had for the last six or seven years. He has been absolutely outstanding – going through tough patches is part of a footballer's career and David will be fine.' He does not want to drop him but may also have an eye on the Spaniard's contract situation – the need to have him sign a fresh one in the coming summer. Since 2 March, mistakes from De Gea have allowed goals from Yan Valery (United 3 Southampton 2), Granit Xhaka (Arsenal 2 United 0), Felipe Anderson (United 2 West Ham 1), Lionel Messi (Barcelona 3 United 0), Gylfi Sigurdsson, Lucas Digne (Everton 4 United 0), Bernardo Silva, and Leroy Sané (United 0 City 2).

Solskjær is asked about the drop-off in his team's form. He said: 'That's football for you. That's human beings for you, that's margins, and of course we've played you can say easy teams in the beginning and more difficult teams now, but it's the whole scenario, the whole season, and it's been an emotional season for players and the club.'

He cites the points yield in each of the completed campaigns since Sir Alex Ferguson retired – asks the room: 'If you look at the team's total points last five seasons – I don't know if you can give me that average?'

No one can.

'Seventy. We're now on 64, that's where we're at, the reality where we've been for the last five seasons and that's not good enough, that's not down to the last six, seven or eight games, that's where we are. We have a great challenge ahead of us.'

He sends out the following XI: De Gea, Young, Lindelöf, Bailly, Shaw, Pogba, Mata, Herrera, Matić, Lukaku, Rashford. Andreas Pereira, who was at his best in the derby defeat to City, is singing a song of hope rather than confidence. 'It's a must-win. We have to show we want the top four and, in these games, we have to show our level and show we are worthy to be in the Champions League.'

Under OGS, Pereira, a Portugal-born Brazil-qualified attacking midfielder, has become more than the fringe player he was. 'Overall, it's been a special season – I got my first start, scored my first Premier League goal and played in my first derby, although the result was disappointing. I'm so grateful to him that he puts his trust in me,' he said.

In answer to Keane's comments about being thrown under the bus, which can be read as a bastardisation of the 'Ole at the wheel' song sung by fans since he arrived, Ole said: 'Of course that is not going to happen. I speak to my players all the time; they know my expectations and standards. I have got three years now and I am going to do whatever I can to make this club successful. It is not like players v managers here. We are all in this together and we are all working hard to improve.'

He is also forced to defend himself against the accusation of being a mini Ferguson, of being stuck in the past. Paul Ince has been scathing again. 'Ole needs to get over Sir Alex Ferguson – he's the United manager now. That's in the past now, we need to move forward from that. All of this "Ole legend" stuff – yeah, he scored the winner in the 1999 Champions League final, we get that. But he's not a legend – he's the manager of Manchester United. Regurgitating how he's going to do it "the Fergie way" is pointless.

'It's doing my head in, and I know others feel the same. Ferguson isn't the gaffer any more – simple.'

Ole offers a response that suggests he is hearing the criticism from Ince and others and gives it some credence. 'Everyone knows that times have changed and what the gaffer did has been unbelievable,' he said. 'But we are doing things differently to all the previous managers. We can't try to copy Sir Alex and think that's going to be successful, because he was unique. We've got a different generation of players and we've got to do it our own way.'

By around 6.30pm on Sunday reality has bitten yet again. United draw 1-1 with Chelsea and De Gea has contributed the latest killer howler. As in the derby, United start well, dominating the opening half, then fade after the break. Juan Mata scores on 11 minutes, to finally register a goal for Ole's side from open play after 538 minutes. They can and should register again but don't and two minutes from half-time De Gea has his shocker. Antonio Rüdiger decides to take a pot-shot from 30 yards and hits the ball straight down the goalkeeper's throat. Somehow, De Gea spills it to his right, and Marcos Alonso reacts quicker than any United defender and finishes off at the far post – to the keeper's embarrassment and Ole's ashen-faced disbelief. Of concern now is how United are deflated and never truly recover. It is not until the seven added minutes of the second half that they threaten to secure the winner, Marcos Rojo's header being cleared off the line by fellow substitute Pedro. There are questions everywhere that require pondering and answering in a close season that is now only two matches away.

What has happened to Marcus Rashford's form and can he spearhead this team? He last scored on 30 March in the 2-1 defeat of Watford: the first of United's last two wins – the run now two victories in 10 outings, having entered the Chelsea match enduring their poorest sequence since 1961. Ander Herrera played for the first time since the Watford win and United looked a better side, but he is leaving – for Paris Saint-Germain – so can Scott McTominay replace him? Romelu Lukaku admits after the draw he does not know if he will stay at the club.

Pogba's future is up for grabs, Anthony Martial is off the boil (again) and, as for De Gea: the latest error makes it nine goal-allowing mistakes in the last two months, since the 3-2 win over Southampton on 2 March.

Ole suggests he will not drop his No. 1. 'David's been unbelievable for this club. There's no chance that anyone can blame him for losing many points for us, so he's been unbelievable. He will admit himself he could have stopped that goal, but that is football.' OGS is doing a fine job of not blurting the frustration surely felt at how his supposedly star goalkeeper is killing the team at the moment, though it is not really about De Gea. It is about the deep flaws in the squad that have to be addressed in the upcoming summer market.

Arsenal had been trounced 3-0 by Leicester earlier in the day, yet Ole's team could not take advantage so the Gunners are a point ahead of United in fifth, with Chelsea in fourth, three points better off, their goal difference superior by eight with only two matches left. As he must, he refuses to give up. 'I don't think we can until it's theoretically over, but of course it's a big mountain to climb. We need to focus on those last two games, do our best for ourselves, win games and see what the other games throw up. The end of a season throws up a few marginal decisions, strange results, so anything can happen. Let's see how many points we can get.'

It has to be six, surely. But even those may not be enough to secure passage to the promised land of Champions League football. Luke Shaw sums it up. 'It's the story of our season really. We've had so many chances and not been able to take them.'

Ahead of Sunday's trip to Huddersfield OGS said: 'We've got to find a way of playing as well – what is the best style: the style should be attacking quickly, playing forward, running forward, chasing back, winning the ball back. I'd love to get to where we have a set system but it hasn't worked that way. You see the teams who get two or three years together, they know each other, they know the relationships, as a football manager or a coach you know the more time you get to work on relations, the better it will be, because then you're a step ahead all the time instead of at the moment we maybe react too much to the opposition.'

This is, indeed, the difference between United and, say, City or Liverpool: stability of management and a coherence of style. For now, the priority is to beat Huddersfield. Tottenham Hotspur have, somehow, lost 1-0 at Bournemouth on Saturday. They have 70 points with the home game against Everton remaining. This is five ahead of United who, after Huddersfield, have the final-day visit of Cardiff City, who are also relegated. Spurs have to beat Everton to be sure, but it remains in their hands so are favourites to take the third Champions League berth with Chelsea (on 68 points) and Arsenal (66) ahead of United. But the Spurs defeat does mean that Solskjær and his team retain an outside chance.

In terms of being given enough time to rebuild the side, Ole Gunnar is confident. 'I have regular meetings with Ed, I've seen Joel Glazer and the rest of the owners, they are very realistic on where we are and what we want to get to and how long that will take,' he said.

And it is notable that when asked for the first time to assess his United tenure, Ferguson was not mentioned: Ole perhaps stung by criticism that he had compared himself to the Scot too often. 'You should ask the players. They should describe me as a manager,' he said. 'I'm a manager who loves to work with people. I've got my values and standards and expectations. I think my players now, if you ask them, know my expectations and standards. I'm an optimist. But then again, I'm a realist. I just love to see people improve. And for the team to improve, individuals have to improve.

'My job is for the club. I have to manage for the club, and manage the players, yes. You give people a chance, but sometimes, you've got to be ruthless and say: "Sorry, but you had your chance." I'm not afraid to do that. It's not me really – sitting here and talking about myself.'

By the end of the match against Huddersfield what is

apparent is that the 1-1 draw means the outside chance of a top-four finish is over. For him and the team it is time to forget the Champions League and say an unwanted hello to the Europa League.

And, if Watford were to beat Manchester City in the FA Cup final, time also to say hello to the prospect of cutting short their summer tour of Australia and Asia to play a Europa League qualifier in late July. Forget playing Tottenham Hotspur in Shanghai in a stroll-a-minute pre-season warm-up, Ole and his team could be going to Israel, Bulgaria, Azerbaijan, Croatia, Albania, Moldova, Georgia, Luxembourg, Latvia, Lithuania, Ireland, Finland or some other lesser-known corner of the continent.

Chelsea's convincing 3-0 victory over Watford means their superior goal difference had all but shoved United out of Champions League qualification. 'What a bunch of chokers,' said the former England striker Chris Sutton of United. Sutton is kind of right and wrong in his assessment.

Really, the bottom line is that the squad Ole inherited was not good enough. It was – and remains – a muddle of average talent, past-their-best footballers, the odd player of potential and only two world-class acts: De Gea and Pogba. This United are several light-years from Manchester City and Liverpool, who are taking their titanic title tussle into the season's final weekend whatever Pep Guardiola's side do against Leicester City in their penultimate match, on Monday 6 May.

The effort the players put in for Ole on his arrival last December also caught up with them. They look a tired bunch and shot – the attrition of being managed by José Mourinho in the opening part of the season sapped energy levels and mental reserves, a view from the club that has some credence. This is also the squad's message to Ole Gunnar and Woodward: that they have found this campaign the 'most challenging' while at the club. The scrutiny of the Mourinho months, having to tiptoe around the unhappy Portuguese, was a drain. And, also, that having prepared in the summer for a Mourinho campaign, his fitness demands being lower, then having to adapt to Ole's: that was where the instant upturn in form came before the crash. The City defeat is assessed as a prime example at the club: the players sent out by Ole just could not sprint and press on a level with Pep Guardiola's. This is a damning indictment of seriously well-paid, supposedly high-end professional footballers.

At the John Smith's Stadium Scott McTominay, Ole's best performer of the past few months, gave the team a lead, his eighth-minute strike squeezing under Jonas Lössl, Huddersfield's goalkeeper, in a hapless manner reminiscent of David De Gea's recent series of howlers. The lead lasts to the hour: United are as under-par (actually par for this late-season rabble) as they have been for Ole, and when Luke Shaw misses a regulation clearance Isaac Mbenza is in and finishes – through De Gea's legs. The way he is playing is hardly the best advertisement for his talents with regard to being offered a lucrative new contract or to attracting a move to Real Madrid or elsewhere. Ole Gunnar's luck has truly turned. This is the poorest De Gea has been since Ferguson left. At the start of his United career, the Scot dropped him but the way he is bombing is worse than then.

Cut to Ed Woodward in the posh seats, stony-faced, the executive vice-chairman knowing this summer really has to be the start of the reset for the club and squad that should have occurred in each of the six previous ones since Sir Alex Ferguson retired. He has known it before and the execution has lacked. This time, surely, lessons will be learned.

Afterwards, Ole Gunnar said: 'We didn't perform to the required level, and though we are all disappointed not to be in the Champions League next season, the Europa League is probably the right place for us at the moment.'

Now, the bottom line. 'I can't talk about individuals now, but there is the chance you have seen the last of players.'

Who and how many Solskjær culls in the close season will be the summer's prevailing narrative. Ashley Young, who signed a one-year contract extension in February, offers words that have been spoken a zillion times after one of the dismal displays Manchester United have put on since the last title of 2012-13. 'A club like this shouldn't be talking about finishing in the top four, we should be talking about winning trophies. Ole and his staff will prepare over the summer and be ready for next season. I'm not sure what it is. It could be a number of things. It's a disappointment now that we can't get in the top four. We'll have to go away and think about how the season has gone and come back ready to go again.'

Ole offers a final word on the disappointment. 'It's a big summer.'

It will be – for the club and for OGS's hopes of success. Before Huddersfield his mantra was: 'We've got to keep playing until 12 May.' But the problem was that, as Pogba faded from the stellar midfield form and goalscoring that saw him voted into the PFA Premier League Team of the Year in spring, no one else could take over. Quality, temperament was lacking. Martial, Rashford, Mata, Lingard and Lukaku were as disappointing a group of forwards as Nemanja Matić and Ander Herrera were in midfield. It is noticeable that McTominay, one player to shine during the dire run, is only 22 and still relatively new to the side.

More of this freshness is required in the summer: fresh blood *and* fresh ideas.

CHAPTER 21

The Start of the Start

'He doesn't have a record of experience as manager, does he?'

GEOFFREY BOYCOTT

This has to be it. The start of the start. Time for Ole Gunnar Solskjær to unveil the blank canvas that will be *his* Manchester United. The turn for fresh vistas, the new and compelling Manchester United of Ole Gunnar Solskjær.

Cardiff City are in town in four days' time for the final game of the 2018-19 season. Sunday 12 May 2019 has to be Day Zero for the Ole Gunnar Solskjær Revolution.

Another turbulent season in the post-Sir Alex Ferguson world of the nation's record 20-time champions is nearly over. Last year José Mourinho's United ended in second place on 81 points, 19 behind Manchester City. This time the best they can possibly do is 69 points, close to the 70-point average of each of the seasons since Ferguson strolled away. It has been

THE START OF THE START

another one in which United have been in disarray – before Mourinho was sacked – and then towards the end when the results became unacceptable.

Cardiff are already relegated so 'should' provide an ideal patsy, a fitting final opponent of another disappointing campaign. United are guaranteed to finish sixth and may overtake Arsenal if Unai Emery's team lose at Burnley and Cardiff are defeated. A fifth-place position and Manchester United will go straight into the Europa League group stage, which would mean no second qualifying round to be played in late July/early August. Instead, the competition would start for them on 19 September 2019. But, really, all Manchester United supporters ask: 'Who cares?' As should Ed Woodward. As should the Glazers.

As *does* Ole Gunnar Solskjær surely, privately.

Now, it is all about the start of *his* Manchester United. Yet the sense of chaos at the club is retained on the Thursday night of the Manchester United Season Awards. This is anti-slick PR that advertises a dysfunctional operation. Luke Shaw wins the Players' Player of the Year and the gong voted for by fans, the Sir Matt Busby Player of the Year award. 'It's obviously nice for me, but I'd rather win no individual trophies and have a better season as a team,' he said.

Shaw is as on-message as the off-message Sir Geoffrey Boycott, who is considered a great England cricketer and keen United fan and who is never, ever circumspect with an opinion, as when being interviewed live on MUTV.

Boycott is just not enamoured of OGS. 'He doesn't have a record of experience as manager, does he? He had a short time at Cardiff then resigned honourably; he's looked after a team in his home country – Molde – but it's not the Premier League.'

OUCH.

Who sanctioned having Sir Geoffrey on air? Which MUTV producer decided it was a great idea? What it does do well is provide a neat summation of United's season: the club's own in-house organ giving a platform for its manager to be slated *live* on air to fans. Ole, being Ole, laughs it off – this characteristic is invaluable in his role, particularly given the club's predicament. His mind is on the summer and next season. 'It's a great challenge, but it's a great responsibility as well, because this club is huge and the media and everyone's criticising us as soon as they've got a chance. We've just got to stick together, know that we've been through tough and difficult periods before. We've got to recruit smart; we've got to keep blooding the youngsters and we'll be fine.'

He is asked to describe his overriding emotion regarding the half-season in charge. 'A mixture because we were so far behind when we came in before Christmas, I could sense the positivity, when you start winning games it was fantastic to be in that group. That showed us the potential and quality in the players; of course we didn't have the consistency. The Premier League is the most competitive league in the world and we just fell short of what would be a miraculous target of fourth back in December. Overall, it's been an adventure for me so far. I've absolutely loved it.'

By 4.50pm on Sunday he is not loving what he has seen: Manchester United 0 Cardiff City 2.

In consecutive weekends, Solskjær's team have drawn and lost to two already relegated sides, United again hapless against the Bluebirds, their best player the 17-year-old forward who shines on his full debut – Mason Greenwood. Afterwards, OGS is sure the Glazers and Woodward understand what is required. 'Definitely,' he said. 'I've had loads of conversations and they've been upfront and honest. We know where we are and our form towards the end of the season makes it clearer. The big plus is the season is over.'

United have gone into freefall since he was given the manager's job permanently at the end of March, managing only two wins with six defeats in all competitions. He is not 'shocked' at this. They end on 66 points, a yawning 32 behind the champions, Manchester City, and the same number they are from Cardiff in third-bottom, and 15 poorer off than last season under José Mourinho. This is some reversal and is reminiscent of how Ferguson signed off with a side that claimed the 20th title by 11 points, before United trailed in 22 points off the champions, Manchester City, the following 2013-14 term under David Moyes (he was sacked with four matches left). Ole Gunnar has to be able to arrest this trend next season.

Before the Cardiff reverse, OGS's adjective of choice was 'adventure' to describe his ride so far. Any adventure has drama and his is being played out in public, in the 4D of real time. The first summer in charge of Manchester United will define his tenure.

CHAPTER 22

Transfer Market Blues

'Manchester United is the only club that I
would have left Bayern Munich for.'

BASTIAN SCHWEINSTEIGER

A word: Recruitment. *Recruitment.* RECRUITMENT.

Wilfried Zaha for £15m, Guillermo Varela (£2.5m),
Saidy Janko (£750k), Marouane Fellaini (£27.5m), Juan
Mata (£37.1m), Luke Shaw (£27m), Radamel Falcao (loan),
Marcos Rojo (£16m), Ángel Di María (£59.7m), Daley
Blind (£13.8m), Memphis Depay (£25m), Matteo Darmian
(£12.7m), Víctor Valdés (free), Sadiq El Fitouri (free),
Timothy Fosu-Mensah (£340k), Bastian Schweinsteiger
(£6.5m), Morgan Schneiderlin (£25m), Sergio Romero
(free), Anthony Martial (£36m rising to £50m-plus), Regan
Poole (£100k), Eric Bailly (£30m), Zlatan Ibrahimović
(free), Henrikh Mkhitaryan (£26m), Paul Pogba (£89.3m),
Victor Lindelöf (£31m), Romelu Lukaku (£75m), Nemanja

Matić (£30m), Alexis Sánchez (swap for Mkhitaryan), Diogo Dalot (£19m), Fred (£47m) and Lee Grant (£1.5m).

This is the list of the 31 major players who walked through the door to the club in the six years since Sir Alex Ferguson left and Ole Gunnar became manager. It tells a glaring tale of dismal and disjointed recruitment. That this has been the fundamental problem at Manchester United of the past six years.

Recruitment was done by Ed Woodward in concert with managers, yet the ability to assemble a balanced squad that was a unified force eluded them, one that did not stumble when players were ruled out by injury because the replacement was of similar quality *and knew* precisely what the team's style and pattern was. No manager has lasted as long as three years. Alex Ferguson took four to win a first pot and *seven* to win a first league title.

The club structure responsible for managers being hired and which footballers were then acquired has been dysfunctional. This points to Woodward, whose role is to ensure the football policy is as successful as the commercial policy so obviously is – if not more so.

In summer 2019 Woodward, Matt Judge – the head of corporate development responsible for getting deals over the line – and their in-house 'football experts' finally acknowledged that recruitment had been disjointed. Defining more than one of the 31 players brought to Old Trafford in 12 transfer windows as an unqualified success is difficult. The sole unqualified successful acquisition was a free transfer: Zlatan Ibrahimović, in summer 2016.

And, brought to the club by Mourinho, he was a lumbering No. 9 who blared how outmoded Manchester United were. If there is an argument for Paul Pogba also being a success – he is the most talented – a hit rate of two from 31 in six years remains dismal.

This was the state Manchester United were in. The club that Ole Gunnar found when he returned. The Glazers had to take responsibility, too. The drift that had occurred indicated owners who were not focused on ensuring United remained English football's dominant force.

All of this meant that Ole Gunnar's mission in summer 2019 was to try to reverse the deep structural malaise during a transfer window that opened on 1 July and would be a major factor in defining his hopes of success as manager.

Ole's cordial manner, ensuring he has good relations with Woodward and the Glazers, would be an asset as he tried to sign players he wanted. Fourteen years before, relations with the owners were different. Then OGS agreed to become a patron of Shareholders United, who were against the Malcolm Glazer-leveraged takeover of the club. On 15 February 2005, as Glazer was putting through the deal, Ole Gunnar said, 'I am honoured [to be a patron]. I think it is important that the club remains in the right hands. I am absolutely on the supporters' side and think the club is in very good hands as it is today. I am a United fan myself and only want what is best for the future.'

Then OGS aligned himself with the many supporters furious at the takeover. Fast-forward to 28 April 2019 and, as he had to, Ole defended the Glazers. 'You can't say that we haven't invested enough money. If you look at the money that's been spent, the owners have invested loads of cash – and will continue that. I've been in meetings and we've had discussions about that. But you can't change the team in one transfer window. We are all realistic enough to see where we are and you just don't go bang and move from 70 points to 90 points.

'It's not like playing *Football Manager* this, you know. There's players that we maybe have expressed an interest in and if they're not available for sale, it's not just like "I'll get him".

'Liverpool didn't do that and City didn't do it. They got to where they are by stability, consistency and steady investment. We have to have the right type of player, with the right quality and the right personality. If they're driven by money or fame then they're not right for Man United or right for my team.'

It was a fair point about the investment. Between Ferguson and Ole Gunnar £788.57m had been invested in players at a net spend of £544.96m. The problem was it had been misspent. If Ole could not arrest this, he would fail. How much agency Woodward and the Glazers would allow him would be crucial. Ole Gunnar *had* to recruit well. Had to be the talent-spotter supreme. Able to identify and then persuade the right players to come and join the club. 'I've been the same at Molde and Cardiff and I've been the same here,' he said. 'I need players who can reflect me as a person as well and my values.'

And with no Champions League football in 2019-20, Ole still had to sell his vision to the footballers who would want to join and try to help finally relaunch the club back into the rarefied air of the elite game. It has to be the stratosphere or nothing at Manchester United.

So what Ole Gunnar does is gaze at the post-Ferguson 31 and know what must be different: to only go for footballers who fit into three criteria he and Woodward and the football department draw up as a prerequisite, the ideal

Manchester United footballer – X factor, respectful yet humble, and arrogant.

The definitions of the these, as drawn up by the club, are: 'X factor' means that the player has one area in which he shines. An example Ole and Woodward work with is that of Darren Fletcher, whose X factor was consistency of performance that ran at a minimum of seven out of 10 virtually every game-day.

'Respectful yet humble' means wanting to sign autographs, understanding how fans are the core of the club. Being the best ambassador for Manchester United.

'Arrogant' means that on the pitch the player wants to take responsibility; Michael Carrick this time the embodiment, as he was, for example, always willing to receive the ball in tight areas.

To take only one illustration of how wrong Woodward and Ole's three managerial predecessors got it in the market, OGS need only look at Bastian Schweinsteiger's arrival from Bayern Munich in July 2015 under Van Gaal's management. The German was 30 so there should have been greater scrutiny of why Bayern would allow a World Cup-winner of the previous summer to leave, a hint of which Schweinsteiger offered when he said: 'Manchester United is the only club that I would have left Munich for.' If this read on one level as regulation footballer-speak when joining a new team, it can also be deciphered as meaning that, despite knowing he was now only a squad player at Bayern, the midfielder would have remained there if not for United's lucrative, and mistake of an offer.

Schweinsteiger duly failed to make an impact at the club and at one stage Mourinho had him training with the kids.

The German had arrived a year after the summer of the Galático at United when Radamel Falcao, on loan, and Ángel Di María for a then British record £59.7m fee were acquired. Neither worked and were gone the following year. Daley Blind was also signed in summer 2014 and stayed for four years, yet his averageness is another example cited within the club as being precisely the kind of player who lacks the X factor a United footballer must have.

Ole's summer window of 2019 was indeed far better than the one of Moyes, the two of Van Gaal and Mourinho's three. It could be deemed a success with qualifications. It was probably the best start he could hope for given the state of the club and the financial limitations he worked under. By the close of the market on 7 August, Ole signed Harry Maguire (for £80m, from Leicester City), Aaron Wan-Bissaka (£50m, Crystal Palace) and Daniel James (£15m, Swansea City). Yet this outlay was offset by the sale of Romelu Lukaku for £74m, so the net spend was £71m – hardly a fortune, especially for a club as cash-soaked as United. Yet all the players signed by OGS fitted the ideal of the identikit United footballer *and* were also a fit for 'my team', Ole said.

Maguire's X factor was his billing as England's first-choice centre-back and his ability to play out from the back. Wan-Bissaka's was his searing pace, attacking verve and defensive prowess along his right-back corridor. James's was even greater pace and a rawness and courage – proven by the attritional demands of the Championship – qualities required in order to have any chance of flourishing in the Manchester United frontline.

The trio embodied a clear vision from Ole Gunnar, and allowed fans to be more optimistic than they had been since May 2013. OGS's plan for them was clear: all were part of his revamp of a Manchester United he wanted to be a fast-thinking and fast-pressing band that would give the opponents zero rest while playing the dazzling stuff.

Maguire, 26, would be the defensive linchpin and provide leadership alongside the youth of Wan-Bissaka (21) on the right, whose vibrancy also made him ideal for the right wing-back berth when Ole wanted to operate with three at the back. James would dovetail with the fleet-footed Marcus Rashford and Anthony Martial in attack, where Jesse Lingard and, to a lesser extent, Juan Mata, would also provide competition for places.

Yet where Ole's transfer business was weaker – poor, really – was in midfield and this was a consequence of not replacing those who left in the position. OGS had already allowed Marouane Fellaini to leave in the January window and, while this was an understandable move as the Belgian's pedestrian style did not suit, it meant being a player light in midfield.

This was compounded when Ander Herrera also departed in the summer and was not replaced, a disappointing outcome for OGS that could be chalked up as his first significant defeat in terms of recruitment. Herrera's case was illuminating. The Spaniard had once wanted to stay but lost patience, becoming disillusioned as a result of the club taking too long to offer fresh terms. This took root when Mourinho was still in charge, the midfielder's contract moving towards him having two years left, in summer 2017. That season Herrera had been named the Sir Matt Busby Player of the Year, the award voted for by supporters. Yet still no fresh terms to extend had been received, and as the two-years-remaining mark is the usual point at which a club signals intent to re-sign talent (or not), the runes were clear to Herrera.

A few days after the awards dinner a fresh offer did arrive for an extension, but this came through the post, which hardly gave Herrera a warm feeling, a sense heightened by the fact that the monies being suggested were far from desirable. Yet when Ole Gunnar took over, Herrera became a key player for him – as he had been for Louis van Gaal, 'important for his mouth', the Dutchman said – and OGS did, 100 per cent, want him to stay. But by then the 29-year-old had decided to leave. This was all very muddled and dysfunctional with a capital D.

Scott McTominay was the natural successor to Herrera, but losing a seasoned operator and not bringing in a player of equivalent profile was an error. Ole may have been constricted by the transfer budget, but the upshot was that he had to look to the thus far misfiring Fred plus Andreas Pereira to step into the two vacated berths: risky as neither had yet convinced.

The next mistake concerned a similar failure to replace Romelu Lukaku with a new striker. The Belgian's battering-ram No. 9 style again did not work to Ole's blueprint, but to sell Manchester United's top scorer of the past two seasons (to Internazionale) and bring no one in was puzzling, as it meant Marcus Rashford and Anthony Martial – yet to become the one-in-two (one goal every two games) marksmen that is the elite-level bare minimum – were also being gambled on.

While Ole stated that Lukaku wanted to go, so it was time for him to leave, OGS did not have the same stance regarding Paul Pogba – who wanted to depart but who Ole publicly declared he wished to stay. And though Lukaku was an ill-fit for plan A, what about when a plan B or C was needed with 25 minutes left of a match? This seemed a failure of judgement from Ole Gunnar, though he would say the right replacement could not be found and he had no wish for a quick fix. This would prove costly during the upcoming season.

Still, the reasoning for not replacing Lukaku was at least credible as it emphasised how clear a vision Ole wanted to have. He could have signed Juventus's Mario Mandžukić but decided against a 33-year-old striker who would be a short-term option only. Was OGS wise in building only for the long term, unlike, say, Mourinho, who brought the 34-year-old Zlatan Ibrahimović to United in July 2016 as a quick fix?

Alexis Sánchez (on loan to Internazionale) was allowed to leave, too: the right call regarding a player who had lost his way. Chris Smalling also went, making a temporary move to Roma, and Matteo Darmian signed for Parma, while Antonio Valencia and James Wilson were released. As it was impossible to clear out all the deadwood at once, Phil Jones, Ashley Young (who was made club captain) and Marcos Rojo remained.

As there was no Champions League involvement in 2019-20, this allowed a valid reason (or excuse) for the star turns of Pogba and David De Gea to want out. Pogba's future had again been thrown into serious doubt when Mino Raiola, the midfielder's hardly palatable agent, went public in early July stating that 'everyone at the club knew his client wanted to leave'.

Yet Raiola's move was a glaring red light: it actually revealed the strength of the club's hand, since Pogba was under contract until summer 2021 with an extra year option, so Raiolo showed his desperation by using the ploy to try to force his client out of United, the desired destination being Real Madrid, whose head coach, Zinedine Zidane, was a long-time admirer.

This followed Pogba's own utterance, which he tried to clothe in double-speak: the language of the player who wishes to leave and yet wants to try to keep fans onside in case it backfires. It may be time for a new 'challenge', Pogba said, just as Christian Eriksen of Tottenham Hotspur had pronounced, too, earlier in the summer, as he agitated for a move to Real Madrid. The clue to why the noise from Pogba and Raiola quietened almost instantly was in what Eriksen was also supposed to have been told by Real: as the club lacked sufficient funds, they would rather take him in summer 2020 when the Dane would be a free agent.

This appeared to be Pogba's situation, too. With Eden Hazard signed from Chelsea, Real could not afford the circa £150m price Manchester United asked for him. The who-could-Pogba-be-replaced-with poser was even more difficult to answer than that of De Gea, as world-class midfielders in their prime and available are a rarity. Even rarer is one who would agree to come to a club with no European Cup on offer. There were certainly no replacements of a Pogba-level talent in the current squad, and for one to emerge fully formed from the home-grown ranks, who was ready for the Premier and Champions Leagues, would be a once-in-a-generation (at best) happening – as with Paul Scholes's emergence in the early 1990s.

After the domestic market closed on 8 August and Pogba was finally confirmed as not leaving (for the 2019-20 season, anyway) he stated, following United's 4-0 win over Chelsea three days later, to a French media outlet that the 'question mark' still remained over his future at the club. This was the latest plot twist in the Pogba summer of 2019 pot-boiler that was surely not yet over.

The question of De Gea's future also ran all close season but, unlike with Pogba, it continued beyond the window closing. When United rolled into Molineux to take on Wolverhampton Wanderers for the season's second Premier League fixture, he was still to sign a new deal, his present one ending in summer 2020.

The club had been ready to sell him rather than lose out on £70-100m. Yet the mood music changed. On tour, Ole Gunnar spoke of the club potentially announcing De Gea having agreed a new contract – one that was thought to be worth a salary north of £350,000 a week, a move that would suit each party. The goalkeeper would receive a sizeable pay hike, while United ensured that, should he try to engineer a move in summer 2020, the best price possible would be extracted due to the new length of contract.

'David's had a summer now where he's been negotiating and thinking about his contract, so we hope that we're going to get it sorted soon,' Ole said in Perth in early July during the first stop on United's pre-season trip. And while it would take two more months before the goalkeeper did agree a new deal – on 16 September – this was more good business by Ole.

CHAPTER 23

The Homecoming

'It will be bigger for everyone in Norway
because of the huge fanbase.'

OLE GUNNAR ON KRISTIANSUND V
MANCHESTER UNITED, PRE-SEASON

Oslo, 30 July 2019. Ole Gunnar is here. At the Ullevaal
Stadium. Back in Norway as Manchester United manager
for their fifth tour match – against Kristiansund, the club
of his beloved home village. What a homecoming. What a
dream. A dream that is the reality that Ole has made happen.
Touch, feel it.

Solskjær's cultural impact on Kristiansund is such that Kjell
Neergaard, the mayor, plans to give him a special tribute
usually reserved until those who have made their mark have
passed away.

'He wants to put up a statue, a monument,' Odd
Williamsen, the local historian, says. 'We like positive news,

and people making success, that's very popular, but it's very unusual to do that with people who are still alive. Everybody loves Ole Gunnar and everybody respects him and thinks he's a very good person.'

It is inevitable that a street will be named for him, too. 'It will come,' says Williamsen. 'It's not usual in Norway to name streets after people until they've been dead some years.'

Neergaard, the mayor since 2015 and a member of the Norwegian Labour Party, says: 'Ole has put Kristiansund back on the world map, with the job as manager in Manchester United. The media exposure around the manager and the team is massive, and much of this includes focusing on Kristiansund. Since Ole got the caretaker job in December, crews from BBC, Israeli TV, Russian TV, along with several others, have been visiting our little town. This gives us publicity we could not afford in any other way and is a unique opportunity for us to show the world this part of Norway. We have also noticed that tourists are more aware of the fact that Kristiansund is Ole's hometown. We hopefully expect a growth in tourism as a result, and we also hope to strengthen the relationship between Kristiansund and the UK. We are very proud of the values that Ole represents – he is down-to-earth and shows a positive attitude and we have the utmost respect for his work and achievements.'

It is a shame that the friendly with Kristiansund is not there rather than in Norway's capital. Commercial imperatives prevailed.

So far there have been four victories from four on a summer tour that began earlier this month. In Australia, Perth Glory were beaten 2-0 and Leeds United 4-0. The win against Perth featured two different XIs in each half and goals from Marcus Rashford and a second academy graduate, the 18-year-old midfielder James Garner. Again changing the whole team at the break, the Leeds win came via Mason Greenwood's debut strike for the first team, then Rashford, Phil Jones and Anthony Martial ensured a slick 4-0 victory. Then Internazionale were beaten 1-0 in Singapore, Greenwood scoring again. 'Mason's a natural finisher,' Ole said of the 17-year-old, who will be understudy to Rashford and Martial in 2019-20.

Part of Ole Gunnar's strategy for the upcoming season is to blood youngsters like Greenwood, Garner, Tahith Chong and Angel Gomes, the latter two also featuring. 'You see the confidence in the kids when they get minutes under their belts and play against very good players. They play with team-mates, first-team players they have maybe been looking up to and now, suddenly, they're with them. They've great skill, all of them, and I know they're ready to perform at this level,' he told manutd.com.

The move to bring in more of the club's own hot-housed players is also due to financial practicalities. For a club that is a virtual licence to print money – as an illustration it is four years into a record £750m kit deal with Adidas – watching the pennies may seem odd. Yet do the maths on Ole's summer spend and this is the only logical conclusion. When the sale of Matteo Darmain (for £3.9m) and Fellaini in January (around £10m) are factored in, it is only circa £58m – £12m less than a single year of the Adidas money.

Next on tour was a 2-1 win over Tottenham Hotspur in Shanghai, the strikes from Martial and Gomes. Five days before this – Ole's homecoming as Manchester United manager, which is a proud day for him and his family and friends, many of whom have travelled from his hometown.

There is much excitement. 'A great day,' Kjetil Thorsen, Kristiansund's top-ranking executive and a childhood friend, says. 'A once-in-a-lifetime experience.' A hope of Kjetil's is that Ole Gunnar, the local hero, might one day return to manage his hometown team, following the rise to the Eliteserien. 'It's been quite special for us as we were once too small for him,' he says. 'So the only way for him to have a job in football before in Norway was to coach the national team or Molde.'

Ole continues to be an inspiration for any young hopeful. 'Everyone in Norway – they want to hear the stories,' says Kjetil. 'And I talk to him many times every year.'

The interest is feverish; Norway's media is in Oslo for the pre-friendly training sessions and press conference, and the match. A documentary is being made about the fixture, Manchester United's fanbase in Ole's native country being particularly sizeable.

'It will be bigger here for everyone in Norway because there is such a huge fanbase following us through thick and thin. We'll be the home team, no doubt about it,' Ole said. 'I'm so proud, privileged and honoured to lead the club and be in charge of the club so to do it in Norway is another little bonus for me, of course.'

Bjarte Valen, UK correspondent of the Scandinavian sup-porters' club united.no, says: 'Solskjær is probably the most famous Norwegian there has ever been. His return as United manager was a massive deal. At the match were families and the atmosphere was very friendly.'

The family feel extended to both of Ole's sons being involved in the actual match, which was a sell-out. Noah, his eldest, was a late replacement, making his senior debut for Kristiansund at 19, and his younger son, Elijah, watched alongside his smiling father on the bench.

Manchester United win at the death courtesy of a late Juan Mata penalty. 'Noah makes his debut in front of 28,000 – it's not very often a Norwegian does that,' Ole Gunnar said. 'Elijah next to me enjoyed it. Their players have been in our dressing room, swapping shirts and taking pictures, and our boys have been outstanding. The camaraderie is good.

'Of course, I enjoyed it. There's been a build-up to this game from the press and in my local hometown, and loads of people from my hometown came.'

From this happy occasion it was back to the UK and the sixth and final tour game, a 2-2 draw with Milan in Cardiff a few days later. Throughout pre-season the pattern of Ole's side has been to press quickly and move the ball quickly, the onus on Aaron Wan-Bissaka and Luke Shaw, the first-choice full-backs, to join attacks.

The following Sunday is the season opener, the visit of Frank Lampard's Chelsea. 'It's gone very quickly but it's what we're waiting for, though, the league games that matter,' Ole said. 'These friendly games are important but, then again, a little edge was missing. When you're playing for three points, the edge will come back.

'It's not about one team for the first game and that's the team for the rest of the season. We've got a strong squad and I feel there's not too big a difference when we make the subs. We're going to have to find the right balance. I've not really picked the first XI yet, but most of the relationships we've tried.'

The early August sun is shining. Before Ole is a first full campaign in charge. When José Mourinho was sacked, the team had played 17 Premier League matches, had won seven, drawn five, lost five, scored 29 times, conceded 29 goals, and had 26 points. Ole's record from then until Cardiff City in the 38th and final league match read: P21, W12, D4, L5, scored 36, conceded 25, 40 points.

Before him is the challenge failed by David Moyes, Louis van Gaal and Mourinho: make Manchester United contenders again. In the Premier League, the Champions League, the FA Cup, the League Cup. Reconstruct them into a winning machine, a band of fantasy football men for the Old Trafford faithful to laud and an ominous presence for opposition fans at away grounds.

Solskjær has improved Manchester United from the greyness of Mourinho's end-days. The 11-point gap to fourth place and the final Champions League berth he inherited became a five-point deficit. But, as Juan Mata wrote on his blog on Monday 6 May after the 1-1 draw at Huddersfield Town, in a message to fans: 'YOU DESERVE BETTER – No more words needed.' OGS improved form, and morale, yet said it will be 'miraculous' for United to be contenders in 2019-20.

Tor-Kristian Karlsen, a countryman of Ole's and sport director at Norway's IK Start, agreed. Karlsen's 23-year career in football began at Switzerland's Grasshopper Zürich, ahead of posts at Watford, Bayer Leverkusen, Fredrikstad, Zenit Saint Petersburg, AS Monaco and Maccabi Haifa before his current position. Despite the febrile reaction to United's plunge in the closing phase of the 2018-19 season, Karlsen says, 'In my view he has performed more or less as anticipated, perhaps even slightly better than expected. It seems to me that OGS is handling most facets of the manager role well.'

In the eight months of his tenure Solskjær has appeared in control – of team matters, of the media, of the constant noise around the club in what is the steepest of learning curves. 'The role of manager is extraordinarily complex and demanding,' says Karlsen. 'Not only are you expected to plan meaningful training weeks aimed at preparing the team to your best ability for the game ahead, come up with an analytical and well-designed tactical game plan, but also to dedicate an ever-increasing amount of energy towards man-management – how to make each and every player tick – and please the fans, "upstairs" and the media as well.

'Then there's all the stuff that is suddenly thrown at you, all the unexpected things that are challenging and time-consuming – injuries, unpleasant events breaking, stories in the media, personal things, to mention a few – but which take up hours and hours and ultimately disrupt your preparations and turn your week upside down.'

Simon Austin, a former BBC journalist and founder of trainingground.guru, which specialises in clubs' back-of-house operations, identifies the challenges facing Ole. A year since *The Observer* reported that the club would appoint a director of football, the role has been renamed technical director and downgraded to one working alongside the manager and the football department, rather than being more senior than even the manager. The reason for this was the acquisitions overseen by Ole this summer, Ed Woodward noting how he worked with Mike Phelan, Jim Lawlor, the chief scout, and the rest of the recruitment department.

Yet Austin believes the position is crucial to Ole's hopes of success for the obvious reasons: football is simply about the players a manager can pick from, having a squad bursting with quality. 'They're crying out for a sporting director,' he says. 'I think 16 of the 20 Premier League clubs have got a sporting director or equivalent – they all call it different names. You have technical director, director of football, sporting director, and they're all slightly different. They are basically trying to do the same thing. It just really stands out that such a big club does not have that position.'

Among the candidates of interest to the club for the post had been Rio Ferdinand, the former captain, whose profile as a prominent player in the supreme United XI that claimed three successive championships, between 2007 and 2009, and the 2008 European Cup, gives him pedigree and a glamour factor. His actual experience relating to the job description was less clear. Austin offers a different kind of candidate:

'Norwich City are the best example really of how it should work. They've got Stuart Webber, who was at Huddersfield, and he has just achieved promotion with Norwich to the Premier League. He's in charge of the whole football side – responsible for the academy, sports science, medical, ultimately for the first team. Then he appoints all the people who are in charge of those departments – he signs them all off. He set out a strategy and a philosophy for the club.

'You look at Man United and there just isn't that strategy, really.'

Woodward was insistent on the subject. 'We've expanded our recruitment department in recent years and we believe this now runs in an efficient and productive way. Player recommendations and decisions are worked on by this department and by the first-team manager and his staff, not by senior management. There is a myth that we have non-football people making football decisions, and it's insulting to the brilliant people who work on the football side in this club,' he said. 'Many of the senior staff on the football side of the club have been in their roles for over 10 years. Some of our scouts have worked with us for more than 25 years.

'The changes we saw over the summer have resulted in a very young squad. But it's also a squad with the players and the culture to provide a base camp for us to build and grow from as we start our new journey. Ole's vision maps exactly to the core three football objectives we have: we must win trophies, we must play attacking football and we must give youth its chance.

'Ole has also instilled the discipline back into an environment where we may have lacked it in recent years. He is building a squad that respects the club's history, in which players work hard and respect their team-mates. No one is bigger than the club.'

Woodward's backing of Ole Gunnar extended to an overhaul of football staff. Neil Wood, a clubmate of OGS for seven years until 2006, was made the under-23 coach, and Quinton Fortune, who won the 2003 championship alongside Ole and was with him at Cardiff, became the assistant. Richard Hartis, a goalkeeping coach under Ferguson, and Ole Gunnar's at Molde and the Bluebirds, was appointed to the senior position; former United defender Michael Clegg became first-team power and strength coach, and Ed Leng the lead sports scientist. Leng has worked with Warren Joyce, who was alongside OGS when he was in charge of the reserves.

OGS's challenge is to make this new staff line-up work in

concert with his players and the rest of the club, as he did for the three successful years at Molde. Karlsen says: 'Leading what is possibly the biggest football club in the world is an extreme challenge, of which just a handful of people are able to do with success. No one comes with any guarantees, but OGS was thrown in at the deep end right in the middle of the season. On that basis I think he did well. For me what's interesting to consider is whether someone else could have done any better and I'm not sure the answer to that question is a roaring "yes".'

Karlsen has an answer for those who may look at Solskjær's time at Cardiff and wonder about his abilities. Karlsen points to the style of Vincent Tan, the owner. 'It was a tough task for a number of reasons. To mention one reason: I've also worked with "hands-on" owners who are relatively new to football. Sometimes the politics and having to justify your choices and thinking before the owner becomes the most time-consuming part. Not only is it energy-sapping and demoralising, but it can even be a disillusioning experience for a young manager or head coach.'

Austin wonders if Ole has enough support staff. 'Manchester City probably have about 30 that travel to games with them working in different areas. A manager just couldn't be across all of that, really,' he says. Of Ole Gunnar's appointments, Austin adds: 'United lost more than 20 years of experience from their performance with the departure of Robin Thorpe, a world-class sports scientist, and fitness coach Gary Walker [both in spring]. They replaced them with two practitioners with no experience at senior level in England – Ed Leng and fitness coach Charlie Owen, who was promoted from the academy. While Mourinho had fitness specialists among

his assistants – in Carlos Lalin and number two Rui Faria –
Solskjær does not have that same support.'

These issues all shine a glaring light on how fundamental
Sir Alex Ferguson was. When he left, it was akin to a director
of football/technical director leaving. And the recruitment
department. Along with the head of scouting. And the
chief psychologist, spiritual leader and all-round club guru.
Ferguson left a black hole of expertise that in the six ensuing
years has sucked in each and every one of his replacements. It
was like the brains, mind, heart and soul were removed from
United, and the club is yet to fully live and breathe again as it
did during the 26 and a half years of the Scot's tenure.

Will United actually fill the technical director position?
There would be no surprise if not. Should the club do so,
Edwin van der Sar, the Ajax chief executive who joined the
Dutch club as marketing director in 2012, is surely the calibre
of candidate required. Not one with Rio Ferdinand's profile.
Van der Sar knows the business side of the game *and* what it
means to be an elite player; and, having been United's No. 1,
from 2005 to 2011, is versed in the club. Whatever occurs
regarding the vacancy, Matt Judge, the head of corporate
affairs and Ed Woodward's de facto number two, will continue as the actual deal-maker, following up on whoever is
recommended by Ole Gunnar, Mick Phelan and the technical
director if appointed. Each has a veto along with Ole, Phelan,
and the recruitment department, which also contains Marcel
Bout, the head of global scouting, Jim Lawlor and Mick
Court, chief technical scout.

In summer 2018 Mourinho encountered the veto after
identifying Yerry Mina, a 23-year-old centre-back, as a signing he wanted to strengthen this area. When the recruitment

department examined his injury record, it decided the Colombia defender was a risk not worth taking. Who was right, who was wrong – the garlanded manager, considered one of the best ever? Or the recruitment department, whose power to veto was never held accountable before fans and the media? Mina did then proceed to have a chequered injury record at Everton the following season.

Given the retreat regarding a sporting/technical director and Woodward's public praise of Ole Gunnar, the onus is now on Solskjær to be the multi-faceted, polymath manager that Ferguson was. Maybe the beginnings of this were in Ole overseeing the appointments of Leng and Clegg. This, done to address the below-par fitness of the inherited Mourinho players, might come to be viewed as OGS successfully starting to build real power and influence over the club.

When recognising the initial success of the side under Ole, Ed Woodward also touched upon how fitness faded and injuries occurred. 'The middle section of last season, after Ole's arrival, feels most relevant to what we want to achieve and where we want to be,' he said, acknowledging privately that players became burned out due to the demands placed on them by OGS. 'We saw a team playing fast, fluid football, with a clear representation of the style and philosophy the manager wants,' he said.

Austin says: 'Even when they were on a good run, Solskjær wasn't rotating the team. He did up the training a bit, but then if you have a spike that's when you could be very susceptible to injuries. They had a big spike in intensity and that probably led to the injuries. I was surprised by Mourinho – they were the only club in the Premier League, probably in the Championship as well, that wasn't using GPS trackers.

That's what gives you your stats for the players – about the distance that you're covering, the speeds, the intensity. Most clubs find that really useful, injury monitoring and other stuff, as I say. It was pretty amazing he wasn't doing that, really. I think he did away with a lot of wellness stuff as well, immunology tests and things like that – basically, tests to find out how healthy you are and how well you are at that point. He just became very anti-science and -data, really, which is surprising. Leng, though, has already made a positive impression, but it's a big leap to step into the shoes of those who were at the club before.'

For this to be true of Mourinho – who raised the bar to Niagara Falls level when becoming Chelsea manager in summer 2004 because of an obsession with every detail – is a surprise: a development that Ed Woodward may not have bargained for when appointing one of the great managers.

This is what Ole Gunnar is tilting at: becoming one of the greats as Manchester United manager. It is ambitious and unlikely, but Ole does not let the odds cow him. Karlsen believes he has the chance of doing *something*. 'I enjoyed watching his Molde teams. When OGS was in charge, Molde more often than not played with pace, power and energy,' he says. 'Interesting patterns combined with occasional variety and freedom in the attacking phase of the game made them unpredictable and exciting to watch. Furthermore, he's never been worried about giving kids a chance or even successfully integrating young Africans with little knowledge of European football.

'I've worked with people who've been members of his coaching staff or played for him, and I understand that he's a good listener, gives people confidence and cares about the human being, not just the football player. In that regard he might stand out slightly from his ex-top player colleagues. And although the media are now poking fun at his references to Sir Alex and a manner of expressing himself that to some may seem somewhat dated, he seems more than prepared to incorporate new methods and ideas into his work. At least in Norway his Molde sides always appeared the most modern and vibrant in the league – in terms of style of play and tactical approach.'

Karlsen, like Austin, warns that Solskjær has to keep modernising. 'On the other hand, this is Manchester United, not Molde. And having had a glance at how their immediate competitors work and what kind of expertise is now associated with the top clubs in the Premier League, one cannot rest a minute – just keeping up, being able to attract the cutting-edge knowledge of the best people in the business, is a daily struggle. The bar is raised to an incredibly high level and closing the 20-odd points gap to runaway title contenders [winners, Manchester City and second-place Liverpool] is not done by chance, but by an immense effort which goes well beyond the manager.

'It looks as though OGS is pretty much – along with his immediate support staff – left to deal with Manchester United himself, whereas the two other obvious rivals – City and Liverpool – have put together huge teams consisting of leading experts and know-how to make Guardiola and Klopp as successful as they possibly can.'

Karlsen knows that if Solskjær is to succeed he has to become as omniscient as Ferguson was. Yet, as Ferguson was no mini Matt Busby, so Solskjær cannot be a diluted Ferguson. 'With time OGS will have to insist on asserting his own identity as a head coach/manager. The respect and esteem he holds for Sir Alex is understandable and highly justifiable, but at some point he needs to develop his own ideas, concept and ideology as a manager – and go on to achieve on his own intellectual work as a coach.

'I know Manchester United have invested heavily in the scouting department, and there's no reason why they shouldn't be able to identify or have indeed reached the same level of intel and knowledge as the other Premier League top clubs. And with my knowledge of OGS, I have every reason to believe that he will work constructively with the in-house staff in terms of assessing and finding suitable candidates.

'On the other hand, personal relations might well be as important as the mere identifying and scouting aspect. Presumably players that may interest Manchester United will probably also be on the radar of other top clubs across Europe – does OGS have the personal relations with the top agents and powerbrokers, and indeed the ability to convince, in order to make his number one target choose Old Trafford ahead of north London or even Dortmund?'

It will not be easy, OGS's challenge akin to driving a Ferrari backwards at 150mph while executing long division in his head: a cocktail of mental dexterity and bravery and resourcefulness.

But, it is possible – for the most talented, the very best number ones. Will this finally be it? Can Ole Gunnar crack the conundrum of moving the club on from the Ferguson era of 13 championships towards number 21? Will summer 2019 prove to be the watershed? The start of a successful overhaul of the squad that should have begun six years before?

Ole Gunnar has the intelligence, brains. But so,

apparently, did two of his predecessors – Van Gaal and Mourinho. He needs something else. This is football. This is Manchester United, the beast that has to roar and not whimper. He needs to have what the Dutchman and Portuguese did not possess while at the club: a grasp on the intangible, the magic that conjures up championship-winning XIs. The kryptonite that weakens all opposing managers and teams and makes Ole and his players supreme.

He has to take the team on an upward trajectory. Show real progress. What he needs is time and for time he needs to survive and to survive he has to win enough games with enough bounce and positivity and feel-good factor. Christian Michelsen has no doubt Ole can pull off this greatest of all challenges.

'To manage Man United, it's not enough just being a great coach. You need to have a little bit of luck,' he says. 'You have to be at the right spot at the right time. But Ole Gunnar, he is that kind of man, when he has to deliver he does. He scored a fantastic goal in a national game – against Azerbaijan – when United were scouting another player in another team, Ronny Johnsen. He scored the Champions League winner in 1999. He was the first manager of Molde to get the gold medal [title win]. This team was always the runner-up behind Rosenborg but Ole Gunnar was the man who won the trophy.

'It's not surprising. He is a winner, but at the same time he is a fantastic human being who creates a team together, gets the best out of every human being. Not only the players but everybody around him. He shows by example that everything is possible in life. He has been a role model in many ways. Of course, we are talking about Man United. In that way, people don't understand how huge it is to manage that kind of club. One of the greatest and one of the biggest in the world.'

Brian McDermott, who got to know Ole during a year spent together on a UEFA coaching course, agrees. Now an Arsenal scout, McDermott managed Slough Town, Woking, Reading (twice) and Leeds United. His time with Ole Gunnar came in 2010 when Reading were a Championship side, the 59-year-old guiding them to promotion to the Premier League two years later.

He says, 'It was for our Pro Licence and my first impression of him sticks in my mind. He came walking in and I was sat down and hadn't met him before. It was the end of the season and he sat next to me and went, "Hello, Brian. I've been watching your work. You're doing really well and I follow you."

'He was really humble. I thought, "Wow. I've been watching you play football at a top club for many, many years and scoring all of these goals, and scoring and winning the Champions League." It was really quite humbling for me to hear that from a man like him, for him to say, "I've been following you." He was such a really top guy and he hasn't changed a bit. What you see is what you get – I'm just struck by his humility more than anything. And he knows his football. I liked that, because he was listening, wanted to learn. He wrote a lot of things down when many other people didn't or whatever. He was studious and it was a constant learning thing for him. He was constantly trying to learn, as we all were, but he was a big part of that and he gave great energy to the group as well.'

McDermott's impression of Ole Gunnar is the same as that of most people. 'He's very open. Very honest. I was impressed with that – I thought there was no side of him where he was cagey about this or cagey about that. He was very happy to share and was open to ideas and I liked that. I really did,' says McDermott.

Michelsen points to the T-word – time – as being imperative if Solskjær is to have a chance of success. 'He has a huge experience that is so important now for United. He knows what it takes to succeed there. I think that's a huge and a very good thing for the club and for him as a coach and the players. At the same time, you know that he can't be a winning team tomorrow. He needs to get the time.'

Ahead of Chelsea's visit on the opening day of the 2019-20 season, Ole mentioned '12 months' as the timeframe in which Manchester United can again be contenders, and he has to hope that Ed Woodward and the Glazers will be patient when the ride becomes as bumpy as he knows it will.

In a longer period – two seasons, at least – Ole will try to replicate the success at Molde in 2011, when he took the team that had finished 11th in 2010 – they flirted with relegation as late as August of the term – to the title.

That feat does not surprise McDermott. 'No – he did really well at Molde and he's come back to United now and now we'll see what happens. It's really important that players want to play for the manager and he's the kind of guy you want to play for,' he says. 'Whatever happens to United in the next few years, time will tell, but he's certainly a guy that you would, as a player, want to play for and trust him and think he'll be a good man.'

A defining difference – perhaps, *the* difference – between Ole Gunnar and all the other post-Ferguson permanent managers is the connection between him and the club and the fans. This does not guarantee success, of course, but it does allow an instinctive grasp of Manchester United and an obvious love for it. The bond meant the feel-good factor was back ahead of the new campaign despite the end to the previous season.

McDermott says: 'From what I can see supporters want him to do well. He's obviously always going to be a hero there and legend for what he's done in the football club. On the coaching course, he would talk about his experiences at United. That was always fascinating – I wanted to hear what Sir Alex was doing and how it worked, because it's all part of a learning curve for us as managers.

'Let's just see what happens over a period of time. Assessing managers over a period of six months is non-sense. I've managed in the Conference and I've managed Reading, I've managed Leeds United. Every single game I managed is a difficult game. It's not easy to win. You have to do the best you can every day and Manchester United is a monster of a club. But he knows that football club better than anybody. He knows what that club is all about and that's key. He knows what the fans want, what they're about. He knows what they've been used to and how they want to play their football.'

Michelsen concurs. 'I was on a vacation in December when the news came that Ole Gunnar was going to be the tempo-rary manager. I was like, "Wow, I can't believe it." Because at last, United are in good hands. I know it means so much for him to be in that club and, at the same time, he has had the best teacher – Sir Alex, of course. Also, great coaches in Norway and he has played with great players.'

Ollie Norwood points to how Solskjær has begun to

restore some of the foundations that the 20-time champions of England are built on. 'I do feel simply baffled that they lost their identity in that humbleness, what it meant to be Man United,' he says. 'This is the biggest club in the world and there's a way to represent the biggest club in the world and there's a demand on the entire players to represent the biggest club in the world.

'The humbleness of the group, that is important – Manchester United is a family club, a humble club. They went away from that a little bit, whereas Ole's now trying to bring it back – I can see Ole's trying to bring that back. You can see it a mile away.'

Ole will be aware that Ferguson needed time to create his unstoppable juggernaut. 'I've been a United supporter my whole life, and I remember Sir Alex: he came to United in 1986,' Michelsen says. 'It was the same situation with a lot of big names playing in the team, but it was not a good team. So give Ole some time because he knows what to do and it takes time to create a winning team. I'm sure that the right leaders above Ole are in the club. Now give him some time, and the club will arise.'

Nils Johan Semb has optimism for his former player's prospects. 'He knows the game, he is intelligent. If you see how he has gone into the job at Manchester United, he has done almost everything right so far. How he treats the media, how he speaks with the players, how he has adapted. He changed the atmosphere at Manchester United.'

Åge Hareide, the manager who kick-started Solskjær's career by taking him from Clausenengen to Molde, believes Ole Gunnar can lead United to the championship. 'It's possible,' he says. 'There's huge competition within the top 10 of the Premier League – and the six top clubs are all fighting for this title. He showed how he can change things around with his attitude, there's nothing wrong with the football he plays, and he has good people around him. He also needs good football players to win the title. It's important that United get the right players to make them even better. They have good players there now, but United need a good-quality scorer. Ole knows that as well and it depends who he is going to get in to make the team even more solid than it is today.'

Goals have been a glaring issue for United since Ferguson went. For the club that boasts about a proud, attacking tradition the drop-off is alarming. In the David Moyes season of 2013-14 (curtailed after 34 matches), the total league strikes was a paltry 64 compared to Manchester City's 102 as champions.

In 2014-15 and 2015-16 under Louis van Gaal, the count was 62 and 49 to the 73 of Chelsea and 68 of Leicester City, the respective champions.

In 2016-17 and 2017-18 under José Mourinho, it was 54 to Chelsea's 85 and 68 to Manchester City's 106. In 2018-19 (17 games under Mourinho, 21 under Ole Gunnar) – 65 to City's 95. The overall average for United – 60.3, for the champions 88.1.

Ferguson ended his final 2012-13 term with Manchester United as champions and the goal found 86 times. The side has not managed 70 since. The finishing positions post-Ferguson have been 7th, 4th, 5th, 6th, 2nd and 6th. Two top-four finishes in six seasons, four times outside the Champions League positions.

Now was the start of his first full season in charge. Chelsea's arrival for a 4.30pm kick-off on the opening Sunday has to be ground zero for Ole Gunnar's new Manchester United. A serious tilt at the title is rated by him as 'miraculous', which is optimistic. Even a top-four finish will be tough.

CHAPTER 24

Twelve Months

'The first half was attacking football as it should be played.'

OLE GUNNAR,
7 DECEMBER 2019 – MANCHESTER CITY 1
MANCHESTER UNITED 2

A pat of José Mourinho's head and a smile from Ole Gunnar. Old Trafford is delirious and Manchester United have just scintillated in a 2-1 victory over Tottenham Hotspur. In 15 days it is 19 December and the one-year anniversary of Ole Gunnar Solskjær's appointment as interim manager.

A memorable 12 months in the life of Ole. A year to measure where his management of Manchester United is at. He began with the 5-1 win at Cardiff City. He is bookending it with the pat on the head of Mourinho, who he replaced.

Do not view the pat of his predecessor as patronising. Read it as OGS being content, at ease. In control. Which for large swathes of this campaign has not been the case. He has looked what he is: a man trying to retain faith while being hurled about in the gale of incessant criticism and craven shrieks that demand he be sacked, that he has to go, is being shown up to be what was expected: not good enough for the job by a long way.

Not tonight. Ole has just seen his team take apart Mourinho's Spurs. Just when Ole Gunnar needed it. Just as the critics were pointing to a league table that showed his team in ninth place with 18 points after 14 games. They had scored 21 goals and conceded 17 and were eight points behind Chelsea in fourth, 22 behind the leaders, Liverpool. José had been sacked by United with the side on 26 points after 17 games. Ole cannot overtake this haul by his 17th game unless Spurs, Manchester City on Saturday and Everton on Sunday week are beaten. After Mauricio Pochettino's removal, Spurs are resurgent under Mourinho, winning their first three outings, and United have just drawn – dismally – 2-2 with Aston Villa: Ole and his side are given no chance.

Not any more. The critics fall silent. Where have they gone? Send out a search party. Victory over Tottenham derives from United's finest display since PSG were dispatched. It follows other fine displays against the Premier League big guns: Chelsea, Leicester City and Liverpool. There will be even better in the 179th Manchester derby three days later. The problem with Manchester United in 2019-20 has been against the lesser sides. Crystal Palace, West Ham United, Newcastle United and Bournemouth: all have been lost to in the league.

Against Tottenham Marcus Rashford has been imperious and unplayable. He scored both goals on an evening when the 22-year-old may have taken his game and status into rarefied air. Rashford was a blur of pace and menace. So dominating was he of a Spurs backline of Serge Aurier, Toby Alderweireld, Davinson Sánchez and Jan Vertonghen, it is like the forward could press pause on them at will and run at the visitors' goal through the freeze-frame.

Rashford is the on-field personification of Ole's side. He can be breathtaking or ineffective. He returned zero goals against Crystal Palace, West Ham, Newcastle and Bournemouth. But this Wednesday night Rashford and Ole's side have been irresistible. Forget those who say he is a manager befuddled by the demands of Manchester United. This is proof that given time Ole Gunnar may have the answers the club have been searching for in these post-Ferguson years. When Paul Tierney blows the final whistle and signals victory, OGS has shown a vital element required for the Old Trafford hot seat: an ability to ward off pressure and come up with a win precisely when needed. This is a platinum-plated resource to possess considering the tight corners he has been in and will be in again. After losing to Newcastle 1-0 on 6 October on Tyneside, the mood was funereal. The display had been moribund. Hope was low. And Liverpool were up next – Jürgen Klopp's barracking outfit play a diamond-encrusted muscular football that would surely crush Ole's team. But, no. Rashford's big-game temperament has him scoring first – on 36 minutes – and Adam Lallana equalises with just five minutes on the clock to give Liverpool a draw.

It had been United's finest performance of the season. Even better than the 4-0 win over Chelsea on the opening day of the season. That was a confidence-boosting, spirits-raising victory in which Ole's XI was the youngest fielded in the opening round of Premier League fixtures. He named three

21-year-olds – Rashford, Aaron Wan-Bissaka and Daniel James – a 22-year-old, Scott McTominay, and two 23-year-olds – Luke Shaw and Anthony Martial. In a side that averaged 23 years and seven months for its outfield players. Chelsea were taken apart by two goals from Rashford, one from Martial and one from James.

Then a dip. A 1-1 draw with Wolverhampton Wanderers, the 2-1 loss to Palace, and 1-1 at Southampton. Brendan Rodgers's Leicester City are next and beaten 1-0 courtesy of a Rashford penalty. But penalties have already been missed – at Wolves by Paul Pogba, and by Rashford against Palace. Pogba and Rashford were racially abused on social media for this and Ole Gunnar shows leadership when stating he is 'lost for words' with regard to the latter player's treatment but offers a muddled message about the Rashford–Pogba penalty-taking farrago. In essence, OGS's stance is that the players can and should decide. Sure, they can and should: if and when whoever decides to take the spot-kick *scores* it.

If there is a lack of leadership here it surprises given his steeliness. It is a prevailing characteristic of Ole's make-up. It was evident in the summer when carpeting Jesse Lingard for a social media video the forward posted in which a friend simulated a sex act, and it is evident in the way he brushed off the proposition that Manchester United can no longer compete with Manchester City.

This is put to Ole Gunnar on the Friday before tomorrow's derby at the Etihad Stadium, 48 hours after the Spurs victory. When in charge of United, José Mourinho had raised the prospect: that City's riches meant United could not get close to them. There is a touch of disdain in OGS's response. An arrogant disdain reminiscent of Sir Alex Ferguson and that all the very best managers have. 'Don't agree,' he said. 'What are you going to do? Are you going to give up? Not challenge them? That's what we've got to get back to. You can't argue that we're [not] too far behind, but it's a chance for us now to challenge them and bridge that gap a little bit. So we're going there to win even though we know it's going to be difficult.'

Despite the win and manner of victory over Spurs – fast and hard and ruthless – this is the conventional wisdom as Ole leads Manchester United across town to the champions' home in Bradford, in the city's north-east: that Pep Guardiola's Manchester City will bulldoze them.

Within minutes of the game starting the wisdom is recast as foolery. Led by the effervescent (again) Marcus Rashford, here is the second serious notice in a few days that Ole Gunnar does know what he is doing and the players are intent on executing his plans. City are framed in black and white in contrast to the vibrant palette in which United paint the contest. Ahead of the Spurs encounter, Ed Woodward had taken briefings from senior players that made clear how much they believed in their manager, which the executive vice-chairman was pleased to hear.

This performance is their words made cast-iron real in the furnace of the derby. On 23 minutes Rashford wins and converts a penalty. Six minutes later Anthony Martial fires a low shot past Ederson and that is 2-0 and contest over. Even when the City substitute Nicolás Otamendi scores on 85 minutes there is no panic and Ole and Manchester United have a first consecutive league win since 2 March, when Southampton were beaten 3-2 at Old Trafford, four days before the PSG victory. They are up to fifth, with 24 points, five behind

Chelsea in a Champions League berth and have lost as many games as City.

'We'll work with the mentality of the boys,' Ole said of the losses to the minor clubs. 'It's been very much about margins in those games. I'm not so worried, so concerned.' Of how United made chumps of City: 'The attitude was spot-on and every time we had the ball it seemed like we could carve them open.'

A week that began with the (seemingly) doom-filled draw with Aston Villa ends as Ole's best in the job. To motivate the players, make them believe they could beat Tottenham and City and do so in the style they did, is a massive boost and a fine way to approach the one-year anniversary.

Since he walked back through the door as the temporary manager, Ole's aims were to transform the profile of the squad and instil in the players and club the true culture of Manchester United after this had atrophied under José Mourinho.

He has pointed Alexis Sánchez, Romelu Lukaku and Chris Smalling to the exit. He has marginalised Nemanja Matić and Phil Jones. Blooded youngsters James Garner and Brandon Williams, promoted Andreas Pereira and made 21-year-old Axel Tuanzebe the youngest captain since Norman Whiteside in 1985 – for September's Carabao Cup shootout win over Rochdale. And started the 18-year-old Mason Greenwood as the No. 9 against Spurs, who performed as admirably as he did when scoring against Astana in September's Europa League game to make him the club's youngest ever at 17 years and 353 days. All of this is evidence of a reboot of the club under OGS.

In the final league match before the one-year anniversary

Everton are drawn with 1-1 at Old Trafford. The pattern continues, the Achilles heel remains: a non–Big Six side are struggled against. The Toffees have Duncan Ferguson as their temporary manager and, despite being a Jaguar F-type to the visitors' JCB, United cannot finish them off and are trailing to a first-half Victor Lindelöf own goal before Ole pulls a stroke by putting Mason Greenwood on and he equalises after 77 minutes. 'We lacked ideas,' is OGS's frank summation after the final whistle.

The draw means that United end with one less point than the 26 accrued by his predecessor José Mourinho after the same number – 17 – of games. Yet they are four points closer to Chelsea in fourth place than the 13 they were adrift of a Champions League spot under the Portuguese.

And after Colchester United are beaten 3-0 on 18 December there is an EFL Cup semi-final to look forward to, which will be the 180th and 181st derbies with Manchester City in the two-leg tie in January. Ole can smell Wembley: he is 180 minutes away from a major final in his first full season as Manchester United manager. On facing City again a month or so after beating them 2-1, OGS said: 'We've looked at that game and are very pleased with the result – there are things we need to do so much better. And you won't beat City twice in a row or three times with the same tactics so we'll have to do something better. Pep will have his team fired up.'

Tomorrow – Thursday 19 December 2019 – it is 12 months since Ole Gunnar's official announcement as the interim manager. He smiles and states he would have taken where the team is at this juncture, a year on. 'Of course,' he said. 'We're in a good place, momentum is there at the moment, taking steps forward. If you take away Astana, which was a great experience, after Bournemouth, won six, drawn three, scored loads of goals, we're on the right track. I've really enjoyed it,' he said after the Everton draw. 'I'm looking forward to going into work tomorrow because these boys want to improve.'

Ole is correct – the Astana game was a 2-1 return-leg defeat played with nine emerging players from the academy in a Europa League dead rubber after his team had already qualified as Group L victors. His team have a last-32 tie with Club Brugge in February. Ole sees the potential, claiming the competition is a real possibility and is one route into the Champions League, as is finishing fourth, and there is also an FA Cup third-round tie with Wolverhampton Wanderers in three weeks.

There is cause for optimism about where OGS will take Manchester United next.

CHAPTER 25

Bruno Fernandes

'We are going to have to create our own
atmosphere.'

OLE GUNNAR SOLSKJÆR

There is a bounce and optimism that were so very absent
previously and, with the team still in the Carabao Cup and
qualified for the Europa League knockout phase, Ole has
given himself a real chance of remaining in place for summer
2020. Do this and he will have a second close-season transfer
window to strengthen his squad further.

This is his mission: survive until the warm months when
the mood will be lighter and naysayers quieter, and he can
add another three players minimum. Yet just four weeks later
the end of January is nearing and the critics are no longer
AWOL. They have reappeared in force to declare a mass 'I-
told-you-so' and say this is mission impossible for Ole and
he surely will not now reach the end of the 2019-20 season.

In a breathless period United have played 10 matches. Seven of these have been in the Premier League: three victories – against Newcastle (4-1 home, Boxing Day), Burnley (2-0 away, 28 December) and Norwich (4-0 home, 11 January). But four have been defeats – to Watford, Arsenal, Liverpool (all 2-0 away) and Burnley (2-0 home). In the FA Cup a draw with Wolverhampton Wanderers (0-0 away) was followed by a 1-0 win in the replay. Plus, Manchester City inflicted a 3-1 humiliation at Old Trafford in the Carabao Cup semi-final first leg. This was on 7 January when for a period in the first half Pep Guardiola's team gave Ole's side a hiding that was the most exposed his United has been. At the break, 3-0 could have been seven or eight on a night when Marcus Rashford captained the side he supports for the first time and Guardiola outfoxed OGS by deploying Bernardo Silva as the falsest of false No. 9s. When the players trotted out for the second half, Old Trafford was sombre and concerned – except for the partying visiting support – but now came a heartening turnaround for Ole as his young team demonstrated courage to fight back, Rashford scoring on 70 minutes. It meant the tie was still alive – just – at 3-1, ahead of the return three weeks later.

By that match, though, United were listing and the latest nadir looked to some on the outside to place Ole's tenure in jeopardy (again). Factor in long-term injuries to Paul Pogba, Scott McTominay and Rashford – the latter suffering his during a truncated 16-minute substitute appearance in the FA Cup replay win over Wolves, which threatened to end the 19-goal top scorer's season – and OGS faced the severest test of his turbulent time in charge.

Yet the message from the club remained constant: that OGS was going nowhere and he was, to use one characterisation offered up by an executive, 'bullet-proof'.

Manchester United's faith was about to be tested in the form of two signings made by Ole Gunnar as the winter window neared closing. These had to work or his judgement would be further questioned. One of the new acquisitions was Odion Ighalo, on loan from Shanghai Greenland Shenhua until the close of the 2019-20 season. This was met by derision from critics: a panic move forced by Rashford's lay-off, as the Nigerian was supposedly a busted Watford reject now playing in the backwater of Chinese football who was landed late on 1 February – deadline day – to show up Ole and the club's scattergun transfer policy.

The other new player was Bruno Fernandes, a 25-year-old Portugal midfielder from Sporting Lisbon bought for an initial £46m the day before Ighalo. The midfielder's record showed 137 games, 63 goals and 52 assists, that he was Sporting captain and two-time Portuguese player of the year, and Ole told the club website: 'Bruno's goals and assists stats speak for themselves, he will be a fantastic addition to our team and he will help us push on in the second part of the season. The winter break is coming at a perfect time for us to integrate Bruno into the squad and for him to get to know his team-mates.'

Fernandes was added to Ole's major summer signings of Aaron Wan-Bissaka, Daniel James and Harry Maguire, and his fee soon rated as a bargain-of-the-season (or any other) given his instant success and how the playmaker electrified the rest of the players, elevating them and thus Ole's team.

And, a closer look at Ighalo's credentials revealed him to

be a prospectively shrewd addition by OGS. This was a 30-year-old striker who had been top scorer at Egypt's Africa Cup of Nations in summer 2019 with five strikes, and who knew the Premier League thanks to three years (two in the top flight) at Watford.

What followed was a managerial Shangri-La for Ole. Before either player's arrival, United went to Tranmere Rovers in the FA Cup and left with a resounding 6-0 win, six different scorers featuring: Harry Maguire, Diogo Dalot, Jesse Lingard, Phil Jones, Anthony Martial and Mason Greenwood.

This was on 26 January and began a run of 11 games unbeaten, which equalled Ole's tally at the start of his caretaker tenure. Fernandes arrived three days later – a Wednesday on which United had the return EFL Cup semi-final leg at Manchester City. The performance at the Etihad Stadium impressed due to Ole's display of in-game tactical flexibility after Guardiola initially outthought him by fielding two holding midfielders in İlkay Gündoğan and Rodri. This was a rarity and meant City overran United, whose main ploy under Ole remained the counterattack. Yet, seeing the team were in danger of another hiding akin to that suffered in the first half of the opening leg, OGS dropped one of his two central forwards, Mason Greenwood, back alongside Jesse Lingard and suddenly City were stymied and United back in the contest. Now, Ole hit pay dirt as the extra man allowed the visitors to camp inside the City half and force a free kick. Fred's delivery was finished by Nemanja Matić and United won the game by his strike. City may still have progressed to the final but here was a second win at the home of the champions – which few teams achieve in a season – and hard evidence of Ole's football brain.

The impressive results followed. A goalless draw with Wolves at Old Trafford was followed by a fine 2-0 win at Chelsea, Anthony Martial and Harry Maguire the scorers. In between the matches came the inaugural winter break, which was notable for Ole and his hopes for the side due to Manchester City being handed a two-year ban from the Champions League by UEFA. As they were second, 12 points ahead of Sheffield United in fifth and United were four points further back, then if City's appeal to the Court of Arbitration for Sport failed, fifth would be high enough to qualify for next season's competition.

Around now came news of an outbreak of a new disease that was given the name Covid-19. It originated in Wuhan in December and began ravaging that city and the Hubei province of China. For the time being, it was not affecting English football but this was to change.

After Chelsea, United drew 1-1 at Club Brugge in the Europa League last-32 first leg, and Watford were beaten 3-0 at home. Fernandes scored his first and created Martial's second, with Mason Greenwood scoring an 11th in 18 appearances, the 18-year-old proving to be one of the major pluses of Ole's first full term in charge, his form repaying the manager's belief in him. Next came a 5-0 rout of Club Brugge in the return – Fernandes with an opening penalty, Ighalo making a first start and scoring – as United reached the last 16 with ease. Their unbeaten sequence was now seven outings with six clean sheets and, of his star man, Ole told the post-match media conference: 'Bruno is fit, in good form and we felt he was something we needed and so it proves.'

On the following Sunday – 1 March – United faced a particular test: a trip to Everton, where in last April's corresponding fixture they were pathetic in a 4–0 reverse that left Ole fuming. 'That was the lowest I've been,' Solskjær said in the preview conference. 'That was a capitulation. We had absolutely nothing about us. I can hand on heart 100 per cent say these boys will never give in and never give up like that team did.'

Ole explained why it had taken close to a year to return to the form of the start of his incumbency. 'We knew when we made the decisions we made in the summer it was going to take time,' he said. 'Rome wasn't built in a day. The culture, the attitude, the fitness, the camaraderie, the team spirit, and maybe even the understanding between players, have improved.'

It is quite an admission for any manager to say of any team that they gave up, but for the Manchester United number one to state that he witnessed a capitulation is a searing indictment of the challenge Ole had before him then.

Now, as averred, this time his team did have backbone at Goodison Park, going behind to a third-minute Dominic Calvert-Lewin opener then equalising through a strike by the effervescent Fernandes just after the half-hour.

The United XIs from the two matches are worth recording.

On 21 April 2019: De Gea, Lindelöf, Jones, Smalling, Dalot, Pogba, Fred, Matić, Lukaku, Rashford, Martial.

On 1 March 2020: De Gea, Lindelöf, Maguire, Shaw, Wan-Bissaka, Fred, Fernandes, Matić, McTominay, Martial, Greenwood.

Of the six changes, three players had become personae non gratae – Jones (a reserve at best), Smalling and Lukaku (the former on loan at Roma, the latter sold to Internazionale) – while one, Dalot, was peripheral, meaning only the injured

Rashford and Pogba would (probably) have started: an illustration of the churn Ole had executed successfully since then.

From here United reeled off three consecutive victories. Three-nil at Derby County in the FA Cup fifth round, Ighalo scoring his first brace for the club. Then, City were beaten again, for a remarkable third time in the season. Anthony Martial scored a 16th of the season – for him to close to within one of his best count for the club – while Scott McTominay crowned a memorable victory with a 96th-minute lob into a net vacated by the hapless Ederson on a night when Old Trafford was the loudest and felt the most hopeful in the seven years since Sir Alex Ferguson stepped away.

Afterwards Ole was jubilant. 'The connection between the fans and the team: that means a lot to me,' he said.

This was on 8 March. United were up to fifth – good enough at this juncture for Champions League qualification – three behind Chelsea in fourth and only another five to Leicester City in third. Manchester City's tally of 57 had Ole's team trailing by a yawning 12, and the challenge to make United true contenders again could be found in the barely believable 37 points they were behind Liverpool: enough in some seasons to avoid relegation.

The win over City was the final league match – number 29 – before the disease from Wuhan began to have a shattering effect on life around the world, and therefore English football and Ole's first full year in charge, as Covid-19 led to the cessation of the game. Before these measures were precipitated by Mikel Arteta, the Arsenal manager, testing positive for the disease, Ole took Manchester United to Linz in Austria to face LASK in the opening leg of the Europa League last 16.

Whether the game would go ahead on 12 March hung in the balance and, in an augury of the postponement of football in Europe – confirmed the following day – while it did take place, it was played behind closed Linzer Stadion doors.

This meant that beyond players and staff and security, there was a small media corps in a position to witness an encounter that was instructive, as the silent stadium allowed an insight into who the most vocal – the leaders – in Ole's team are. There was scant surprise that Bruno Fernandes was loud – think booming Brian Blessed volume – with Scott McTominay also in evidence, but it was intriguing to find that Harry Maguire was quieter, given his billing as captain.

Versus a side put together with a budget akin to an English League Two club, Ole was pleased with a 5-0 win, goals coming from Odion Ighalo, Daniel James, Juan Mata, Mason Greenwood and Andreas Pereira.

One of Ole's final comments at what was to be the last post-match media conference before coronavirus took over was a quip to the *Times* correspondent when he asked when Paul (Pogba) might return. The writer is also called Paul and, with a gleam in his eye, OGS shot back: 'You mean yourself?' It caused laughter from the media corps plus a follow-up. 'I thought you were talking about yourself in the third person,' he joked.

The win was the 11th match unbeaten and was the best way for Ole and his team to sign off – with no one knowing precisely when football would return.

CHAPTER 26

The Renaissance Continues

'Sixteen games unbeaten is nowhere near
what Man United should strive towards.'

OLE GUNNAR SOLKSJÆR

The answer was three months later: in mid-June.

Stadiums were empty as matches were staged behind closed
doors to try to contain the spread of coronavirus. Players and
club staff in the 'red zone' were tested three times a week for
the illness. Media were allowed entrance to games and kept
in the 'amber zone', temperatures checked on arrival and face
masks mandatory.

Marcus Rashford became a national – and folk – hero for
forcing the government into a U-turn regarding the granting
of free school meal vouchers to the poorest of families over
the summer holidays: Boris Johnson went from a blanket
rejection of Rashford's campaign to an unabashed about-face
in which the prime minister tried to co-opt the 22-year-old

from Wythenshawe as a standard-bearer for precisely the kind of policy he'd advocated for in the first place.

And what became clear was that Ole and the backroom staff had ensured the squad were mentally and physically primed when football restarted. Also: available again were Rashford, out since mid-January, and Paul Pogba, who had last featured on Boxing Day as a substitute and whose last start was in September. Each would prove a boon to what unfolded for OGS and his team.

As, too, would Mason Greenwood, because the resumption was to feature the forward tearing up opposition defences with a swash, a buckle and a lethal goal threat that cast the 18-year-old as the season's break-out footballer.

United were even better than in the 11 unbeaten outings before lockdown: a slicker unit whose in-game thought, vision and execution was on a more elevated plane. Eight of the 11 had been victories. In the opening eight post-lockdown, six were wins, two draws. The sequence set up a final eight days of the domestic season that began with an FA Cup semi-final against Chelsea at Wembley on Sunday 19 July and Champions League qualification that was in Manchester United's control.

Beat West Ham on the Wednesday and Leicester City on Sunday's final day and Ole would have taken the torrid times of his nascent tenure, plus the two nadirs – last season's 4-0 rout by Everton and late-January's 2-0 home loss to Burnley – and recast them as dark points before the dawn of a gleaming new hope, a look skywards to the stars again. A fourth-place finish was the minimum required to qualify for the Champions League after Manchester City won their appeal to the Court of Arbitration for Sport against their two-year ban from Europe, thus ruling out any chance of the team finishing fifth, taking City's place, and squeezing in through the back door.

The first matches of the restart had kicked off on 17 June: Aston Villa drew 0-0 with Sheffield United; Manchester City beat Arsenal 3-0. Then Ole took his team to Tottenham Hotspur on Friday 19 June. Manchester United were rusty and went behind to a Steven Bergwijn strike on 27 minutes. Then, just after the hour, Ole brought on Paul Pogba. It proved a clever substitution, the playing of a trump card: Pogba – as all A-list acts should – turned the contest. The Frenchman's 81st-minute surge along the right panicked Eric Dier, who pulled Pogba down as he skated past, and a penalty was awarded by the referee, Jonathan Moss. Bruno Fernandes – soon to be viewed as United's player of the season despite only signing in January – smashed home, and Ole had guided his team to a 12th match without loss.

Two points, though, had been dropped in the race for a Champions League place, and David De Gea was culpable, having allowed Bergwijn's regulation shot to squirm in. While Ole subsequently backed the Spaniard as 'the best keeper in the world', United remained in fifth, their 46 points leaving them, crucially, five behind Chelsea in fourth, while a better goal difference of five separated them from Wolverhampton Wanderers in sixth. Tottenham slipped to eighth, four points behind Ole's team.

Five days later when Sheffield United arrived at Old Trafford, Fernandes and Pogba started together for the first time. Ole dropped Dan James and started Mason Greenwood, while the stand-out performer was Anthony Martial. His hat-trick had United coasting and was the first in the league for the club since Robin van Persie's in April 2013 (also at Old Trafford) when Aston Villa were beaten 3-0 on the night United last clinched the title.

Next came an FA Cup quarter-final, extra-time win at Norwich City: 2-1. Odion Ighalo scored in normal time before Harry Maguire's 118th-minute winner. Then, on 30 June, Brighton & Hove Albion were dispatched 3-0 away, at a ground where United had lost on their last two visits – a Mason Greenwood strike and two from the ever-impressive Bruno Fernandes confirming the win.

The latter's second stemmed from a move that swept possession from inside United's area to the opposite one at lightning pace, the ball being pin-balled via a Maguire header and a Nemanja Matić chest-down-and-pass to Greenwood, whose race along the left and cross found Fernandes, who scored. Here was a rapier-like move and goal reminiscent of the Sir Alex Ferguson-vintage Wayne Rooney–Cristiano Ronaldo spearheaded sides.

'Everyone can see the team is improving and we are still in with a shout in the FA Cup and Europa League, as well as the battle for a Champions League place,' Ole told a press conference.

When Bournemouth arrived at Old Trafford on Saturday 4 July – the date of pubs opening again across England as the easing of lockdown continued – Chelsea and Leicester City had lost their previous matches, allowing Ole's side to gain ground. The Cherries were routed 5-2, and until Chelsea won later the same day Manchester United were fourth, their highest position since September. OGS selected the same United XI for a third successive league outing, the first time this had occurred in 14 years.

Other records tumbled: a first Old Trafford league five-goal haul in nine years, which was also the last time two players returned 20 for the club (Dimitar Berbatov and Javier Hernández), just as Anthony Martial, with a curler before the break, and Marcus Rashford, with an earlier penalty, had managed to do. These goals followed a Mason Greenwood equaliser, the 18-year-old's ability to connect with the ball with a striking purity even more discernible due to the *THWACK!* reverberating around the empty stadium.

Fernandes and Greenwood (again) completed the drubbing in the second half, and Ole offered no doubt regarding the latter's status as a teenaged marksman. 'I have seen Wayne Rooney at the same age and Mason is a specialist goalscorer,' he said, placing the boy from Wibsey in Bradford above his former team-mate.

Ole's nurturing of Greenwood is further evidence of the natural he is at managing the differing demands of Manchester United: in this case, expectations placed on precocious, home-grown talent. OGS gave Greenwood his debut in the final three minutes of last March's Champions League victory at Paris Saint-Germain. 'Huge' is how Marcus Rashford describes the value of this experience for Greenwood. The starlet's full debut then came two months later, in the final-day 2-0 loss to Cardiff City, Ole viewing Greenwood as his best player that day. The forward's maiden senior strike was the winner against Astana in September's Europa League group game, and after those against the Cherries, which took Greenwood to 15 in all competitions, OGS could be satisfied with his development of the teenager.

'He's coped really well with the demands on him; we've managed him as well as we could and he's come back from lockdown flying,' Ole told reporters. 'His sharpness is there, he's gained a few kilos, a lot of experience and has confidence in his own abilities.'

De Gea and his (permanently?) waning form remained a live issue, though. Junior Stanislas's opener for Bournemouth was created from a tight angle at close range, the keeper allowing the ball to pass him at the near post when the minimum he should have done was throw his body in the way. 'David's working hard and I've got no worries about him,' Ole argued, though he could hardly say anything else.

United's next outing was game number 17 without defeat: a 3-0 cruise at Aston Villa. Bruno Fernandes – who else – began proceedings with a penalty, Greenwood and the revitalised Pogba completing the damage. In a sign of how United were performing under Ole, Fernandes was voted Premier League Player of the Month for June and Pogba was moved to call his side a 'proper team'. The club, unsurprisingly, agreed, tweeting, 'We are first in Premier League history to win four consecutive games by 3+ goals.' Which made Ole Gunnar the first manager to do so.

Now came a golden – and spurned – chance to leapfrog Leicester and Chelsea, move on to 61 points and take third place. With three matches left, Southampton motored into Old Trafford on Monday 13 July for the late-evening kick-off.

At 90 minutes plus five of added time, United had seemingly pulled it off. With deadlines closing, match report intros had been filed to national sports desks reflecting how Rashford's and Martial's 21st goals of the term had United 2-1 up after Stuart Armstrong opened the scoring for the visitors, before a chaotic few minutes ensued. Brandon Williams's head injury meant United went down to 10 men as

Ole had already used his three allotted slots for substitutions. At a James Ward-Prowse corner, Harry Maguire marked one of his team-mates – Aaron Wan-Bissaka – rather than a Saints attacker, the ball went to Michael Obafemi and he grabbed a late, late equaliser.

As intros were frantically rewritten (and filed) by reporters, United had dropped from third to fifth: cue the camera panning to Ole slumping in his socially distant seat on the touchline.

Caveat time, though. Southampton were a roughhouse side who got in United's faces, pressed hard, and could play. A draw was actually a good result for Ole's ever-improving side. A measure of their growing maturity and solidity was that they had gone toe-to-toe with their visitors and remained unbeaten.

And, then, they bounced back at Crystal Palace three days later. As United kicked off at Selhurst Park, Chelsea and Leicester had won their latest matches over Norwich City and Sheffield United, respectively, the former on Tuesday and the latter earlier on Thursday evening, so Ole's men had to beat Roy Hodgson's outfit to keep pace.

They did – 2-0 – Rashford and Martial scoring to take their tally to 22 goals apiece, the duo plus Greenwood being compared by OGS to the Wayne Rooney–Carlos Tevez–Cristiano Ronaldo triumvirate that powered United to the 2008 Champions League/Premier League double. Martial is another of OGS's successes – his man-management rehabilitating the Frenchman from persona non grata under José Mourinho to a United No. 9 who has become a powerhouse forward, who carries a team ethic and is now more self-demanding.

Victory in south London, achieved without the injured Brandon Williams and Luke Shaw, made it 62 points for United from 36 games, with 63 goals scored and 35 conceded – the latter the joint second lowest in the division.

While Leicester remained a place above Ole's team thanks to a superior goal difference, a gauge of the team's trajectory was that it had fewer weak points, though there were still areas of concern. Shaw was not as potent a left-back as Ole Gunnar would like. The first-choice centre-backs, Harry Maguire and Victor Lindelöf, required competition due to a lack of pace and a propensity for errors. The forward line, too, lacked depth.

Rashford, Martial and Greenwood had become genuine Manchester United quality under Ole's management. But the callow Dan James, the misfiring Jesse Lingard – who had suffered personal problems – and the solid yet stardust-lacking Odion Ighalo were at least a class below. Such issues were the catalyst for OGS's interest in Borussia Dortmund's Jadon Sancho, the 20-year-old England forward who had left Manchester City in summer 2017 in a bold move that precipitated a stellar rise to become the level of performer that OGS – and the United executive – were willing to consider a £100m-plus bid for.

But, before a summer transfer window that would begin on 27 July and run until 5 October (plus 11 days for top-flight clubs to trade with EFL counterparts) came the final eight days of the domestic season. Sunday 20 July was a classic illustration of a day in the life of a Manchester United manager. It began with the best of results as Leicester City were beaten 3-0 by the Mourinho-managed Tottenham Hotspur. It meant the Foxes remained on 62 points, like United, and their goal difference was now equal: 28.

Except. Ole's team had two matches left, Leicester one. If West Ham were beaten at Old Trafford on the Wednesday then a draw – at the very least – at Leicester on the final day of the season would seal Champions League qualification.

First, though, came a dire display and result at Wembley in the FA Cup semi-final against Chelsea. This was due to team selection, the scheduling of the match and an off-day for Ole's players, as tiredness plus defensive and goalkeeping fragilities were again exposed: a smorgasbord of factors that came together to produce United's poorest outing since the loss to Burnley in January. Ole Gunnar had complained – correctly – that Chelsea had two days' more rest after winning 1-0 at Norwich on Tuesday, United playing 48 hours later at Palace. He made five changes – the key ones placing Paul Pogba, Anthony Martial and Mason Greenwood on the bench – and switched to a 3-5-2 that had the fit-again Brandon Williams and Aaron Wan-Bissaka as wing-backs, and Daniel James partnering Marcus Rashford up front.

It backfired. United were sluggish and directionless. The shape neutered Rashford. James again showed how he had gone sideways – a rarity for an Ole signing. Victor Lindelöf, not for the first time, allowed an attacker to make him their patsy: Olivier Giroud, when moving goal-side to score the opener as the break neared. De Gea might have done better, his hand was too soft, and he certainly should not have allowed Mason Mount's speculative 20-yard shot to go through his gloves like they were porcelain for Chelsea's second. Harry Maguire's own goal completed the scoring, while Bruno Fernandes's late penalty was consolation-only, though it was his impressive ninth goal since signing.

The unbeaten run was over. Ended at 19. The best for a

decade, since the 29 of April–November 2010: another fact that augured well for where Ole is taking the side. Afterwards, the manager sent a clear message to his players regarding West Ham and Leicester. 'That's the way of a footballer's life, you need to get over this,' he told MUTV. 'We'll be ready for Wednesday. We know how huge those two games are, they're going to be massive and we're looking forward to it.'

For the visit of David Moyes's West Ham on Wednesday, Ole reverted to his 4-2-3-1. David De Gea was retained – a big call – Anthony Martial and Paul Pogba were restored, Aaron Wan-Bissaka was replaced by Timothy Fosu-Mensah, and the equation ran like this: a win or draw would not affect what was required at Leicester – a point – but if the Hammers were handed a defeat by a margin of three or more goals this would mean that any loss by less than this at the King Power would still have United finishing fourth, ahead of the Foxes.

Yet while not quite punch-drunk, Ole's team staggered through the match. After a bright(ish) start, West Ham were as dogmatic and defensive as United were under Moyes's management in his fated 2013-14, 34-league-games season. And as half-time neared Paul Pogba acted in a way that infuriated fans and caused widespread bemusement. From a free kick 20 yards out, Declan Rice smashed the ball at the wall, Pogba raised his arms to protect his face and committed a needless handball. The penalty was awarded and Michail Antonio beat De Gea.

Cue the interval, Pogba apologising to team-mates, and Ole saying afterwards that the midfielder knows he should have taken it in the 'mush'. By then Mason Greenwood had rescued United – his 17th of the season drawing him alongside George Best, Wayne Rooney and Brian Kidd as the club's most prolific teenagers in a campaign. 'He's bailed us out again,' was Ole's verdict. Just as welcome was Chelsea's 5-3 loss at Liverpool later that night, which lifted United up to third place on the same points, 63, but with a better goal difference than Frank Lampard's side, 28 to 13.

The bottom line had become this: if Ole's side drew with Leicester they were guaranteed fourth place and the riches – financial, status, squad development – of Champions League football next season. If their non-losing result were to equal Chelsea's versus Wolverhampton Wanderers, they would be third. What Ole and his side dared not do was go down to Leicester. Because if they did, they'd require Chelsea to lose too.

It was set up for a grandstand finish.

CHAPTER 27

Premier League Final Day, 2019–20

'We've not ended up anywhere yet.'

OLE GUNNAR SOLSKJÆR

THIS IS IT.

Can he do it? *Can Ole Gunnar Solskjær reveal a red dawn rolling onto the horizon?*

After the dark and dismal days of winter. The uneven form, the bad games and results. Being questioned and doubted and pounded by the critics. Can OGS take his team to Leicester City and depart with the required result? Be calm and clinical and guide Manchester United to Champions League football? Take a giant step in a rescue act that is already leading the club away from befuddlement, dismay and stagnation?

Sunday 25 July 2020 is mild, and for the 4pm kick-off at the King Power Stadium Ole names his strongest side bar the injured Luke Shaw, who is out until next season, to face the Foxes. It reads: David De Gea; Aaron Wan-Bissaka; Harry Maguire; Victor Lindelöf; Brandon Williams; Nemanja Matić; Paul Pogba; Mason Greenwood; Bruno Fernandes; Marcus Rashford; Anthony Martial.

Brendan Rodgers's team is without the injured Ben Chilwell, Christian Fuchs, James Maddison, Ricardo Pereira and Daniel Amartey, plus the suspended Çağlar Söyüncü. His is a decimated Leicester XI.

Except: Ole's side stutters and is tentative. As if the last half-year has a been a mirage. A ghost team. What unfolds is an unwanted return to the United XIs witnessed on too many match days since Sir Alex Ferguson retired. And to the Ole Gunnar Solskjær XI of the closing phase of last season and the first half of this, until the last league defeat, to Burnley in January, seven long months ago.

Then he was a P45-in-waiting, apparently. A man who was sacked but did not know it yet. Now, here, his team are 13 Premier League games unbeaten since then, yet they are freezing, suffering stage-fright. It isn't meant to be like this. The script is rogue, the storybook ending twisted by ogres who are causing Bruno Fernandes – *Bruno Fernandes!* – to hit passes awry. Gremlins that make Nemanja Matić, who has been in fine form post-lockdown, pass across his area to Kelechi Iheanacho, who, thankfully, cannot punish the slip. Harry Maguire is allowing balls to go under his foot. Paul Pogba, Anthony Martial, Mason Greenwood are distant presences.

Jamie Vardy, whose 23-goal tally casts him as Golden Boot winner-presumptive, spoons a chance straight to David De Gea.

On 32 minutes the under-par yet still irrepressible Fernandes takes a Pogba pass on his chest and volleys past

Kasper Schmeichel, but the strike is ruled offside by VAR. United are in a fugue. Have forgotten the lethal attacking force they are.

Vardy misses a chance – United breathe. Rashford misses a chance – United shake a collective head. Rashford smashes a half-volley and Schmeichel beats the ball away.

At half-time 0–0 is the score and the news from Stamford Bridge will not help Ole or his players' nerves: Chelsea are 2–0 up against Wolves.

The second half starts. Bruno Fernandes misses. Leicester dominate possession. Victor Lindelöf clears a Marc Albrighton ball that threatens De Gea's near post.

58 minutes: Rodgers changes Iheanacho for Ayoze Pérez.

60 minutes: Vardy hits the bar.

67 minutes: Fernandes, looking exhausted, cannot put Rashford in with a regulation pass.

70 minutes: PENALTY TO MANCHESTER UNITED!

Jonny Evans, once of United, and Wes Morgan collide into Anthony Martial who is put through by Fernandes, and Martin Atkinson, the referee, awards the spot-kick. After a prolonged VAR wait, the decision is confirmed. This is a record 14th penalty awarded to Manchester United this season. Meaning it is all now on Bruno Fernandes. Who has been tired, lacking his usual spark . . .

Up the Portuguese strides, he *hops*, as usual, just in front of the ball – showing *cojones* of steel – and, after a split-second pause, rolls it home cooler-than-cool to Schmeichel's right, the keeper diving left. 'Bruno Fernandes – makes the difference,' says the commentator. He has done it yet again: this his 10th strike in 20 appearances. Now, surely, United are to finish third.

Jesse Lingard, the forgotten man of Ole Gunnar's Manchester United renaissance, replaces Mason Greenwood with 13 minutes left. Ten minutes later Fernandes gives way to Scott McTominay.

There are three – *three* – minutes left plus the five of added time that Atkinson awards. United have to concede two to have a top-four finish smash-and-grabbed from them. Then it all becomes so, *so* enjoyable. Evans is sent off for a horrible challenge on McTominay – a straight red card – and now Lingard – *Lingard?* – who has not scored a league goal for two years since the 5-1 win at Cardiff City in December 2018, Ole's inaugural match as caretaker manager, breaks his drought. Schmeichel decides to dribble near goal, Lingard hunts him down, mugs the Dane of the ball, and fires home into an empty net.

Ole and United *EXPLODE*.

They have done it. Ole Gunnar Solskjær has done it.

Seconds later, Atkinson blows the whistle and Ole Gunnar Solskjær has taken Manchester United from fifth place and 14 points behind Leicester in second position on New Year's Day to third, ending with 66, four more than the Foxes, who finish fifth instead.

Ole is delighted yet calm afterwards. He is seeing the big picture, taking the long view of where his team should be. Beating Leicester is billed as breaking a 'mental barrier' from players who have now won a 'big game' after losing Carabao and FA Cup semi-finals this season. OGS tells reporters: 'It's a wonderful achievement from the boys. These boys are looking more and more like a Man United team – the Man United way. You play with no fear, you go for it. Qualifying for the Champions League means better opposition and bigger games next year. We need to step it up, definitely, because we can't rest players like we could in the Europa League. We need to get fitter, stronger and more robust.

'The club know what I feel we need in the transfer market, and we're going to pursue it. Let's see where we end up.'

The last comment is the headline. A telegram to Ed Woodward and the Glazers. Back the manager. Look what I did this season. *Back me in the transfer market.*

This is what is next. The next challenge, the next test. What will define Ole's second full season in charge: if his team can truly challenge Liverpool and Manchester City. So, while the players have a couple of days off ahead of the Europa League resuming in a fortnight, OGS starts the process of pruning and strengthening his squad.

He does so with his status and power at Manchester United confirmed. He is stronger than he ever was, even after *that* winner against Bayern Munich 21 years ago.

The Red Dawn is HERE.

CHAPTER 28

Red Horizons

'We might look at it today and see where we
need to improve.'

OGS, AFTER DEFEAT TO SEVILLA

The challenge for the Europa League ends where the League
Cup and FA Cup did: in the semi-finals. Sevilla, five-time
winners of the competition, are too savvy on this hot
Cologne evening where the work-in-progress limitations of
Ole's team and squad are illuminated during a 2-1 loss.

Yet another Bruno Fernandes penalty opens the scoring
but twice the United back four – Aaron Wan-Bissaka, Harry
Maguire, Victor Lindelöf and Brandon Williams – is exposed,
highlighting the positioning and pace fault lines Ole has to
address. Factor in the spurning of several chances – another
point of concern – and Ole's first full season in charge ends
on 16 August 2020: precisely a year and a day after it started.

The challenges ahead for OGS are clear. Despite a

collective 74 strikes between Fernandes (12), Anthony Martial (23), Marcus Rashford (22) and Mason Greenwood (17), Ole's front line could be more ruthless. Missed chances were costly against Sevilla; they were costly at other times in the season. Bringing in Borussia Dortmund's Jadon Sancho, for around £100m, is the strategy to solve this problem. This is Ole's great hope for his number one summer target: that the addition of a 20-year-old who is two-footed, creates and scores all types of goals can elevate the attack into a shock-and-awe proposition that will overrun domestic and Champions League opposition.

Ole also wants more goals from his engine room. If the 12-finish contribution of Fernandes as a No 10 is discounted, then the eight combined from midfield of Paul Pogba (one), Scott McTominay (five), Fred (two), Nemanja Matić (one) was paltry.

Then there is the defence. Despite a definite improvement since Harry Maguire was acquired, he and Victor Lindelöf can be creaky against pace, and as a collective Ole's rearguard has to erase dodgy positioning.

As the truncated month-or-so close season begins, the stance from Ed Woodward in United's purser's office is that if Sancho is bought there will not be any more serious money in the kitty for, say, a Kalidou Koulibaly, the Napoli centre-back who is fast and formidable, but is priced in the region of £80m and is also being tracked by City.

Ole's full-backs are another poser. The first-choice Wan-Bissaka and Luke Shaw: can they fly into space and create in the mode of Liverpool's Trent Alexander-Arnold and Andy Robertson and, actually, are they as accomplished defensively? Again, with finances being tight, Ole may have to pull a Robertson-style acquisition (£8m, from Hull) from the hat in order to add quality here.

Depth is another burning issue. Despite his team conceding Luuk de Jong's second for Sevilla on 78 minutes, OGS waited until the final moments at the RheinEnergieStadion to make any changes to try to pull the tie round: a glaring sign that he looked at a bench occupied by an attack corps of Juan Mata, Jesse Lingard, Odion Ighalo and Andreas Pereira and questioned their abilities to do so.

Once more, this is all about finance, finance, finance. After losing to Sevilla, Ole told reporters: 'We need quality, the right player, the right personality. We might look at it today and see where we need to improve.'

This again sounded like a telegram to Woodward: *Look at how and why we failed here and in the two other semi-finals and how admirably I have done in taking us to third and the Champions League, so now is THE time to really invest.*

On 2 September, as the first day of pre-season training officially began, Ole had a first new addition of the window and the fifth major one of his incumbency. Donny van de Beek was announced as a 39 million Euro (plus 5 million Euro) signing, a 23-year-old who fitted the profile of an OGS/United footballer: hungry, talented, and team-first-centred, who would also – the hope was – add the weight of goals missing from midfield.

The self-described 'box-to-box' operator's eight strikes for Ajax in the 2019–20 coronavirus-truncated Eredivisie season was the same as Matić, McTominay, Fred and Pogba managed in all competitions. Van de Beek's acquisition is also Ole in long-term planning mode: as a message to Pogba to up his game to match-upon-match brilliance rather than sporadically or Van de Beek will become first-choice; and as insurance should the Frenchman revive his former want-away desire when next summer arrives.

Ole will also have to watch the Harry Maguire situation after his captain was convicted in a court in Syros of assaulting a police officer, swearing, resisting arrest and attempting bribery following an incident on the neighbouring Greek island of Mykonos. For this the 27-year-old received a 21 month and 10 day suspended sentence.

The unsavoury episode occurred before training resumed and while Maguire continued to protest his innocence and immediately launched an appeal this is not to be heard for some time and so how Ole's nominated leader performs with his future unresolved will be scrutinised: by fans, the media and, most vitally, OGS.

All of this is, of course, part of the greater picture – the grand challenge before Ole. Can he claim a 21st championship for Manchester United? Even making them true contenders in 2020-21 by closing the gap to Manchester City (15 points) and Liverpool (a yawning 33) appears a Rubik's cube ask, but this is what he must do.

Can he? This is the dream. Why he was employed. To go toe-to-toe with Jürgen Klopp at Liverpool, with all-comers, and prosper.

If he does so, Ole will become the fourth member of United's most venerated managerial group. Ernest Mangnall was Bolton-born and managed Burnley for three years before taking over in 1903, the club then 25 years old. As 'secretary' in 1906, he oversaw promotion to the First Division and two seasons later – 1907-08 – made Manchester United champions for the first time. When he left in 1912 (to manage

Manchester City), Mangnall had also won the FA Cup (1909) and a further title (1910-11).

Sir Matt Busby took over in October 1945 and left in June 1969, and had a second tenure between December 1970 and June 1971. The Scot won five championships (1951-52, 1955-56, 1956-57, 1964-65 and 1966–67), the European Cup of 1968, plus the 1948 and 1963 FA Cups.

Ferguson, manager between November 1986 and May 2013, won 13 titles (1992-93, 1993-94, 1995-96, 1996-97, 1998-99, 1999-2000, 2001-02, 2002-03, 2006-07, 2007-08, 2008-09, 2010-11, 2012-13). Five FA Cups (1990, 1994, 1996, 1999, 2004). Two Champions League titles (1998-99, 2007-08). One Cup Winners' Cup (1990-91). Four League Cups (1992, 2006, 2009, 2010). One European Super Cup (1991). One Intercontinental Cup (1999). And, one FIFA Club World Cup (2008).

This is the lineage Solskjær must emulate to become the next great manager at the club where the story of the post-Ferguson managers *and* management is a Brexit-like farrago of missteps, mistakes and misdemeanours. David Moyes was the home-educated, 11-year veteran of Everton, who would continue the Ferguson way. Louis van Gaal arrived with a glittering CV that included the triumphant 1995 Champions League youth-studded Ajax XI. José Mourinho arrived as arguably *the* best manager of his generation. None of this trio could conjure the magic required.

In microcosm, the Manchester United of Moyes, Van Gaal and Mourinho performed as though the last rites had been read to the players as they pulled on the red strip, laced their boots and left the changing room for the game. Ole's challenge is to have the side perform in the polar opposite manner – achieved thus far – and add English championship number 21, thereby finally filling the Ferguson-sized hole created when he left.

This is what occurred after the post-Mangnall, 1912-45 hiatus ended with Busby's appointment. And between 1969 and Busby's original retirement and 1986, when Ferguson entered the club. Five years after Ferguson stepped down, Ed Woodward stumbled on the formula for renewal and regeneration at United and it was simple: look within.

Manchester United, at heart, can feel a family affair. Place aside the Glazers' controversial ownership and the mountains of interest on loans they continue to pile on the club and the disaffection and fury this causes: on a day-to-day basis engaging with United has a warmth, a soulful feel. Go in and out of the training ground at Carrington or the stadium on match days and there is a friendly welcome on offer from this multibillion-pound corporation, as embodied by Kath Phipps, who has worked at the club for 50-plus years and seen Busby, Wilf McGuinness, Frank O'Farrell, Tommy Docherty, Dave Sexton, Ron Atkinson, Ferguson, Moyes, Ryan Giggs, Van Gaal, Mourinho and now Ole sitting in the hottest of seats.

Woodward has asked an adored member of the family back in to head it and, after Ole's season and a half in charge, he has given himself a real chance of ultimate success. He has the backing of players, fans and executive. His team plays the Manchester United way. He has a smile and a steeliness. The eternal optimist who is no gentle touch.

And he also has a relaxed media persona that can be traced to the legacy of his champion wrestler father, Øyvind, Ole's own profile as Norway's most famous native, and the 14 years at Old Trafford as player and coach before departure in 2010. OGS may not want the incessant, feverish scrutiny of being Manchester United manager, but he handles it with charm.

Childhood friend Arild Stavrum says: 'The press has been part of his life in the last 25 years or something, so he has got used to it and he's so good at it. He's an intelligent guy. When you lead a football club – if it's in the Premier League of Norway or England – it's the same principles. But, of course, at United the pressure and interest is much, much higher and the focus on behaviour in the press conference that much higher too. There is much more pressure in England.'

What truly matters is what is put on the pitch. OGS characterises the demand thus: 'The United way is about taking the game to the opposition, always believing in yourself,' he told UEFA.com. 'If you asked other managers who played against Sir Alex's teams, the pace and the tempo going forward was key. And the surge, that last 15 to 20 minutes towards the Stretford End – it was almost like the ball was just sucked into the goal. There will be a lot of Sir Alex Ferguson I will take into management. He has transformed me into the professional I have been. He has drip-fed things into me all the time.'

How OGS can draw upon this tutelage will be key. Raimond van der Gouw says of Ole and Ferguson: 'Solskjær was the type of player [who'd] never let you down, he was working hard, he was giving everything to the manager – he knew exactly his place, and if there was somebody better than him, he would be frustrated, he would be disappointed but he kept going.

'And that's why he played for Man United and that's why

he was a very important player for Man United. If you work with Alex Ferguson for 14 years as a player then coach then it becomes in your genes, it enters your blood – how Sir Alex Ferguson works. I think he took everything in and that's a big part of how he's managing Man United.'

Rob Swire, the physiotherapist who saw Ole up close over the three-plus years of his serious knee injury, points to how adversity was an invaluable lesson. 'Not at all am I surprised about him at United,' he says. 'He's probably benefited regarding Cardiff City and how he didn't do too well. It was a very difficult situation as a manager, the circumstances there would be very difficult for anybody. He was summed up then as being no good for management after a few months there, but he did well in Molde, didn't he?'

It all remains before him – the red horizons of next season. Can he who bombed at Cardiff City and has 'only' won trophies in Norway succeed? Can he prove the Renaissance man, football polymath required to deliver at Old Trafford? Can he return the glory days to Manchester United? Make them champions of England? The emperors of Europe?

Can OGS establish himself in the lineage of great Manchester United managers?

Will the Red Apprentice become the Red Master?

ACKNOWLEDGEMENTS

Massive thanks to:

Jon Wood: a gent and brilliant agent.

Matthew Brook and Scott Fletcher: fine muses and brothers.

Ian Marshall and Frances Jessop: great editors.

Mum: obvious reasons.

All the writers I've read and will read.

And: anyone who ever danced to disco anywhere.

XXX

INDEX

OGS indicates Ole Gunnar Solskjær.

INDEX

Y033228

The item should be returned or renewed
by the last d